LA BONNE CUISINE

COOKING NEW ORLEANS STYLE

Compiled by
The Women of All Saints' Episcopal Church
New Orleans, Louisiana

I

Copies of La Bonne Cuisine may be obtained from:

La Bonne Cuisine
100 Rex Drive
New Orleans, Louisiana 70123
(504) 737-1416
Toll Free 1-800-375-1416
Fax (504) 738-7829

First Printing 1980	10,000 copies
Second Printing 1981	10,000 copies
Third Printing 1981	10,000 copies
Fourth Printing 1982	15,000 copies
Fifth Printing 1983	25,000 copies
Sixth Printing 1985	15,000 copies
Seventh Printing 1988	15,000 copies
Eighth Printing 1990	15,000 copies
Ninth Printing 1992	15,000 copies

Printing by Mercury Printing Company, Memphis, TN 38132

Contents

The Louisiana Seafood Promotion Board can provide you with a complete list of seafood processors who will ship fresh seafood to you.

To obtain this free list, write:

    Louisiana Seafood Promotion Board
    P.O. Box 15570
    Baton Rouge, LA 70895

or telephone: (504) 383-7710.

Acknowledgments

Book Layout and Design
John Green

Creative Writing
The Rev. William C. Morris

Photographs
Cover Photograph by Will Crocker
Photographs by John Donnels, 31, 51, 87, 205, 293
Photographs by Will Crocker, 1, 73, 109, 145, 171
Photographs by Syndey Byrd, 121, 229

*The board of directors of La Bonne Cuisine
wish to thank the many people who submitted
their favorite recipes for inclusion in this
book and those who contributed their time
and talents to its creation.*

TOUT ENSEMBLE
How New Orleans Cooking Came To Be

Visitors to New Orleans often get a wrong idea of New Orleans cooking — that it is all rich, French, difficult, and expensive. However, many favorite dishes are distinctively local, simple, and frugal, designed to use leftovers and whatever is available. Some are even better warmed-up than when first cooked. Many can be endlessly varied. In a good New Orleans kitchen, food is never thrown away. The aim is to make something good out of everything you have. Indeed, learning to do that is what created New Orleans cooking.

South Louisiana itself is a major contributor to New Orleans cooking. The land is wet. The climate is subtropical. Seafood is abundant and easy to catch. Fresh vegetables grow all year long. Pigs and chickens flourish with little care. On the other hand, the land does not lend itself to cattle or to root crops, and, without refrigeration, food spoils very quickly. The land created a crisis in the cooking customs of the first European settlers. Used to a more temperate climate and to different ingredients, they were unable to use what they found. After subsisting for as long as they could on corn-meal mush, they turned, in desperation, to the Indians, who taught them how to make lye hominy and grits, how to cook rice, fish, crabs, crawfish, and shrimp, how to prepare gumbo, jambalaya, and corn bread. So began the happy blending of diverse elements which makes New Orleans cooking different and delightful.

The dish called gumbo is a good example of how this blending has taken place. The basic recipe comes from the Indians, who thickened it with the powdered sassafras leaves called *filé* (pronounced *feelay*) and served it with rice. The *roux* (pronounced *roo*), composed of carefully browned fat and flour, is French. This is what lends the dish such dark mystery, and also retards spoilage. The okra which is used as an alternative thickening came with the slaves from Africa — and some say the name of the dish is African as well. The peppers which sharpen it come from the Indians of Central America, and were, perhaps, first brought to South Louisiana by the Spanish. Into the gumbo you may put anything and everything in any combination — game, chicken, crabs, shrimp, greens, ham, sausage, oysters. The

(continued on next page)

result is often sublime, but it is never quite predictable.

The cooking of the first European settlers was, more or less, country French. However, once New Orleans was well-established, determined attempts were made to import aristocratic cooking as well, along with wines, opera, and architecture. It added butter, sauces, French bread, delicately-cooked fish, candies, and pastry to local preferences. However, except in a few restaurants and great houses, it did not remain separate, but married local cooking and settled down happily in the New World.

The Acadians — a name quickly corrupted to *Cajuns* — settled in the swamps and bayous west of the city, and brought a more rollicking and inventive influence to the cooking. To this day, there is a difference between the Creole cooking of the city and the Cajun cooking of the country. Creole cooking tends to be more delicate and restrained, and Cajun cooking more robust. Often, the dishes are the same, and the difference lies in the cook, who puts in more of this and less of that, depending on where she — or he — lives.

After the Louisiana Purchase, Americans began to populate what had been a French and Spanish city. They seem to have adopted Creole cooking wholesale — at least, it is difficult to find any identifiable English influences in the local cooking, unless it is a liking for beef. Even the beef is more likely to be simmered in a sauce, prepared as a *daube*, or roasted with garlic, than grilled plain over a fire.

The Blacks of New Orleans have always been among the city's best cooks. Their special contribution is knowing how to put together what everyone brings — and, over the years, that has amounted to a great deal. All during the nineteenth century, successive waves of immigration brought new people, new customs, and new dishes to the city. The Irish came, and the Germans, the Orientals, and the Italians. The Italians, particularly, shared with the whole city their love of pasta, olives, tomato sauces, more solid bread, fancy desserts, and the round muffulatta sandwich. More recently, many people have come from Central and South America and from the Far East. Already some of their customs and ideas are being taken into the local cooking. That's how we like it — *tout ensemble*, all together.

APPETIZERS AND BEVERAGES

The Greek philosopher Socrates thought that hunger is the best appetizer. That's true—if hunger and dinner arrive in the right sequence. When they don't, a good introduction awakens the slumbering appetite, and something good to drink may help make the difference between having eaten and having eaten well. That is why, from ancient times, recipes for some special extras have been cherished.

1

This flowing fountain surrounded by brick flagging, magnolia and mimosa trees, and the beautiful arched openings and galleries of a serene French Quarter Courtyard, are typical of the beauty and privacy of such enclosed gardens.

Canned shrimp or crab meat may be substituted for fresh shrimp

Shrimp Fritters

½ cup water
¼ cup butter
½ cup flour
3 eggs
1 cup cooked shrimp, minced
Salt and pepper to taste
1 tablespoon Worcestershire sauce
Cooking oil

In a saucepan bring the water to a boil and add the butter. When the butter melts, add the flour all at once, stirring constantly. Cook until the dough leaves the sides of the pan and forms a ball. Remove the mixture from the heat and cool it slightly. Add the eggs, 1 at a time, and beat well after each addition. The dough will be stiff, smooth, and shiny. Add the shrimp, salt, pepper, and Worcestershire sauce. Heat the oil in a deep fryer to 360°F and drop the batter by teaspoonfuls into the oil. Fry the fritters until they are golden.

Shrimp Butter

1 small onion, finely chopped (preferably in food processor)
1 (8 ounce) package cream cheese (at room temperature)
½ cup margarine (at room temperature)
4 tablespoons mayonnaise
2 tablespoons bottled lemon juice concentrate
1 teaspoon lemon pepper seasoning
1 teaspoon butter flavoring
salt and pepper to taste
garlic salt to taste
2 cups fresh shrimp (boiled & peeled; measure after peeling) (NOTE: 2 (4½ ounce) cans shrimp, drained, may be substituted)
Melba toast

Cut small onion in half, place in food processor and chop finely. Remove and set aside. Add cream cheese, margarine and mayonnaise to processor and blend well. Add lemon juice, seasonings, flavorings, shrimp and onion. Run processor just long enough to mix well and to chop shrimp; do not overblend at this stage. Chill for at least 2 hours. Remove from refrigerator and allow to soften at room temperature for 30 minutes. Serve spread on small rounds of bread or Melba toast. (Freezes well in covered container. Thaw overnight in refrigerator, then bring to room temperature as above.)

Bacon Surprise

8 fresh oysters (reserve liquor)
4 thin slices bacon, halved
2 slices hot toast, buttered (each cut in 4 squares)

In a saucepan simmer the oysters in their own liquor over low heat for 4 minutes and drain them. Wrap each oyster with a piece of bacon and secure the bacon with toothpicks. Place the oysters under a hot broiler, or grill them over charcoal until the bacon is crisp. Serve the oysters on squares of hot buttered toast. Serves 4.

Can be used as an hors d'oeuvre if small patty shells are used.
Especially attractive in a chafing dish surrounded by patty shells

Oyster Patties

½ cup butter
1 large onion, chopped
4 ribs celery, chopped
1 bunch green onions, chopped
2 cloves garlic, chopped
¼ cup chopped parsley
2 pints oysters (reserve liquor), chopped
Salt and pepper to taste
1 teaspoon Worcestershire sauce
Cayenne to taste
3 cups thick White Sauce (see Index)
1 dozen large patty shells

In a heavy saucepan melt the butter over medium heat. Add the
onion, celery, green onion, garlic, and parsley and sauté until limp
and translucent. Add the oysters and cook until the oysters are curled.
Add the salt, pepper, Worcestershire sauce, and cayenne. In
another saucepan make a thick White Sauce. Add the White Sauce to
the oyster mixture gradually. Thin the mixture with oyster liquor if
necessary. Heat the patty shells at 350°F until they are piping
hot. Fill the shells with the hot oyster mixture and serve them
immediately. Serves 12.

Spicy Cheese Straws

1 cup butter
½ pound sharp Cheddar cheese, grated
2 cups flour
1½ teaspoons red pepper

In a large bowl combine the butter and cheese. Add the flour
which has been sifted with the pepper, mix together with your hands,
and work the mixture into a smooth dough. Press the dough
through a cookie press into strips. Bake the straws at 325°F on an
ungreased cookie sheet on the bottom rack of the oven for 5
minutes. REDUCE OVEN TEMPERATURE to 300°F, move
the pan up to the middle rack, and continue cooking for 5 minutes.
Turn the oven OFF and allow the straws to stay in the oven
for 2 to 3 minutes, or as long as possible without browning. DO
NOT BROWN. Bake only 1 pan at a time so the oven heat can
circulate freely. Remove the straws from the pan immediately,
transfer them to unwaxed paper, and sprinkle them generously with
salt. Cool the straws and store them in a tin can. Makes 36.
VARIATION: Dough may be rolled out, cut with a cookie or
biscuit cutter, and a pecan placed on top.

Cheese Pastries

1½ cups sifted flour
1 cup grated provolone or Cheddar cheese
½ cup butter or margarine
3 tablespoons milk
1 egg, slightly beaten

In a bowl combine the flour and cheese and cut in the butter. Stir in the milk until it is well blended. Divide the dough into 24 pieces. Roll each piece into a 5-inch strip. Shape the strips into wreaths on an ungreased cookie sheet. Brush the tops of the pastries with the egg. Bake the pastries for 20 to 25 minutes at 300°F, or until they are lightly browned. Makes 24.

Artichoke Squares

1½ (8 ounce) cans refrigerated crescent dinner rolls
4 tablespoons margarine
½ cup finely chopped onion
1 tablespoon flour
½ cup half-and-half cream
½ cup sour cream
4 eggs, beaten
1 teaspoon salt
½ teaspoon pepper
¼ teaspoon dill weed
¼ teaspoon nutmeg
1 tablespoon chopped parsley
2 (9 ounce) cans artichoke hearts, cut in small pieces
1 cup grated Cheddar cheese, firmly packed
1 cup grated Swiss cheese, firmly packed
½ cup grated Parmesan cheese

Unroll the pieces of dough and form a flat crust over the bottom and halfway up the sides of an 11"x13" pan. Bake the crust at 350°F for 7 minutes and flatten it down with a spoon. Return the crust to the oven for 5 minutes, remove it, and allow it to cool. In a saucepan melt the margarine. Add the onion and cook until it is tender. Stir in the flour, add the half-and-half, and cook the mixture until it has thickened. In a bowl combine the sour cream, eggs, salt, pepper, dill weed, nutmeg, and parsley. Add this mixture to the onion mixture and mix well. Place a layer of artichoke hearts in the bottom of the pie shell and sprinkle the Cheddar cheese on top. Add another layer of artichokes and top them with the Swiss cheese. Pour the egg mixture over the artichokes and cheese. Top the dish with Parmesan cheese and bake at 325°F for 45 minutes. Cool the dish completely before cutting it. To serve as hors d'oeuvres, cut in small bite-size squares. To serve as an appetizer, cut in 2-inch squares. Serves 12.

Canapé Royale

PASTRY:
3 (3 ounce) packages cream cheese
1½ cups margarine
3 cups sifted flour
BEEF FILLING:
1 pound ground beef
1 onion, minced
1 clove garlic, minced
Prepared beef stew seasoning mix
¼ cup red wine
1 (4 ounce) can chopped mushrooms
Salt and pepper to taste
½ cup water
Paprika

In a bowl blend together the cream cheese, margarine, and flour.
Chill the pastry. In a skillet brown the beef, add the onion, and sauté
until soft. Add the garlic, seasoning mix, wine, mushrooms,
salt, pepper, and water. Simmer the mixture until it is thick
and the meat is well done. Roll the dough out thin on a
well-floured surface. Work with only ¼ of the dough at a time,
keeping the remainder chilled. Cut the dough in 2-inch rounds.
Place ½ teaspoon of beef filling in each round and fold it over.
Press the edges with a fork and prick the pastry. Sprinkle the
canapés with paprika and bake them at 400°F for 20 minutes.
Makes 200.

Crab Meat Mornay

1 small bunch green onions, chopped
⅓ cup chopped parsley
½ cup butter, melted
2 tablespoons flour
1 pint half-and-half cream
½ pound Swiss cheese, grated
1 tablespoon sherry
Red pepper to taste
Salt to taste
1 pound white crab meat
Melba rounds

In a heavy pot sauté the green onion and parsley in the butter.
Blend in the flour, cream, and cheese, stirring, until the cheese
is melted. Add the sherry, pepper, and salt and gently fold in
the crab meat. Serve the dish hot in a chafing dish with Melba
rounds or in individual ramekins.

Cover Brie cheese with brown sugar and chopped pecans.
Broil just until the brown sugar melts. Serve with crackers.

Lumpia

½ pound ground pork
½ pound raw shrimp, finely chopped
½ cup finely chopped mushrooms
¼ cup finely chopped water chestnuts
2 tablespoons chives
½ teaspoon salt
⅛ teaspoon pepper
1 egg yolk
1 tablespoon soy sauce
36 Won Ton wrappers
1 tablespoon cornstarch
½ cup water
Cooking oil

In a bowl thoroughly combine the first 9 ingredients. Place 1 tablespoon of the mixture on each wrapper. Mix the cornstarch with the water, brush the mixture on the edges of the wrappers, and fold the wrappers over the filling. The cornstarch acts as a glue. Deep fry the lumpia until they are golden brown and drain them well. You may prefry the lumpia and reheat them at 400°F for 10 minutes. Serve with Lumpia Dip. Makes 36.

LUMPIA DIP:
1 cup pineapple juice plus 1 teaspoon vinegar
2 tablespoons ketchup
1 tablespoon brown sugar
1 tablespoon cornstarch
1 tablespoon chili sauce

In a saucepan combine the sauce ingredients and heat the sauce over low heat until it is thick and clear. Serve the dipping sauce hot.

Hot Crab Spread

1 tablespoon milk
1 (8 ounce) package cream cheese (at room temperature)
1 (8 ounce) can flaked crab meat
2 tablespoons minced green onion
½ teaspoon horseradish
¼ teaspoon salt
Pepper to taste
Dash of Tabasco sauce
⅓ cup sliced almonds, toasted
Crackers

In a bowl blend together the milk and cream cheese. Mix in the next 6 ingredients. Transfer the mixture to an ovenproof dish and sprinkle the top with the almonds. Bake the dish at 350°F until the mixture bubbles. Serve the spread with crackers. Makes 1 pint.

Oysters Rockefeller Hors d'Oeuvre

4 ribs celery, chopped
4 bunches green onions, chopped
3 large cloves garlic, chopped
1¼ cups butter, melted
2 (10 ounce) packages frozen chopped spinach, cooked until thawed and drained
4 tablespoons chopped parsley
2 teaspoons salt
⅛ teaspoon cayenne
½ teaspoon ground anise seed
1 tablespoon lemon juice
3 tablespoons Worcestershire sauce
3 tablespoons ketchup
2 teaspoons anchovy paste
½-1 cup bread crumbs
4 dozen oysters, drained
Crackers

In a large heavy saucepan or Dutch oven sauté the celery, green onion, and garlic in the butter until transparent. Remove the mixture from the heat, add the next 9 ingredients, and mix well. Purée the mixture, ¼ at a time, in a blender. Mix all of the purée together and add the bread crumbs until the mixture is of medium consistency. Place the oysters in a single layer in a shallow pan and bake them at 400°F for 5 to 6 minutes, or until the edges are just curled. Using a slotted spoon transfer the oysters to a chafing dish and combine them with the heated sauce. Serve the dish with crackers.

Stuffed Mushrooms

12 large mushrooms
2 tablespoons butter
1 medium onion, chopped
¼ cup finely chopped bell pepper
1 clove garlic, minced
12 crackers, crushed
½ cup diced pepperoni sausage
3 tablespoons grated Parmesan cheese
1 tablespoon chopped parsley
½ teaspoon salt
¼ teaspoon oregano
Pepper to taste
⅓ cup chicken broth

Remove the stems from the mushrooms and chop them. In a skillet melt the butter and sauté the stems, onion, bell pepper, and garlic until limp. Add the cracker crumbs, pepperoni, cheese, and seasonings. Add enough of the chicken broth to moisten the mixture to stuffing consistency. Fill the mushroom caps with the mixture. Place the stuffed mushrooms in a shallow baking dish with ¼-inch water and bake them, uncovered, at 325°F for 25 minutes. Serves 6.

Lettuce Package Appetizer

1 large head iceberg lettuce
10 fresh mushrooms, finely chopped
½ cup finely diced bamboo shoots
16 water chestnuts, finely diced
1 pound coarsely ground pork
1 egg, lightly beaten
2 tablespoons soy sauce
4 teaspoons cornstarch
2 tablespoons dry sherry
1½ teaspoons sugar
¼ teaspoon MSG
1 teaspoon salt
½ cup chicken stock
3½ tablespoons cooking oil
1 cup finely diced celery

Split the lettuce in half with a knife. Place the largest leaves on a platter. In a bowl combine the mushrooms, bamboo shoots, and water chestnuts. In another bowl combine the pork, egg, soy sauce, and 3 teaspoons of the cornstarch. In a small bowl mix together the sherry, sugar, MSG, and salt. In a measuring cup blend the remaining cornstarch with ¼ cup of the chicken stock. Heat 2 tablespoons of the oil in a wok or on high heat in an electric skillet. When the oil is nearly smoking, add the pork mixture, stirring quickly, to separate the bits of pork until it is cooked. Add the mushroom mixture, stirring, for 2 minutes. Add the sherry and sugar mixture and the remaining chicken stock, stirring, for 15 seconds. Blend the cornstarch mixture into the pork mixture, stirring rapidly. Mix in the celery. Stir in the remaining oil. Serve the pork mixture in a chafing dish. Place a spoonful of the mixture on a lettuce leaf, roll it, and secure it with a toothpick. Serves 8.

Tipsy Weiners

1½ pounds weiners
1½ pounds smoked sausage
1 cup brown sugar
1 cup bourbon
1 cup chili sauce

Slice the weiners and sausage in 1-inch pieces, place them in a 2-quart casserole, and add the remaining ingredients. Bake the dish, uncovered, at 350°F for 3 hours. Stir the mixture well after the first hour and again after the second hour. Provide toothpicks for serving. Serves 15-20.

Hors d'oeuvres are usually served with cocktails.

Appetizers

Delicious! May be served as a party dip or as an entrée

Crawfish Elegante

1 pound crawfish tails or 1 pound raw peeled shrimp
½ cup margarine
1 bunch green onions, chopped
½ cup chopped parsley
3 tablespoons flour
1 pint half-and-half cream
3 tablespoons sherry
Salt and red pepper to taste

In a skillet sauté the crawfish in ¼ cup of the margarine for 10 minutes. In another skillet sauté the green onion and parsley in the remaining margarine and blend in the flour. Gradually add the cream, stirring constantly, to make a thick sauce. Add the sherry, crawfish, salt, and red pepper.

Stuffed Artichoke Hearts

2 (14 ounce) cans artichoke hearts, drained
1½ cups Italian bread crumbs
3-4 cloves garlic, crushed
Salt and pepper to taste
1½ cups grated Parmesan cheese
¼ cup olive oil
½ cup Italian salad dressing
3 tablespoons lemon juice
Paprika

Remove the pulp from the center of the artichoke hearts and cut each in half. In a bowl combine the bread crumbs, garlic, salt, pepper, and cheese. Moisten the mixture with olive oil, salad dressing, and lemon juice. Stuff the artichoke hearts with the mixture. Place the hearts in a greased baking dish and sprinkle them with paprika. Bake the dish at 350°F for 15 minutes.

Artichoke Bits

1 (14 ounce) can artichoke hearts, drained
2 lemons
½ cup olive oil
1 cup seasoned bread crumbs

Quarter the artichoke hearts and squeeze the lemon juice over them. Dip them in the olive oil and roll them in the bread crumbs. Bake at 400°F on a greased cookie sheet for 10 to 15 minutes. Makes 32.

Artichoke Balls

2-3 cloves garlic, mashed
6 tablespoons olive oil
1 (14 ounce) can artichoke hearts, drained and mashed
2 eggs, well beaten
1½ cups seasoned bread crumbs
1 cup Parmesan or Romano cheese
Salt and pepper to taste

In a skillet sauté the garlic in the olive oil. Add the artichoke hearts and simmer for 2 minutes. Fold in the eggs and simmer for 2 minutes. Add the bread crumbs and cook for 2 minutes. Remove the mixture from the heat, add the cheese, mix well, and cool. When the mixture is cool, form it into bite-size balls. Roll the balls in the bread crumbs and bake them at 350°F for 10 minutes. Makes 24.

Pickled Shrimp

SAUCE:
1½ cups vegetable oil
2 teaspoons salt
¾ cup vinegar
3 teaspoons celery salt
2½ tablespoons capers with sauce
Dash of Tabasco sauce
1 onion, sliced in rings
8 bay leaves
TO BOIL SHRIMP:
3 quarts water, boiling
2½ pounds raw shrimp, peeled and deveined
3 teaspoons salt
¾ cup sliced celery
¼ cup pickling spices or 2 bags crab boil

In a bowl combine the sauce ingredients and refrigerate the mixture. To the boiling water add the shrimp, salt, celery, and pickling spices and cook for 2 minutes after the water returns to a boil. Drain the shrimp and rinse them with cold water. In a glass container combine the shrimp and sauce. Refrigerate the mixture for 24 to 30 hours. Remove the shrimp from the marinade to serve. Serves 10-12.

Cream ¼ cup butter with anchovy butter, chives, capers, chili sauce, garlic, horseradish, Parmesan cheese, parsley, or tarragon for a quick, easy spread for crackers.

Hot Chili Roll

½ pound Velveeta cheese (at room temperature)
1 (3 ounce) package cream cheese (at room temperature)
2 cloves garlic, minced
¼ teaspoon onion juice
Red pepper to taste
¼ teaspoon salt
¼ teaspoon Worcestershire sauce
¾ cup finely chopped pecans
Chili powder

In a bowl cream together the Velveeta and cream cheese. Add the next 5 ingredients and mix well. Stir in the pecans. Shape the mixture into 4-inch long rolls, approximately 1½ inches in diameter, and roll them in chili powder. Wrap the rolls in plastic wrap and chill them for 1 hour. Makes 3-4 rolls.

Cold Pepper Steak

1 (4 pound) eye of round or flank steak
Garlic powder to taste
1 (1.87 ounce) bottle peppercorns
MARINADE:
½ cup soy sauce
1 (12 ounce) bottle cooking sherry
¼ cup Worcestershire sauce
¼ cup corn oil

Generously cover the meat with garlic powder. With a small paring knife pierce the entire surface of the meat and stuff each hole with a peppercorn. Prepare the marinade. Place the meat in a deep dish and pour the marinade over it. Refrigerate the meat in the marinade for 24 hours, turning periodically. Remove the meat from the refrigerator and allow it to come to room temperature. Place the meat and the marinade in a roasting pan. Bake the meat at 500°F, uncovered, for 30 minutes. REDUCE OVEN TEMPERATURE to 350°F and continue cooking, basting occasionally, for 1½ hours. Remove the meat from the oven, allow it to cool to room temperature, and refrigerate it. Serve the meat thinly sliced.

Bleu Cheese Ball

1 (8 ounce) package cream cheese (at room temperature)
4 ounces bleu cheese (at room temperature)
6 ounces sharp Cheddar cheese, grated (at room temperature)
1 small onion, minced
1 tablespoon Worcestershire sauce
¾ cup shopped walnuts or pecans
Parsley sprigs

In a bowl cream together the cheeses. Add the onion and Worcestershire sauce and mix well. Shape the mixture into a ball, roll it in the nuts, and chill it thoroughly. Serve the cheese ball garnished with parsley sprigs.

Use a firm fish such as trout, redfish, or drum

Ceviche

(Marinated Raw Fish)

2 pounds fish fillet, cut in bite-size pieces
2 cups lime juice
1 large onion, minced
20 pitted green Spanish olives
3 ripe tomatoes, peeled, seeded, and minced
1 cup tomato juice
½ cup olive oil
½ cup water
½ cup ketchup
2 teaspoons salt
1 teaspoon oregano
1 teaspoon Tabasco sauce

In a glass container marinate the fish in the lime juice for
3 hours. This "cooks" the fish. To serve the fish, drain
off the lime juice and add the remaining ingredients. Serves 20.

Marinated Mushrooms

⅔ cup olive oil
⅓ cup wine vinegar
1 tablespoon Worcestershire sauce
1 teaspoon lemon juice
1 tablespoon salt
1 teaspoon Tabasco sauce
8 cloves garlic, crushed
Pepper to taste
4 (4 ounce) cans whole button mushrooms, drained

In a 1-quart jar combine all of the ingredients. Allow the
mushrooms to marinate for 3 weeks, shaking the jar gently every
few days.

Tuna and Anchovy Pâté

1 (7 ounce) can tuna
1 (2 ounce) can flat anchovy fillets, chopped
6 tablespoons butter or margarine, melted
2 tablespoons lemon juice
Pepper to taste

In a bowl thoroughly combine all of the ingredients. In a
blender process the mixture until it is smooth, switching the blender
on and off, and pushing the mixture down. Refrigerate the pâté for
24 hours in a 1-pint covered dish. Serves 4.

Marinated Artichoke Ball

1 (14 ounce) can artichoke hearts, drained and chopped
1 (6 ounce) jar marinated artichokes (reserve liquid), chopped
3 tablespoons grated Parmesan cheese
1 cup seasoned bread crumbs
1 egg, beaten
Cocktail crackers

In a bowl combine the artichoke hearts, marinated artichokes, and liquid. Add the cheese, bread crumbs, and egg and mix the ingredients by hand until they are well blended. Form the mixture into a ball and chill it. Serve the artichoke ball on an attractive tray surrounded by cocktail crackers.

Also good served on romaine lettuce as a salad

Caponata

2 medium eggplants
½ cup olive oil
2 large onions, chopped
1½ cups sliced celery
2 bell peppers, cut in chunks
2 cloves garlic, minced
2½ pounds tomatoes, peeled, seeded, and diced
⅓ cup red wine vinegar
2 tablespoons each salt, sugar, and basil
3 tablespoons tomato paste
½ cup chopped parsley
1 teaspoon pepper
¾ cup sliced stuffed olives
French or Italian bread, sliced
OPTIONAL:
4 tablespoons capers, drained
2 carrots, thinly sliced
2-3 zucchini, sliced

Cut the unpeeled eggplant in 2-inch cubes. Heat the olive oil in a 6-quart enameled cast iron casserole or Dutch oven. Add the eggplant and onion and sauté for 5 minutes. Add the remaining ingredients except the bread and stir gently. Simmer the mixture, covered, for 1½ hours. Serve the dish at room temperature with slices of French or Italian bread.

Cream ½ cup butter with 2 tablespoons prepared mustard to make mustard butter. Spread toast rounds with mustard butter and top with caviar.

Chipped Beef Ball

1 (8 ounce) package cream cheese (at room temperature)
1 (2½ ounce) jar dried beef, finely chopped
3 green onion tops, finely chopped
2 tablespoons pickle relish
Crackers

In a bowl cream together the cream cheese and ½ of the chipped beef. Add the green onion and pickle relish and mix well. Chill the mixture for 1 hour in a round container. Remove the ball from the container and roll it in the remainder of the chipped beef. Allow the ball to stand at room temperature for 30 minutes. Serve the beef ball with crackers.

Cheese Ball

2 (8 ounce) packages cream cheese
1 (8 ounce) Gouda cheese
1 pound muenster cheese
1 pound Swiss cheese
1 pound American cheese
½ cup grated onion
Chopped pecans

Grate all of the cheeses into a bowl and mix them together by hand very well. Add the onion and pecans. Shape the mixture into a ball and refrigerate it, covered.

Chopped Liver

1 pound chicken livers
2 tablespoons shortening
1 large onion, sliced
3 hard-boiled eggs
1 tablespoon chicken fat, melted
Salt to taste

In a skillet sauté the livers in the shortening. Remove the livers, add the onion, and sauté until soft. In a bowl combine the pan drippings, onion, liver, and eggs. Grind the mixture in a meat grinder fitted with the fine blade or in a food processor fitted with the chopping blade. Repeat the process until the mixture becomes very pasty. Add the chicken fat and salt. Serve the liver at room temperature or chilled. Serves 15-20.

Completely cover cream cheese with Pickapeppa sauce and serve with crackers.

Shrimp Mold

1½ envelopes unflavored gelatin
¼ cup water
1 (10½ ounce) can tomato soup
1 (8 ounce) package cream cheese, quartered
2 cups cooked shrimp, chopped
1 cup mayonnaise
1 teaspoon Chinese mustard
Salt and pepper to taste
¾ cup finely chopped celery
¾ cup finely chopped onion
½ cup finely chopped bell pepper
Crackers

In a small bowl dissolve the gelatin in the cold water. In a saucepan bring the soup to a boil and add the cream cheese, stirring, until the cheese is melted. Remove the mixture from the heat and add the gelatin. Add the next 7 ingredients and mix thoroughly. Pour the mixture into a 2-quart mold and refrigerate it until it is firm, preferably overnight. Serve the dish with crackers. Serves 30-40.

Makes a delicious salad or a spread served with crackers

Broccoli Ring

1 (10 ounce) package frozen chopped broccoli
1 envelope unflavored gelatin
½ cup water
1 (10½ ounce) can condensed chicken broth
⅔ cup mayonnaise
⅓ cup sour cream
1 tablespoon minced onion
1 tablespoon lemon juice
3 hard-boiled eggs, chopped

Cook the broccoli, drain it, and chop it finer, if desired. In a medium saucepan soften the gelatin in the water, add the broth and heat the mixture, stirring, to dissolve the gelatin. Add the mayonnaise, sour cream, onion, and lemon juice and heat the mixture until it is smooth. Chill the mixture until it is partially set. Fold the eggs and broccoli into the gelatin mixture and turn it into a lightly oiled 1-quart ring mold. Chill the mold for 4 hours.

Fill 1 lettuce leaf with any savory spread, roll, and fasten with a toothpick, chill thoroughly, and slice in ½-inch pieces.

Curried Sherry Pâté

1 (8 ounce) package cream cheese (at room temperature)
1 cup grated Cheddar cheese
½ teaspoon curry powder
½ teaspoon garlic powder
¼ teaspoon salt
4 teaspoons sherry
1 (9 ounce) jar Major Grey's chutney
½ bunch green onions, chopped
Unflavored crackers

In a bowl blend together the first 6 ingredients thoroughly by hand. Form the mixture into a flat bottomed round shape on an attractive serving plate. Chill the pâté for 1 hour, cover it with the chutney, and top it with the green onion. Serve the pâté with crackers.

Mushroom Pâté

1 pound fresh mushrooms, finely chopped
¼ cup margarine
⅓ cup minced onion
⅓ cup finely chopped celery
1 (3 ounce) package cream cheese
2 eggs, beaten until creamy
¾ cup dry bread crumbs
1 teaspoon salt
¼ teaspoon each basil, rosemary, oregano, thyme, marjoram, and pepper
1 teaspoon Worcestershire sauce
¼ teaspoon Tabasco sauce
1 bell pepper, sliced in rings
1 (2 ounce) jar pimiento-stuffed olives, sliced
Crackers

In a bowl blend together the first 11 ingredients. Bake the pâté in a foil-lined buttered pan, covered with foil, at 400°F for 1½ hours. Garnish the pâté with pepper rings and olives and serve it at room temperature with crackers.

Tangy Cauliflower Dip

1 cup mayonnaise
1 (8 ounce) carton sour cream
2 teaspoons celery seed
1 (0.6 ounce) package garlic salad dressing mix
Cauliflower florets

In a bowl combine the first 4 ingredients. Refrigerate the dip for 24 hours. Serve the dip with fresh cauliflower florets. Makes 1 pint.

Crab Pâté

1 (16 ounce) can lump crab meat (reserve liquid)
1 teaspoon unflavored gelatin
2 tablespoons chili sauce
½ cup chopped celery
1 cup chopped green onion
2 teaspoons chopped parsley
½ teaspoon Tabasco sauce
½-1 cup mayonnaise
Crackers

In a saucepan heat the crab liquid. Stir in the gelatin until it is dissolved. Stir in the remaining ingredients, starting with ½ cup mayonnaise and adding more if needed. Serve the pâté chilled with crackers.

Shrimp Dip

1 (8 ounce) package cream cheese (at room temperature)
1 lemon, juiced
2 pounds Boiled Shrimp (see Index), peeled, deveined, and coarsely ground
10 green onions, minced
1 cup mayonnaise
Salt and pepper to taste
Worcestershire sauce to taste
Tabasco sauce to taste

In a bowl soften the cream cheese with the lemon juice. Add the shrimp, green onion, and mayonnaise. Season the mixture with the remaining ingredients and mix well. Refrigerate the dip for 2 hours.

Raw Vegetable Dip

1½ cups mayonnaise
⅔ cup chili sauce
1½ tablespoons finely chopped parsley
1½ tablespoons chopped chives or green onion
Salt and pepper to taste
½ teaspoon sugar
Tabasco sauce to taste
Assorted crisp vegetables: celery, carrots, cucumbers, cauliflower

In a bowl or jar combine the first 4 ingredients. Add the salt, pepper, sugar, and Tabasco sauce. Serve the dip with raw vegetables. Makes 2½ cups.

Top cream cheese with pepper jelly as a cracker spread.

Smoked Oyster Dip

1 (8 ounce) package cream cheese (at room temperature)
1 (4 ounce) can chopped black olives, drained
2 (3¾ ounce) cans smoked oysters, drained and chopped
1½ cups mayonnaise
7 dashes Tabasco sauce
3 teaspoons lemon juice
Melba toast or wheat thins

In a bowl combine the first 6 ingredients and chill the dip. Serve the dip with Melba toast or wheat thins. Makes 2 cups.

Guacamole Dip

1 large ripe avocado, peeled and pitted
1 lemon, juiced
½ small white onion, minced
1 clove garlic, pressed
½ teaspoon Tabasco sauce
¼ teaspoon salt
1 medium ripe tomato, peeled
¼ cup mayonnaise

In a bowl mash the first 7 ingredients together until the mixture is smooth and fold in the mayonnaise.

Roasted Pecans

3 cups shelled pecans
1 tablespoon Worcestershire sauce
¼ cup margarine
Seasoned salt to taste

Melt the margarine in a shallow pan. Add the Worcestershire sauce and stir in the pecans, coating them thoroughly with the margarine. Roast the pecans at 275°F on a cookie sheet for 45 minutes, or until the desired crispness is reached, being careful not to scorch them. Stir the pecans every 15 minutes. Transfer the pecans to absorbent paper towels to drain and salt them. When they are cool, store them in an airtight container. Makes 3 cups.

Sausage Cheese Balls

1 pound bulk hot sausage
3 cups biscuit mix
1 pound sharp Cheddar cheese, grated (at room temperature)

In a bowl combine the ingredients by hand. Roll the mixture into bite-size balls. At this point, the cheese balls may be frozen to be baked later. Bake the cheese balls at 300°F on ungreased cookie sheets for 20 to 25 minutes. Cool the cheese balls on a rack. Makes 120 walnut-size balls.

Use in cocktails such as Old Fashioneds and Whiskey Sours

Bourbon Orange Slices

4 seedless oranges
2½ cups sugar
1 cup water
1 cup light corn syrup
1 lemon, juiced
⅓ cup bourbon

Wash the oranges and cut them in ½-inch slices. Cut each slice in half. Combine the sugar, water, corn syrup, and lemon juice. Bring the mixture to a boil and boil it rapidly for 5 minutes. Add the orange slices and simmer them slowly for 5 minutes without stirring. Transfer the orange slices to a jar, arranging them in overlapping layers. Stir the bourbon into the syrup and spoon the syrup over the orange slices, covering them completely. Seal the jar and store it in the refrigerator.

Simple Syrup

1 cup sugar
1 cup boiling water

Fill a 1-pint jar approximately ½ full of sugar. Add the boiling water and stir the mixture quickly until it is clear. When the syrup is cool, store in the refrigerator. Makes 1 pint.

Storyville Surprise

1 jigger rum
1 jigger vodka
1 jigger Simple Syrup
2 jiggers pineapple juice
½ teaspoon lemon juice
Pineapple chunks
Maraschino cherries

Pour all of the liquid ingredients over crushed ice and shake well. Garnish the cocktails with pineapple chunks and cherries. Serves 4.

When storing large quantities of ice for a party, don't overlook using your washing machine.

Margaritas

6 large lemons, juiced
¾ cup triple sec
1 cup tequila
¼ cup water
8 ice cubes, crushed

Blend all of the ingredients in a blender with crushed ice.
Serve each cocktail in a 4-ounce wine glass which has been
dampened on the rim and rubbed across a plate of salt. Serves 10.

Dream Sicle

1 ounce half-and-half cream or vanilla ice cream
1 ounce orange juice
¾ ounce Bols crème de noyaux
2 ice cubes, cracked

Place all of the ingredients in a blender and process, covered,
at frappé for a few seconds. Strain the mixture into a glass.
Serves 1.

Old Fashioned

2 ounces bourbon
1 tablespoon Simple Syrup (see Index)
1 dash bitters
1 teaspoon maraschino cherry juice
Orange slices
Cherries

Combine the first 4 ingredients and stir well. Add ice
cubes. Garnish the cocktail with an orange slice and a cherry.
Serves 1.

Whiskey Sour

1 (6 ounce) can frozen lemonade
6 ounces bourbon
1 (10 ounce) can beer
Cherries
Orange slices

In a shaker combine the first 3 ingredients and serve over ice.
Garnish each drink with a cherry and an orange slice. Serves 6.

Daiquiri

1½ ounces light rum
¾ tablespoon lime juice
1 teaspoon sugar

In a cocktail shaker combine all of the ingredients with cracked ice. Shake the mixture well and strain it into a chilled cocktail glass. Serves 1.

FROZEN DAIQUIRI:

In a blender combine the Daiquiri ingredients with 8 ounces of cracked ice. Process the mixture, covered, on high speed until the desired consistency is obtained. Serve the Daiquiri in a champagne glass. Serves 1.

FRUIT DAIQUIRI:

To the Daiquiri ingredients blend in 2 ounces of fruit before adding the ice. Bananas, peaches, strawberries, apricots, pineapple, or cherries may be used. If sweetened fruit is used, omit the sugar. Serve the Daiquiri in a champagne glass. Serves 1.

Absinthe Frappé

1½ ounces absinthe
2 dashes anisette or Simple Syrup (see Index)
Soda or water

Fill an 8-ounce highball glass with shaved ice and add the absinthe and anisette. Slowly add the soda and stir vigorously until the outside of the glass becomes frosted. Serves 1.

Chablis Cassis

4½ ounces Chablis wine, chilled
½ teaspoon crème de cassis
Lemon peel

Pour the Chablis into a champagne glass. Add the crème de cassis. To this mixture add a twist of lemon peel and stir gently. Serves 1.

Boiled and cooled water is essential for making a clear ice ring.

Piña Colada

1 ounce Coco Lopez concentrate
2 ounces pineapple juice
1 ounce rum
1 ounce half-and-half cream or vanilla ice cream
2 ice cubes, cracked

In a blender combine all of the ingredients and process, covered, at frappé for a few seconds. Strain the mixture into a glass. Serves 1.

Grasshopper

2 ounces green crème de menthe
2 ounces white crème de cacao
2 ounces heavy cream
4 ice cubes, cracked

In a blender combine all of the ingredients and process, covered, at frappé for a few seconds. Strain the mixture into glasses. Serves 2.

Pineapple Passion
(An after-dinner drink)

1 (13½ ounce) can pineapple tidbits
½ cup light rum
¼ cup lime juice
1 tablespoon sugar
1 teaspoon grenadine
6 ice cubes

In a blender combine the first 5 ingredients. Process the mixture, covered, on high until the pineapple is finely crushed. While the blender is running, add the ice cubes, 1 at a time. Serves 3-4.

Amaretto Sour

2 ounces amaretto
1 ounce Lemon Joy cocktail mix
1 ounce Simple Syrup (see Index)
4 ice cubes, cracked

In a blender combine all of the ingredients and process, covered, at frappé for a few seconds. Strain the mixture into glasses. Serves 2.

Gin Fizz "Ramos"

1 teaspoon confectioners' sugar
3 dashes orange flower water
1½ ounces gin
½ ounce fresh lemon juice
¼ ounce fresh lime juice
½ ounce egg white
2 ounces half-and-half cream

Fill a cocktail shaker with ice cubes until ⅓ full. Add all of the ingredients. Thoroughly shake the mixture, covered, to mix and blend all of the ingredients to a creamy, frothy smoothness. Strain the mixture into an 8-ounce highball glass. Serves 1.

Sazerac

1 teaspoon Simple Syrup (see Index)
1 dash Angostura bitters
2 dashes Peychaud bitters
1¼ ounces rye or bourbon whiskey
3 dashes absinthe
Lemon peel

In a cocktail shaker combine the first 4 ingredients. Put the absinthe in a chilled Old Fashioned glass and thoroughly coat the inside of the glass by twirling the absinthe. Discard the excess absinthe. With a cocktail spoon stir the ingredients that are in the shaker. DO NOT SHAKE. Strain the mixture into the chilled, coated glass and garnish it with a twist of lemon peel. Serves 1.

Bloody Mary

8 ounces tomato juice
1-1½ ounces vodka
1 teaspoon Pickapeppa sauce
1 teaspoon Worcestershire sauce
¼ teaspoon sugar
¼ teaspoon salt
1 lemon or lime, juiced
Dash of Tabasco sauce
2 celery sticks

In a cocktail shaker mix all of the ingredients except the celery. Pour the mixture into 8-ounce cocktail glasses ½ filled with ice. Garnish the Bloody Mary with a celery stick. Serves 2.

Mint Julep

2½ ounces bourbon

5 sprigs mint

½ ounce Simple Syrup (see Index)

In a mint julep glass combine the bourbon, 4 sprigs of the mint, and the Simple Syrup. Fill the glass with shaved ice and stir vigorously. Garnish the drink with the remaining sprig of mint and serve it with a short straw so that the aroma of mint will be savored while sipping. Serves 1.

Party Frozen Daiquiri

1 cup sugar

½ cup water

1 fifth light rum

1 (46 ounce) can pineapple juice

5 (10 ounce) bottles 7-Up

1 (6 ounce) can frozen orange juice

1 (6 ounce) can frozen limeade

2 tablespoons lemon juice

3 cups water

In a small saucepan mix the sugar and ½ cup water. Bring the mixture to a boil and continue boiling for 1 minute to make a syrup. Remove the syrup from heat. In a 1-gallon plastic container, which has a lid, mix the rum, pineapple juice, 7-UP, orange juice, limeade, lemon juice, and 3 cups water. Add the syrup and stir well. Freeze the mixture in the covered container for 24 hours, stirring at least 3 times. This procedure is essential in order for the liquid to be frozen in small crystals. Spoon the mixture into saucer champagne glasses.

Creole Creepers

1 fifth bourbon (reserve ½ cup)

1 pint gin

4 (6 ounce) cans frozen pink lemonade, thawed

2 (20 ounce) cans grapefruit juice

1 (20 ounce) can pineapple juice

3 tablespoons grenadine or honey

1 (9 ounce) jar maraschino cherries with stems (reserve juice)

In a large container combine the bourbon, gin, lemonade, grapefruit juice, pineapple juice, and grenadine. Pour the juice from the cherries into the mixture. Pour the reserved bourbon over the cherries remaining in the jar and marinate them for 24 hours. Serve the drink over crushed ice. Top each glass with a marinated cherry. Makes 1 gallon.

Beverages

Fantastic for a Saturday night fish fry

Swamp Water

1 pint peach brandy
1½ quarts brandy
1 pint rum
1½ quarts carbonated water
1 dozen lemons, juiced
1 (1 pound) box confectioners' sugar

In a punch bowl combine all of the ingredients and stir well.
Serve the punch over ice.

Sangría

2 quarts Burgundy wine
1 quart orange juice
3 lemons, juiced
5 limes, juiced
1 cup sugar (to taste)
1 quart club soda
Slices of orange, lemon, and lime

In a large container combine the wine, orange juice, lemon juice,
lime juice, and sugar. Chill the mixture thoroughly. Add the club
soda just before serving. Serve the Sangría in tall glasses over
ice garnished with slices of fruit. Makes 1 gallon.

When serving children, substitute club soda for champagne

Holiday Punch

2 (6 ounce) cans frozen orange juice
1 (6 ounce) can frozen lemonade concentrate
6 cups cold water
1 fifth champagne
1 (10 ounce) package frozen sliced strawberries, thawed

In a large container combine the orange juice, lemonade, and
water. Chill the mixture for 12 hours. Pour the combined juices
into a punch bowl. Add the champagne and stir the punch well. Serve
the punch with strawberries floating on the top. Serves 24.

Tomato-based drinks sparkle with a dash of lemon juice
or Tabasco. Mint compliments tea and most fruit-based
drinks. Nutmeg, cinnamon, and vanilla are welcome additions
to most milk-based drinks.

Cranberry-Apple Punch

3 quarts water

2 cups sugar

2 cups strong tea, cooled

2 (6 ounce) cans frozen lemonade concentrate, thawed

2 quarts cranberry juice cocktail

1 quart apple juice

2 cups orange juice

In a large pot or kettle heat the water and sugar to boiling, stirring constantly, until the sugar is dissolved. Cool the syrup thoroughly. Chill all of the ingredients. Just before serving, combine all of the ingredients in a large punch bowl. Serves 60.

Hot Spiced Apple Cider

6 cinnamon sticks

16 whole cloves

1 teaspoon allspice

3 medium oranges

3 quarts apple cider

¼ cup sugar

1 teaspoon aromatic bitters

1 cup rum

¼ teaspoon butter per cup (optional)

¼ teaspoon brown sugar per cup (optional)

Place the cinnamon sticks, 16 whole cloves, and allspice in cheesecloth and secure the cloth. Combine all of the ingredients in a saucepan and simmer the mixture, covered, for 10 minutes. Serve the cider in cups as it is, or place butter and brown sugar in the cups before ladling in the cider. Serves 12.

Hurricane Punch

1 (46 ounce) can Hawaiian punch

1 (12 ounce) can frozen orange juice

1 (6 ounce) can frozen lemonade

¾ cup sugar (optional)

4 ounces amber rum per glass

Orange slices

Maraschino cherries

In a large pitcher combine the punch, orange juice, lemonade, and sugar. Fill 16-ounce glasses with crushed ice and add 4 ounces of rum per glass. Fill the glasses with the punch mixture. Serve the drinks garnished with the orange slices and cherries.

Warm Cranberry Punch

1 quart fresh cranberries
4 quarts water
3 cups sugar
1 cup cinnamon candies
12 whole cloves
3 oranges, juiced
3 lemons, juiced

In a saucepan boil the cranberries in 1 quart of the water until they pop open. Strain the cranberries and discard them, reserving the liquid. In a separate pot boil together 3 quarts water, sugar, cinnamon candies, and cloves for 10 minutes. Strain the mixture and discard the cloves. Mix the cranberry liquid and sugar mixture together. Add the citrus juices and keep the punch warm, but do not allow it to boil. Serve the punch from a glass carafe. Serves 40.

Milk Punch

2 ounces cracked ice
1½ ounces bourbon
4 ounces half-and-half cream
1 teaspoon confectioners' sugar
Dash of vanilla
Nutmeg

In a cocktail shaker combine the first 5 ingredients. Shake the mixture for 20 to 30 seconds and strain it into an 8-ounce highball glass. Serve the punch topped with nutmeg. Serves 1.

After the Ball Eggnog

6 eggs, separated
1½ cups sugar
1 pint bourbon
1 quart whipping cream, whipped
Nutmeg

In a large bowl combine the egg yolks and sugar until the sugar is dissolved. Add ½ of the bourbon and blend well. Fold in the whipped cream. Beat the egg whites until they are stiff, but not dry, and fold them into the eggnog mixture. Refrigerate the eggnog overnight. Add the remaining bourbon the next morning. Serve the eggnog with nutmeg sprinkled on top. Makes ½ gallon.

Eggnog

1 quart eggnog ice cream

2 quarts eggnog

1 pint or more bourbon

1 pint whipping cream, whipped

Nutmeg (optional)

In a punch bowl combine the ice cream with 1 quart of the eggnog, stirring, until the ice cream is melted. Add the bourbon and slowly stir in the remainder of the eggnog. When ready to serve, fold in the whipped cream. Serve the eggnog sprinkled with nutmeg, if desired. Serves 10-12.

Irish Coffee

1 ounce Irish whiskey

1 tablespoon sugar

4 ounces coffee

Whipped cream

In a coffee cup or Irish coffee glass combine the first 3 ingredients and top the coffee with the whipped cream. Serves 1.

Creole Dripped Coffee

A French drip coffee pot is essential in making dripped coffee, Creole-style. Traditionally coffee and chicory is used in the homes and coffee stands of New Orleans. If you cannot obtain coffee and chicory, use the darkest roast pure coffee available, finely ground. Have boiling water ready. Allow 2 heaping tablespoons of coffee and chicory for each cup of water. Every 2 or 3 minutes, pour 2 tablespoons of the boiling water over the grounds until the desired quantity of coffee is made.

CAFÉ AU LAIT:

Into a coffee cup pour together ½ cup boiling milk and ½ cup hot strong coffee. This is the coffee that is so popular at the coffee stands in New Orleans.

Kahlúa

4 cups sugar
2 ounces instant coffee
2 cups boiling water
1 vanilla bean, cut up
1 fifth brandy

In a dark 1-gallon jug or jar combine the sugar, coffee, and boiling water. Add the vanilla bean and brandy. Let the Kahlúa stand, covered, for 1 month. At the end of the month, pour the Kahlúa off carefully leaving the residue in the bottom of the container to be discarded.

Cherry Bounce

½ gallon wild black cherries
1 fifth straight bourbon
2 fifths vodka
2 pounds sugar

Wash the cherries and remove their stems. In a wide-mouth gallon jar combine the cherries with the remaining ingredients. Cover the top of the jar with cheesecloth. Store the jar in a cool, dark place for 6 months. At the end of that time, squeeze the cherries and pour the mixture through a strainer to remove the seeds. Bottle the cordial in pint jars.

SOUPS AND GUMBOS

Soups and gumbos are a very useful element in cooking.
They are easy to make, inexpensive, and versatile.
Clear soups are excellent appetizers. Cold soups are
just right for a summer evening. A hot, thick soup or
a salad, makes an excellent simple supper. Many soups
improve with age and cooking, and can be kept on
hand for busy days, unexpected company, or a
quick hot lunch. Best of all, they make good use of
otherwise perplexing leftovers.

31

SOUPS AND GUMBOS

The romantic streets of the French Quarter of New Orleans, as those of Paris, have their beauty enhanced by rain falling on cobblestones, greenery and street lights.

Gazpacho

1 large bell pepper, chopped
2 cucumbers, peeled, seeded, and chopped
8 ripe tomatoes, peeled and mashed
3 teaspoons salt
1½ teaspoons paprika
1 clove garlic, peeled and mashed
1 small mild onion, peeled and chopped
¼ cup olive oil
9 tablespoons wine vinegar
1½ cups cold tomato juice

Blend all of the ingredients in a blender or food processor.
Run the blender until the vegetables are smoothly
blended. Chill until very cold. Pour into chilled
bouillon cups. May be served with additional chopped
cucumbers, tomatoes, bell pepper, and croutons. Serves 6-8.

Onion Soup

8 tablespoons butter
2 pounds white onions, thinly sliced
3 tablespoons flour
8 cups beef stock
Salt and pepper to taste
8 (1-inch) slices French bread
Garlic butter
Parmesan cheese, grated

In a 6-quart soup kettle melt the butter and stir in the
onion. Cook, uncovered, over low heat for 20 to 30
minutes, or until the onion is a rich golden brown. Sprinkle
the flour over the onion and cook, stirring, for 2 to 3
minutes. Remove from the heat. In a saucepan heat the beef
stock. Gradually stir the stock into the onion mixture.
Simmer the soup for 30 to 40 minutes. Add the salt and
pepper. Place the slices of French bread on a cookie
sheet and bake at 350°F for 15 minutes. With a pastry
brush, lightly coat each side of the bread with the
garlic butter and return it to the oven for 15 minutes.
Just before serving, pour the soup into individual
oven-proof bowls. Top the soup with a bread slice and
sprinkle heavily with the Parmesan cheese. Brown under
the broiler. Serves 8.

Cream of Broccoli Soup

1 medium onion, chopped
3 tablespoons butter
1 (10 ounce) package broccoli, cooked and drained
4 tablespoons chopped parsley
4 tablespoons flour
2 cups chicken broth (at room temperature)
2 cups half-and-half cream (at room temperature)
1 teaspoon salt
2 tablespoons lemon juice
⅛ teaspoon nutmeg
Lemon-pepper, garlic salt, and cayenne to taste
Parsley, chopped

In a heavy pot sauté the onion in butter until limp. Add the broccoli and parsley and simmer for about 3 minutes, stirring, to prevent scorching. Sprinkle the mixture with the flour and stir until the flour is absorbed, approximately 2 minutes. Transfer the mixture to a blender. Add enough chicken broth to fill blender to ¾ capacity and blend until liquified. Return the blended mixture to the pan and add the remaining liquids and the seasonings. Simmer the soup for 5 minutes. Serve hot, garnished with parsley. Serves 6.

Cream of Spinach Soup

1 medium onion, chopped
2 tablespoons butter
1 (10 ounce) package frozen spinach, thawed
5 cups chicken broth
⅓ cup uncooked rice
2 egg yolks
½ cup heavy cream
⅛ teaspoon grated nutmeg
Salt and pepper to taste
Lemon juice to taste

In a soup kettle melt the butter. Add the onion and sauté until tender. Stir in the spinach and cook, covered, over medium heat for 5 minutes. Add the broth and bring to a boil. Stir in the rice and simmer until the rice is tender. In a blender purée the mixture. Blend the egg yolks with the cream and stir into the soup and simmer briefly. Add the seasonings and lemon juice. Serve hot or cold. Serves 6.

If desired serve cold in chilled bowls

Cream of Cucumber Soup

¼ cup chopped green onion
2 tablespoons butter
2 (1 pound) cucumbers, peeled and sliced
4 cups chicken broth
1 teaspoon wine vinegar
½ teaspoon dill or tarragon
Salt and pepper to taste
3 tablespoons quick-cooking farina
1 cup sour cream
Cucumber slices
Fresh snipped dill

In a heavy saucepan sauté the green onion in the butter for 1 minute. Add the cucumbers, chicken broth, vinegar, dill, salt, and pepper. Bring the mixture to a boil and add the farina. Simmer, uncovered, for 20 minutes, or until the farina is tender. Purée the mixture in a blender and return it to the saucepan. Blend in the sour cream and heat the soup until it is hot. Ladle it into heated soup bowls and garnish with cucumber slices and dill. Serves 6-8.

Cream of Artichoke Soup

3 (14 ounce) cans artichoke hearts
6 tablespoons butter
½ cup finely chopped onion
½ cup finely chopped celery
6 tablespoons flour
6 cups chicken broth
¼ cup lemon juice
1 bay leaf
1 teaspoon salt
¼ teaspoon white pepper
¼ teaspoon thyme
2 cups half-and-half cream
2 egg yolks, beaten
1 lemon, sliced
Parsley, chopped

In a blender purée the artichoke hearts. In a soup kettle melt the butter. Add the onion and celery and sauté for 5 minutes. Add the flour, stirring constantly, and cook for 1 minute. Add the broth and lemon juice, stirring, until well blended. Add the bay leaf, salt, pepper, thyme, and artichoke purée and cook, covered, for 20 minutes or until slightly thickened. Remove the kettle from the heat. Beat together the cream and egg yolks and stir into the soup. Keep warm over hot water. If serving cold, chill. Garnish with lemon slices topped with parsley. Serves 8-10.

Simplified Crawfish Bisque

STEW:
¼ cup cooking oil or olive oil
½ onion, finely chopped
½ clove garlic, finely chopped
1 (6 ounce) can tomato paste
Red pepper to taste
Salt and pepper to taste
2 teaspoons sugar
3 tablespoons Roux (see Index)

In a Dutch oven heat the oil. Add the onion and garlic and sauté until soft. Add the tomato paste. Cook over medium heat until thick and dark, stirring constantly. Stir in the seasonings and sugar. Add the Roux and 1½ cups water, stirring constantly, until well blended. Reduce heat to low.

CRAWFISH BALLS:
1 pound cooked crawfish tails, finely chopped
1½ cups Progresso seasoned bread crumbs
¼ cup chopped green onion
1 clove garlic, minced
1 large onion, finely chopped
2 ribs celery, finely chopped
Red pepper to taste
Salt and pepper to taste
2 eggs
½ cup cooking oil
2 cups rice, cooked

In a large bowl combine the crawfish, bread crumbs, and chopped vegetables. Add the seasonings and 2 eggs and blend the mixture. Add more bread crumbs if needed until the mixture is the consistency of thick dressing. Shape into 1½-inch balls. In a large skillet heat the oil. Add the crawfish balls and sauté until they are browned. Transfer the browned crawfish balls to the stew. Add water to cover. Bring the bisque to a boil. Reduce the heat and simmer, covered, for 1½ hours. Serve the bisque in heated soup bowls over rice. Serves 8-10.

At the center of the table, this delightful soup served
in its own pumpkin shell creates an interesting conversation piece

Sarah's Pumpkin Soup

1½ cups white crumbs from non-sweetened bread (French)
1 (6-inch diameter) pumpkin with 2-inch stem
1 tablespoon butter (at room temperature)
Salt
⅔ cup finely chopped onion
6 tablespoons butter
½ teaspoon salt
Nutmeg to taste
Pepper to taste
½ teaspoon ground sage
½ cup coarsely grated Swiss cheese
2 cups chicken broth
1 bay leaf
½ cup heavy cream
Parsley, chopped

Spread the bread crumbs in a roasting pan and dry them out in 300°F
oven, stirring occasionally, for approximately 15 minutes. Cut a
4-inch diameter crown in the pumpkin. Remove the seeds and strings
and rub inside of the pumpkin with 1 tablespoon butter and salt.
Cook the onion in 6 tablespoons butter for 8 to 10 minutes over low
heat until transparent. Stir in dried crumbs. Cook about 2 minutes
until crumbs absorb butter. Stir in the salt, nutmeg, pepper, and
sage. Remove from the heat. Stir in the cheese, and spoon the
mixture into the prepared pumpkin. Pour in the broth, adding
enough so that the mixture comes to ½ inch from the rim of the
pumpkin. Lay the bay leaf on top of the mixture and replace the
pumpkin top. Place the pumpkin in a buttered baking pan. Bake at
400°F for 1½ hours. REDUCE OVEN TEMPERATURE to 350°F and
continue baking for 30 minutes. Remove top and slightly scrape
inside of pumpkin. Stir mixture to blend. Just before serving, stir in
the cream and garnish with parsley.

Vichyssoise

3 cups potatoes, peeled and sliced
1 ham bone or 1 thick slice ham
6 cups chicken stock or broth
3 cups sliced leek (white only), or green onion (white only)
1 cup heavy cream
Salt and white pepper to taste
3 tablespoons minced chives

In a soup kettle combine the potatoes, ham bone, chicken
stock, and leeks. Simmer for about 30 minutes, or until the
potatoes are soft. Purée the soup either in a blender
or a food processor and then through a fine sieve. Stir in
the cream. Season with salt and pepper. Chill. Serve in
chilled cream soup cups. Top with minced chives. Serves 6-8.

Blender Borscht

1 cup chicken bouillon
1 cup canned beets and liquid
2 tablespoons sour cream
2 teaspoons lemon juice
½ teaspoon salt
Lemon-pepper to taste
TOPPING:
Sour cream
Chopped chives

Combine all the borscht ingredients in a blender. Blend, covered, for 2 minutes. Refrigerate the soup until thoroughly chilled. Serve in chilled bowls. Garnish each serving with a dollop of sour cream and chopped chives. Serves 4.

Cream of Lettuce Soup

1 iceberg lettuce, coarsely chopped
5 tablespoons butter
3 green onions, thinly sliced
1 medium onion, chopped
2½-3 cups milk
2 whole cloves
2 tablespoons chopped parsley
1 bay leaf
1-1½ cups chicken broth
2 egg yolks, beaten
3 tablespoons flour
Salt to taste
½ teaspoon lemon-pepper
Croutons

Blanch the lettuce in boiling, salted water for 5 minutes and drain. In a medium saucepan melt 2 tablespoons of the butter. Add the green onion and onion and sauté until tender. Add the milk, cloves, parsley, and bay leaf. Over low heat bring the mixture to a boil. Remove from heat, drain, and discard the cloves and bay leaf. In a blender or food processor process the strained onion, green onion, parsley, and lettuce with the chicken broth until liquified. Into this mixture stir the egg yolks. In a Dutch oven melt the remaining butter. Add the flour, stirring constantly, for 2 minutes. Stir in the scalded milk, salt, lemon-pepper, and chicken broth mixture. Heat the soup, stirring constantly, until thoroughly heated. Top with croutons. Serves 6.

Red Bean Soup

2 cups dried red kidney beans
¼ cup butter
1 medium onion, finely chopped
3 cloves garlic, finely chopped
2 ribs celery, finely chopped
1 tablespoon Worcestershire sauce
1 bay leaf
1 teaspoon dried thyme leaves
½ pound ham, finely ground
Salt and pepper to taste
½ cup claret wine
2 hard-boiled eggs, finely chopped
1 lemon, thinly sliced

Soak the beans overnight in 1 quart of water. In a heavy
Dutch oven melt the butter over medium heat. Add
the onion, garlic, and celery and sauté until brown.
Add 2 quarts of water, beans, Worcestershire sauce,
bay leaf, and thyme. Simmer for 2 hours, or until
the water has reduced to 1 quart. Strain the mixture
and reserve the liquid. Force the beans through a sieve.
Return the beans and liquid to the pot. Add the ham,
salt, and pepper and simmer for 5 to 10 minutes.
Pour the soup into a heated tureen. Stir in the
wine and garnish with the chopped egg and lemon slices.
Serves 6-8.

Oyster Stew

½ cup butter
6 green onions, finely chopped
1 rib celery, chopped
1 small clove garlic, pressed
⅛ teaspoon cayenne
⅛ teaspoon thyme leaves, crushed
¼ cup chopped parsley
Salt and pepper to taste
3 tablespoons flour
2 dozen oysters (reserve liquor)
2 cups milk
2 cups cream
Tabasco sauce to taste

In a large heavy saucepan melt the butter. Add the
green onion, celery, and garlic. Sauté for 10 minutes
or until soft. Add the cayenne, thyme, parsley, salt,
and pepper and continue cooking for 3 minutes. Stir in
the flour, stirring constantly, until blended. Add the
oysters, liquor, milk, cream, and Tabasco sauce, stirring
gently, until thoroughly heated. Serve immediately. Serves 4-6.

Shrimp Bisque

3 pounds raw shrimp, peeled and deveined
4 quarts water
1 large onion, quartered
1 rib celery, quartered
1 clove garlic, chopped
¼ teaspoon thyme leaves
3 tablespoons chopped parsley
1 tablespoon lemon juice
1 lemon rind, grated
2 tablespoons butter
2 tablespoons flour
Cayenne to taste
Salt and pepper to taste

In a large pot boil the shrimp in the water for 2 minutes
or until just tender. Remove ⅓ of the shrimp and
reserve for the shrimp balls. Add the onion, celery,
garlic, thyme, parsley, lemon juice, and lemon rind.
Allow this mixture to boil slowly for 2 hours. Remove from
heat and allow to cool. Put through a sieve or purée in
a blender. Transfer the purée to the pot and over medium
heat bring to a simmer. In a small heavy skillet over
medium heat melt the butter. Gradually add the flour,
stirring constantly, until the roux is golden brown. Stir
the roux into the soup. Season with cayenne, salt, and pepper.
Simmer for 20 minutes. Serve with shrimp balls. Serves 10-12.

SHRIMP BALLS:
2 tablespoons butter
2 tablespoons chopped green onion
¼ cup minced bell pepper
1 tablespoon chopped parsley
1 clove garlic, minced
Reserved shrimp, finely chopped
Salt and pepper to taste
½ cup French bread crumbs
1 egg yolk
1 teaspoon paprika

In a heavy skillet melt the butter. Add the green
onion, bell pepper, parsley, and garlic and sauté
until soft. Stir in the shrimp. Season with salt and
pepper. Blend in the bread crumbs and egg yolk. Form the
mixture into small balls. Place the balls on a greased
baking sheet and sprinkle with paprika. Bake at 350°F for
10 minutes. Place 2 shrimp balls in each heated soup bowl
and ladle the bisque into the bowls.

Cold Cream of Shrimp Soup

1 pound Boiled Shrimp (see Index), reserve 3½ cups strained stock
4 tablespoons butter
4 tablespoons flour
1 tablespoon tomato paste
1 teaspoon curry powder
1 cup half-and-half cream
Salt and pepper to taste
Pimiento strips
Tomato slices

Peel and devein the shrimp. Finely chop all but 6
shrimp. In a soup kettle melt the butter over medium
heat. Gradually add the flour, stirring constantly, for
1 minute. Gradually stir in the shrimp stock. Bring the
mixture to a boil, stirring constantly, for 15 minutes.
Reduce the heat and simmer. Add the chopped shrimp to the
soup and continue cooking for 10 minutes. Add the tomato
paste, curry powder, and cream. Season with salt and pepper.
Simmer for 3 minutes, cool, and chill. Garnish each serving
with the pimiento strips, tomato slices, and 1 whole shrimp.
Serves 6.

Oyster and Artichoke Soup

½ cup butter
2 bunches green onions, chopped
3 ribs celery, chopped
3 cloves garlic, pressed
2 (14 ounce) cans artichoke hearts, washed, drained, and quartered
3 tablespoons flour
1-1½ quarts chicken stock
Cayenne to taste
1 teaspoon salt
1 tablespoon Worcestershire sauce
¼ teaspoon thyme
1 quart oysters, drained and chopped (reserve liquor)
⅓ cup sherry
1 cup half-and-half cream
1 cup milk

In a heavy 4-quart pot melt the butter over medium heat.
Add the green onion, celery, and garlic and sauté
until soft. Add the artichokes. Sprinkle the mixture with the
flour and stir to coat the vegetables well, but do not let
the flour brown. Gradually add the stock, stirring constantly.
Add the cayenne, salt, Worcestershire sauce, and thyme. Simmer
the mixture, covered, for 1 hour. Add the oysters, oyster liquor,
and sherry and simmer for 10 minutes. Do not allow the soup to
boil. Stir in the cream and milk. Cool and refrigerate for
at least 8 hours. Before serving, heat the soup slowly over
low heat. Serves 8 bowls or 16 cups.

Chicken Soup

1 (5 pound) hen, cut in pieces, trimmed of fat
3 quarts water
1 tablespoon salt
1 large onion, chopped
8 small onions, optional, X cut in root end
½ cup chopped parsley
2 bay leaves
2 teaspoons thyme leaves
2 teaspoons lemon pepper
½ pound carrots, sliced
6 tops of celery ribs, chopped
White pepper to taste
4 ounces egg noodles

In a soup kettle combine all the ingredients except
the noodles. Bring the mixture to a boil. Reduce the heat
and simmer for 2 hours, or until the chicken is tender.
Remove the soup from the heat and allow to cool. Transfer the
chicken to a large plate. Skim the fat from the top of the
broth and discard it. Skin and bone the chicken and return
the meat to the broth. Bring the soup to a boil, add
the noodles, and continue boiling for 10 minutes. Serve
in large soup bowls. Serves 6-8.

Cream of Shallot Soup

5 tablespoons butter
4 bunches green onions, finely chopped
2 tablespoons flour
1½ cups chicken broth
1½ cups half-and-half cream
½ cup milk
½ cup vermouth
½ cup water
¼ teaspoon Tabasco sauce
¼ teaspoon white pepper
Salt to taste

In a Dutch oven melt 3 tablespoons of the butter over
medium heat. Add the green onion and sauté until soft. Using
a slotted spoon remove the green onion and reserve it. In
the same Dutch oven melt the remaining butter over
low heat. Add the flour, stirring constantly, until
the mixture is frothy but not brown. Gradually add
the chicken broth, cream, milk, vermouth, and water,
stirring constantly, until blended. Add the green onion,
Tabasco sauce, pepper, and salt. Bring the mixture to a
boil, reduce the heat, and simmer the soup for 30 minutes.
Ladle the soup into heated soup bowls and serve immediately.
Serves 4-6.

Turtle Fricassee

2 pounds turtle fillet, cut in 3-inch pieces
3 tablespoons shortening
3 tablespoons flour
1 large onion, finely chopped
Salt and pepper to taste
½ teaspoon ground cloves
⅛ teaspoon thyme
¼ teaspoon allspice
½ cup tomato sauce
3 quarts boiling water
3 cloves garlic, finely chopped
1 cup sherry
2 hard-boiled eggs, chopped
Parsley and lemon slices

In a Dutch oven parboil the turtle in salted water for
40 minutes. Reserve the liquid. Remove the turtle meat and
pat it dry. In a large skillet heat the shortening and brown the
turtle meat. Add the flour and stir until browned. Add the
onion, salt, pepper, cloves, thyme, allspice, tomato sauce, and
3 quarts boiling water, including any reserved liquid from
parboiling the turtle. Boil for 40 minutes. Stir thoroughly.
Add the garlic, cover, and simmer gently at least 3 hours or until
tender, adding a little water if needed. 30 minutes before serving,
add the sherry. Garnish with the egg, parsley, and lemon slices.
Serves 6-8.

Oyster Soup

2 tablespoons butter, melted
2 tablespoons flour
2 tablespoons chopped green onion
3 tablespoons chopped celery
1 clove garlic, minced
4 dozen small oysters (reserve 2 cups liquor)
2 cups hot water
1 bay leaf
Salt and pepper to taste
Lemon juice (optional)
Tabasco sauce to taste (optional)
Parsley, chopped

In a heavy saucepan combine the butter with the flour but
do not brown. Add the onion, celery, and garlic and
sauté until soft. Gradually add the oyster liquor and
water, stirring, until well blended. Season with the
bay leaf, salt, pepper, lemon juice, and Tabasco sauce.
Add the oysters and parsley 10 to 15 minutes before
serving. Serves 6.

Devilishly Good Black Bean Soup

2 pounds dried black beans
½ pound bacon, cut in 1-inch strips
2 large white onions, chopped
2 cloves garlic
2 bay leaves
1 teaspoon oregano
1 teaspoon cayenne
1 tablespoon celery salt
½ cup chopped celery
½ cup olive oil
1 teaspoon thyme
1 tablespoon pepper
1 bell pepper, finely chopped
Salt to taste
1 (14-inch) link smoked sausage
2 hard-boiled eggs, chopped
1 lemon

Wash the beans thoroughly and soak overnight. Drain and discard water. In a large pot, fry the bacon until crisp. Sauté the onion and garlic in the bacon grease. Add the soaked beans and fill the pot with water. Boil rapidly for about 4 hours, replenishing water as needed. Add the bay leaves, oregano, cayenne, celery salt, celery, and olive oil. Continue cooking for 2 hours. Add the thyme, pepper, bell pepper, and salt. At this point begin mashing the beans and checking frequently to make certain they have not stuck to the bottom of the pot. Stir occasionally, mashing the beans as you stir. An hour before serving, place the beans in a blender filling blender to ¾ capacity at a time. Blend until a thick and creamy consistency is reached. Return the beans to the pot. Add the sausage and cook over low heat for 1 hour. (The sausage is not served with the soup.) Serve the soup in heavy bowls. Garnish with chopped egg or a twist of lemon. Freezes very well. Serves 12-16.

Easy Corn-Mushroom Soup

4 slices bacon
1 medium onion, chopped
1 (17 ounce) can cream-style corn
1 (10¾ ounce) can cream of mushroom soup
1 soup can of milk
¼ teaspoon lemon-pepper
2 tablespoons lemon juice

In a heavy pot fry the bacon until crisp and drain. Sauté the onion in the bacon grease. Add the remaining ingredients, stirring occasionally. Crumble the bacon over each serving. Serves 4.

When making Gumbo, okra or filé is used as a thickening agent. Filé is the powder obtained from ground sassafras leaves which was first used by the Indians of this region. If okra is used, it is added according to the recipe instructions, and cooked. When filé is used, it is NEVER cooked. It is added at the last minute before serving and the gumbo must never be brought to a boil again. Another way of using filé is to have it on the table, letting each person add it to the gumbo. This means the pot of gumbo not used may be frozen or reheated easily.

Following the above instructions for use, okra and filé may be substituted interchangeably for each other. The substitution proportions are approximately 1 pound of okra is equal to 1 tablespoon filé. Since filé is difficult to obtain outside of the New Orleans region, feel free to substitute okra. Do experiment with the filé. It is a unique taste.

Roux

"First you make a Roux" — this phrase is repeated in almost all Creole and Cajun recipes. A Roux is a mixture of fat and flour, cooked together until the flour has turned an even, nut-brown color. It is important that the Roux be cooked in a heavy pot, slowly and evenly. If the flour is burned, it will not thicken the sauce. It will also impart an unpleasant taste.

Accepted methods of making a Roux call for equal parts of flour and fat (oil, bacon grease, shortening, butter, or margarine). For an ordinary sauce (such as gumbo, daube, grillades, etc.) bacon grease or oil is used. For more delicately flavored dishes (poultry, fish, and eggs), butter or margarine is usually preferred.

In a heavy saucepan melt the butter, or slightly heat the oil, over low heat. Stir in the flour. Cook over low heat, stirring constantly, until a rich brown Roux is formed (about 20 to 25 minutes).

Roux may be made ahead and refrigerated or frozen, tightly covered, for long periods of time.

Potato flour is an excellent thickener for soups.

Gumbos

Basic Creole Stock

2 tablespoons bacon grease
¼ pound smoked ham, diced
1½ tablespoons flour
2 pounds onions, finely chopped
1 medium bell pepper, finely chopped
Rind and pulp of 1 lemon, minced
3 cloves garlic, pressed
⅛ teaspoon Worcestershire sauce
Dash of Tabasco sauce
1 teaspoon salt
Pinch of thyme
2 cups water
2 bay leaves

In a heavy saucepan melt the bacon grease over medium heat. Add the ham and sauté until light brown. Remove the ham and reserve it. Blend the flour into the grease and cook, stirring, until the flour is browned. Add the onion and mix well. Cook over low heat, stirring occasionally, until the onion is soft and lightly browned. Stir in the reserved ham and remaining ingredients. Continue cooking over low heat, uncovered, stirring occasionally, for 30 minutes. Remove the bay leaves. Makes 2-3 cups.

Duck Gumbo

1 cup cooking oil
½ cup flour
1 cup chopped onion
¼ cup chopped green onion
3 quarts boiling water
Tabasco sauce to taste
Salt and red pepper to taste
4 small or 2 large ducks, cut in pieces
¼ cup chopped parsley
½ cup chopped green onion tops
2 cloves garlic, pressed
½ pound smoked sausage, cut in ½-inch rounds
2 cups rice, cooked

In a large heavy pot heat ½ cup of the oil over medium heat. Add the flour, stirring constantly, until dark brown. Add the onion and green onion and cook until tender. Add the boiling water and season with Tabasco sauce, salt, and red pepper. Season the duck with salt and red pepper. In a large skillet heat the remaining oil over moderately high heat. Add the duck pieces and fry until brown, turning occasionally. Transfer the duck pieces and pan scrapings to the gumbo. Simmer, uncovered, over low heat for 2 to 2½ hours, or until the meat is tender. More water may be added if needed. Correct seasonings. Add the parsley, onion tops, garlic, and sausage. Cook, covered, for 20 to 30 minutes longer. Serve in gumbo bowls over rice. Serves 8.

Chicken Gumbo

1 (4-6 pound) hen
Salt, pepper, and cayenne to taste
⅓ cup cooking oil
2 large onions, chopped
2 ribs celery, finely chopped
½ bell pepper, chopped
2 large cloves garlic, minced
⅔ cup flour
2 gallons water
⅓ cup dry red wine
¾ pound smoked sausage, sliced
1 pint oysters, drained and rinsed
Parsley, chopped
1 tablespoon gumbo filé
3 cups rice, cooked

Cut up the hen and season generously with the salt, pepper, and cayenne. In a heavy pot fry the hen in oil until golden brown. Remove the oil and reserve it for making the roux. Add the onion, celery, bell pepper, and garlic to the chicken. Cover and cook over low heat. Make a dark brown Roux (see Index) using ½ cup of the reserved oil and the flour. Cool the roux slightly and add to the chicken. Continue cooking over low heat, adding the water in small amounts and add the wine. When the chicken is fork tender, add the smoked sausage. Add the oysters and parsley 10 minutes before serving. Immediately before serving, remove from the heat and add the filé. Serve in heated gumbo bowls over rice. Serves 12.

To skim fat from soup quickly, dip a lettuce leaf in soup. The lettuce will pick up the fat.

Bayou Gumbo

1 ham hock
2 quarts water
1½ pounds okra, sliced
¼ cup bacon grease
1 bell pepper, chopped
2 large onions, chopped
½ cup chopped parsley
3 ribs celery, chopped
6 cloves garlic
3 ripe tomatoes
Salt, pepper, cayenne to taste
½ teaspoon mace
¼ teaspoon ground cloves
½ teaspoon allspice
2 pounds peeled, raw shrimp
1 pound crab meat
1 pint oysters
2 cups rice, cooked

Place the ham hock in the water and simmer for 1
hour. In a large skillet fry the okra in the bacon grease
until soft and the texture is no longer ropey. Add the
bell pepper, onion, parsley, celery, and garlic and simmer
for 30 minutes. Remove the garlic and add the tomatoes. Cook for
3 minutes. Remove the meat from the ham hock bone
and return the meat to the ham stock pot. Place the
vegetables in the ham stock and cook over moderate heat
for 3 hours. Add the salt, pepper, cayenne, mace, cloves,
and allspice. Add the shrimp 30 minutes before serving. Add
the crab meat and oysters 10 minutes before serving. Serve
in gumbo bowls over rice. Freezes beautifully. Serves 8-10.

For use in thickening gumbos, soups, sauces, and gravies,
thoroughly blend together equal parts of softened butter and
flour, form into small balls, and store in the freezer.

A traditional "after Thanksgiving" dish in New Orleans

Turkey Gumbo

1 turkey carcass
2 turkey legs or thighs
½ cup bacon grease
½ cup cooking oil
1 cup flour
8 ribs celery, chopped
3 large onions, chopped
1 bell pepper, chopped
2 cloves garlic, minced
½ cup chopped parsley
1 pound okra, sliced
1 cup smoked sausage, sliced
½ cup Worcestershire sauce
Tabasco sauce to taste
1 (12 ounce) can tomatoes
1½ tablespoons salt
4 slices bacon, cut in 1-inch pieces
1-2 bay leaves
Cayenne to taste
1 teaspoon brown sugar
1 tablespoon lemon juice
4 cups rice, cooked

Crack the turkey carcass into several pieces. Place the turkey carcass and legs in a soup kettle with 3 quarts of water and 1 teaspoon salt. Boil for 1 hour. Remove the carcass and legs and cool. Remove the meat from the bones and discard the bones. Reserve the stock and meat. In a heavy Dutch oven over medium heat, heat the grease and oil. Add the flour, stirring constantly, and cook until dark golden brown. Add the celery, onion, bell pepper, garlic, and parsley. Cook for 15 to 20 minutes, stirring constantly. Add the okra and sausage and continue cooking for 5 minutes. Add 2 quarts of the turkey stock and 2 quarts of water, Worcestershire sauce, Tabasco sauce, tomatoes, salt, bacon, bay leaves, and cayenne. Simmer, covered, for 2½ to 3 hours, stirring occasionally. Add the turkey meat and simmer for 30 minutes. Just before serving, add the brown sugar and lemon juice. Serve in heated gumbo bowls over rice. Serves 16-18.

Soup becomes thicker when chilled; if too thick to serve chilled, add consommé or thin cream to thin the soup.

This Gumbo breaks all the rules as it uses neither okra
nor filé, and when originally prepared contained
no meat, seafood, or game

Gumbo Z'Herbes
(Green Gumbo)

1 bunch each, in any combination, but use at least five: spinach, collard, mustard or turnip greens, watercress, chicory, beet tops, carrot tops, pepper grass, radish tops
1 bunch parsley, chopped
½ bunch green onions, chopped
1 small green cabbage, chopped
1 gallon water
4 tablespoons flour
4 tablespoons shortening
1 large onion, diced
1 pound boiled ham, diced
½ pound Creole or Polish smoked sausage, cubed
2 bay leaves
2 sprigs thyme
¼ teaspoon allspice
Salt and pepper to taste
Cayenne to taste
2 cups rice, cooked

Wash the greens, parsley, green onion, and cabbage thoroughly
and remove the stems and hard centers. Boil in water for
2 hours. Drain the greens and reserve the water. Chop
the greens finely. In a soup kettle make a brown roux of the
flour and shortening. Add the onion, ham, and sausage
and sauté for 5 minutes or until soft. Add the greens
and simmer for 15 minutes. Add the reserved cooking water,
herbs, spices, and seasonings. Simmer for 1 hour. Serve
over rice. Serves 8.

In clear soups and stocks, the vegetables are added at the
beginning of the cooking period.

SALADS

Green salads, for most of us, are another benefit of modern ways. Once available seasonally, and only to those with a garden near by, we may now enjoy them all through the year. They are easy to make, but are often made wrong. Sliced lettuce drowned in a heavy dressing is not what a salad is meant to be. Rather, a variety of greens, with a little bright color coated with—but not swimming in—a zesty dressing, is what's wanted. With meat, cheese, or fish added, or based upon pasta or potatoes rather than greens, the salad becomes a fine make-ahead meal in itself.

SALADS

Parades and New Orleans! They are synonymous in the minds of tourists and residents alike. Many of the parades are made more colorful by the addition of "second-liners," a tradition of umbrella-carrying, dancing people who follow the bands in the "second-line" behind a parade. Many second-liners are simply uninhibited on-lookers who cannot resist joining the parade; others have made a profession of being colorful participants as "second-liners."

Super Avocado Salad

2 chilled avocados, sliced
Lettuce leaves
DRESSING:
½ cup chili sauce
2 tablespoons sherry
1 teaspoon horseradish
½ teaspoon Worcestershire sauce
1 tablespoon lemon juice
1 tablespoon mayonnaise
½ teaspoon salt

In a bowl combine all of the dressing ingredients and transfer the dressing to a jar, cover, and refrigerate. When ready to serve, place the avocados on the lettuce leaves and top them with dressing. Serves 4-6.

This dressing is excellent combined with chopped hard-boiled eggs and onion and served over fresh spinach

Asparagus Teriyaki

2 (15½ ounce) cans asparagus spears, drained
Romaine lettuce
DRESSING:
1 cup finely chopped walnuts
2 tablespoons light salad oil
¼ cup cider vinegar
¼ cup teriyaki sauce
2 tablespoons sugar
Pepper to taste

In a bowl mix together all the dressing ingredients. Pour the dressing over the asparagus 1 hour before serving and serve on romaine lettuce. Serves 6.

Cauliflower Salad

1 head lettuce, shredded
1 head cauliflower, thinly sliced
2 (10 ounce) packages frozen small green peas, thawed
1 pint mayonnaise
2 (1.3 ounce) packages dry Italian dressing mix
Parmesan cheese

In a salad bowl layer the lettuce, cauliflower, and peas. Cover the vegetables completely with the mayonnaise and sprinkle the top with the dry dressing mix and cheese. Cover the salad and refrigerate it overnight. Serves 8-10.

Fancy Green Bean Salad

2 (15½ ounce) cans whole green beans
1 (8 ounce) bottle Wishbone Italian dressing
Lettuce leaves
DRESSING:
¼ cup coarsely chopped onion
1 green onion, coarsely chopped
1 tablespoon chopped bell pepper
1 tablespoon chopped parsley
1 cup mayonnaise
1 teaspoon Worcestershire sauce
2 tablespoons horseradish
3 tablespoons Creole mustard
1 tablespoon ketchup

In a bowl marinate the beans in the bottled dressing overnight. Chop the first 4 dressing ingredients in a blender, add the remaining dressing ingredients, and blend. Drain the green beans and place them on the lettuce leaves. Pour the dressing over the beans. Serves 6-8.

Crunchy Bean Salad

1 (16 ounce) can Chun King bean sprouts
1 (15½ ounce) can French-style green beans
¼ cup stuffed olives, sliced
1 cup thinly sliced celery
1 cup thinly sliced green onion
DRESSING:
¼ cup salad oil
¼ cup tarragon vinegar
1 tablespoon soy sauce
½ teaspoon paprika
½ cup confectioners' sugar

Drain all the vegetables and in a bowl combine them. In a 2-cup bowl mix together the dressing ingredients and pour the mixture over the vegetables. Cover the salad and chill it. Serves 10-12.

Marinate sliced, raw mushrooms in your favorite Italian salad dressing. They provide a tempting taste treat alone or mixed in a salad.

Creamy Coleslaw

1 medium head cabbage, grated
1 small onion, grated
1 large carrot, grated
1 bell pepper, chopped
3 tablespoons vinegar
1 teaspoon salt
½ teaspoon celery seed
1 tablespoon sugar
⅛ teaspoon pepper
1-2 tablespoons mayonnaise

Combine all the ingredients except the mayonnaise in a large bowl, toss well, and refrigerate the salad for 1 hour. Add the mayonnaise to the salad and mix well. Serves 8-10.

A lovely carrot salad

Gold Doubloons

2 pounds carrots, sliced crosswise
1 medium white onion, sliced in rings
1 medium bell pepper, chopped
3 ribs celery, chopped
1 (10½ ounce) can tomato soup
1 cup sugar
½ cup Mazola oil
¾ cup apple cider vinegar
1 teaspoon dry mustard
1 tablespoon Worcestershire sauce

In a saucepan cook the carrots in salted water until they are tender and drain them. In a bowl combine the onion, bell pepper, and celery. In a salad bowl alternate the carrots and the onion mixture in layers. In a separate saucepan mix together and bring to a boil the remaining ingredients and pour the mixture over the layered vegetables. Refrigerate the salad at least 8 hours before serving. Serves 6.

To shred cabbage for slaw, use your blender. Fill ⅓ to ½ full of cold water, add ⅓ of the cabbage, cut into chunks, chop, and drain.

Potato Salad

5 large russet potatoes, boiled and peeled
2 tablespoons pickle juice
1 cup finely chopped sweet pickle
1 large white onion, chopped
4 ribs celery, chopped
4 hard-boiled eggs, chopped
1½ tablespoons prepared yellow mustard
1¼ cups mayonnaise
Salt and pepper to taste
Paprika

Cut the potatoes into 1-inch cubes and place them in a salad
bowl. Sprinkle the potatoes with the pickle juice. To the
potatoes add the other ingredients except the paprika, in order,
and mix the salad well. Sprinkle the top with the paprika
and chill it well before serving. Serves 6.

Macaroni Salad

1 cup uncooked elbow macaroni
½ cup chopped celery
¼ cup chopped bell pepper
1 carrot, sliced
¼ cup chopped onion
¾ cup chopped dill pickle, sweet pickle, or olives
½ teaspoon Worcestershire sauce
1 teaspoon salt
⅛ teaspoon pepper
1 teaspoon sugar
¼ cup Miracle Whip salad dressing
2 hard-boiled eggs, chopped

In a saucepan prepare the macaroni according to package directions,
rinse, and drain it. In a salad bowl combine the cooked macaroni,
celery, bell pepper, carrot, onion, and pickle. In a separate
bowl combine the remaining ingredients and pour the mixture
over the macaroni mixture, toss the salad gently, and chill it.
Serves 8-10.

Select a crisp lettuce that is heavy for its size. Spinach
should have dark, small, tender leaves. If it has coarse
stems, it will be tough.

Green Pea Salad

2 (10 ounce) packages frozen peas, thawed
1 cup chopped green onion
1½ cups chopped celery
1 (8 ounce) can water chestnuts, drained and sliced
1 pint sour cream
1 pound bacon, crisply fried and crumbled

In a salad bowl mix all the ingredients except the bacon.
Refrigerate the salad until it is ready to serve. Just before serving,
add the bacon. Serves 10-14.

Broccoli Salad

2 (10 ounce) packages frozen broccoli
2 hard-boiled eggs, chopped
1 small red onion, sliced
Salt to taste
3-4 tablespoons mayonnaise

In a saucepan boil the broccoli until it is just tender.
Drain the broccoli, transfer it to a salad bowl, and cool it.
Sprinkle the eggs over the broccoli, cover it with slices of
onion, and season it with salt. Fold in the mayonnaise and
serve the salad at once. Serves 6-8.

Spinach Salad

2 bunches fresh spinach, deveined and torn
½ head lettuce, torn
2 hard-boiled eggs, chopped
4 slices bacon, fried and crumbled
6 large fresh mushrooms, sliced

In a large bowl toss the spinach and lettuce. To the greens
add the egg, bacon, and mushrooms. Pour the dressing over
the salad, toss, and serve. Serves 8.

DRESSING:
1 cup salad oil
5 tablespoons tarragon vinegar
4 heaping tablespoons sour cream
2 tablespoons sugar
1½ teaspoons salt
1 tablespoon pepper
5 heaping teaspoons dried parsley
¼ teaspoon garlic purée
3 small green onions, chopped

In a bowl mix the dressing ingredients well and refrigerate.
This dressing is delicious on other green salads.

Disappearing Salad

1 (15¼ ounce) can unsweetened pineapple chunks (reserve juice)
5 cups torn spinach leaves, chilled
6 slices bacon, crisply fried and crumbled
2 hard-boiled eggs, chopped
¼ cup sliced green onion
Pineapple dressing

Prepare the dressing. Place the spinach in a salad bowl.
Top the spinach with the pineapple and garnish it with the
bacon, egg, and green onion. Just before serving the salad,
add the dressing and toss it lightly. Serves 8.

DRESSING:
¼ cup salad oil
2 tablespoons sesame seed
Reserved pineapple juice
3 tablespoons white wine vinegar
½ teaspoon garlic salt
½ teaspoon ground ginger

Heat the salad oil in a skillet. Add the sesame seed and brown.
Add the remaining ingredients and mix well. Transfer the
mixture to a jar, cover, and refrigerate several hours. Shake well
before using. Makes 1 cup.

Egg-Spinach Salad

1 pound fresh spinach
½ cup salad oil
2 tablespoons sugar
2 tablespoons wine vinegar
1 teaspoon finely grated onion
½ teaspoon salt
¼ teaspoon dry mustard
6 slices bacon, crisply fried and crumbled
4 hard-boiled eggs, chopped
1 hard-boiled egg, sliced

Wash and drain the spinach. Transfer it to a large bowl and chill
it. In a separate bowl combine the oil, sugar, vinegar, onion,
salt, and mustard. Beat the dressing or mix in a blender until
it becomes thick and syrupy. Tear the spinach and
add the bacon and chopped eggs. Pour the dressing over the
salad. Let it stand for 1 hour. Toss the salad to mix it
and garnish with the egg slices. Serves 6.

Cut or tear the greens into bite-size pieces. Cutting makes
them lose moisture and wilt much faster.

Caesar Salad

1 clove garlic
½ cup salad oil
1 cup French bread cubes, crusts removed
¾ teaspoon salt
¼ teaspoon dry mustard
¼ teaspoon freshly ground pepper
1½ teaspoons Worcestershire sauce
6 anchovy fillets, drained and chopped
1 egg
1 large head romaine or leaf lettuce, chilled
2 tablespoons Parmesan cheese
¼ cup crumbled bleu cheese
2 tablespoons lemon juice

Crush ½ clove of the garlic and combine it in a jar with the salad oil. Cover the jar and refrigerate the garlic oil at least 1 hour. Heat 2 tablespoons of the garlic oil in a medium skillet. Add the bread cubes and sauté them until they are browned, stirring often, and set them aside. Add the salt, mustard, pepper, Worcestershire sauce, and anchovies to the remaining garlic oil and shake it vigorously. Continue refrigerating it until it is needed. Coddle the egg (by submerging in simmering water) for 1 minute and set it aside to cool. Just before serving, rub the inside of a wooden salad bowl with the remaining ½ clove of the garlic and discard it. Tear the lettuce into the salad bowl. Shake the dressing well and pour it over the greens. Sprinkle the salad with the cheeses and toss it until it is well coated. Break the egg over the center of the salad. Pour the lemon juice directly over the egg and toss the salad well. Add the bread cubes, toss gently, and serve immediately. Serves 6.

French Bread Croutons

Stale French bread, diced
Melted butter or olive oil
Garlic powder to taste

In a bowl toss the diced bread with melted butter and garlic powder. Brown the bread cubes in a shallow baking dish at 325°F for 30 to 45 minutes, stirring 2 or 3 times during browning.

To clean spinach, add 4 tablespoons of salt to each gallon of water, soak the greens a few minutes, and rinse them well. Shake off the excess water and refrigerate to crisp.

Garden Potpourri

1 bunch romaine, torn in bite-size pieces
1 large head iceberg lettuce, torn in bite-size pieces
3 heads Bibb lettuce, torn in bite-size pieces
1 stalk Chinese cabbage, top half only, thinly sliced
1 cup finely shredded red cabbage
¼ bunch curly endive
1 large white onion, sliced in rings
1 cup crisp croutons
Poppy Seed Dressing (see Index)
2 hard-boiled eggs, sliced

In a large salad bowl combine the vegetables. Add the croutons and dressing and toss gently. Serve the salad garnished with the egg slices. Serves 16.

Excellent accompaniment for assorted finger sandwiches

Party Fruit Salad

1 cup pineapple chunks, drained
1 cup mandarin oranges, drained
1 cup pitted Queen Anne cherries, drained
1 cup apricots, drained and quartered
1 cup pecans, chopped
1 cup sour cream

In a bowl mix all the ingredients well. Refrigerate the salad for 24 hours. Serves 6-8.

Extraordinary, colorful centerpiece

Watermelon Basket

1 large watermelon
2 cantaloupes
2 honeydew melons
1½ pounds white grapes
1½ pounds dark grapes
2 pints fresh strawberries, stemmed
½ cup orange or pineapple juice
Mint sprigs (optional)

With a large knife remove the top ⅓ of the watermelon. (The bottom portion is used as the basket for serving.) Remove the seeds from all of the melons. Using a melon-ball cutter, scoop the fruit from the melons and place them in a bowl. Gently mix all of the fruits and the juice. Transfer the fruit to the melon basket. Garnish it with the mint.

NOTE: For special effect cut the top edge of the watermelon basket in a zigzag pattern.

Deep South Ambrosia

8 navel oranges
1 small coconut, finely grated
Confectioners' sugar to taste

Peel the oranges and cut them in sections, removing all membranes. In a large bowl mix together the orange sections and grated coconut. Sweeten the fruit with confectioners' sugar. Chill for several hours before serving. Serves 6-8.

VARIATIONS:

2 tart red apples, sliced and sprinkled with lemon juice
¼ cup maraschino cherries
¾ cup chopped pecans
1 cup crushed pineapple

One or all of these ingredients may be added for variety. However, the true Southern Ambrosia is oranges and coconut alone.

Bloody Mary Aspic

1 (15½ ounce) can tomato wedges (reserve liquid)
8 small cocktail onions
2 tablespoons cocktail onion liquid or vinegar
½ teaspoon dill seed
Salt and pepper to taste
Dash of celery salt
½ teaspoon onion powder
1½ envelopes unflavored gelatin
1 (6 ounce) can Tabasco Bloody Mary mix

Arrange the tomato wedges and cocktail onions in a lightly oiled 1-quart mold. In a saucepan combine the onion liquid, dill seed, salt, pepper, celery salt, onion powder, and reserved tomato liquid and heat. In a measuring cup dissolve the gelatin in ¾ cup cold water and add it to the hot juice and cool. Add the Bloody Mary mix to the juice mixture and pour it over the tomatoes and onions in the mold. Refrigerate the aspic until it is firm. Serves 4.

Our most common types of lettuce are iceberg, Boston, and Bibb, but endive, chicory, escarole, and romaine are nice variations.

Especially good with game

Black Cherry Salad

2 (6 ounce) packages black cherry gelatin
2 envelopes unflavored gelatin
2 (17 ounce) cans pitted dark sweet cherries (reserve liquid)
2½ to 3 cups water
2 cups port wine
4 cups pecans
Lettuce leaves
Mayonnaise

To reserved cherry liquid, add enough water to measure 4 cups of liquid. Bring to a boil. In a bowl, dissolve black cherry and unflavored gelatin in the boiling liquid. To the gelatin, add the port wine, cherries, and pecans. Pour the mixture into a lightly oiled or sprayed 9″ × 13″ pan. Refrigerate the salad until it is firm. Cut it in squares with a hot knife. Serve the salad on lettuce leaves and top it with mayonnaise. Serves 12.

Congealed Beet Relish Salad

2 (16 ounce) cans whole beets, shredded (reserve 1½ cups liquid)
2 envelopes unflavored gelatin
½ cup sugar
1 teaspoon salt
⅔ cup vinegar
5 tablespoons prepared horseradish
¼ cup chopped onion
1 cup finely chopped celery
½ cup finely chopped bell pepper

In a saucepan dissolve the gelatin in the beet liquid over low heat, stirring constantly, for 3 minutes. Stir in the remaining ingredients and pour into a 1½-quart mold. Chill the salad until it is firm. Serves 8-10.

Tropical Fruit Salad

1 (3 ounce) package lemon gelatin
¾ cup boiling water
½ cup mashed banana
½ cup crushed pineapple (reserve liquid)
¼ cup sliced maraschino cherries
⅓ cup mayonnaise
½ cup whipped cream

In a large bowl dissolve the gelatin in the boiling water. Chill the gelatin until it is slightly thickened. Fold in the fruit, fruit liquid, mayonnaise, and whipped cream. Pour the mixture into a 1-quart crystal bowl. Refrigerate the salad until it is firm. Serves 6.

Cranberry Christmas Salad

I (6 ounce) package cherry gelatin
1½ cups boiling water
2 teaspoons grated orange rind
I (16 ounce) can whole cranberry sauce
I (8 ounce) can crushed pineapple, drained
½ cup finely chopped celery
½ cup chopped pecans
Bibb lettuce

In a saucepan dissolve the gelatin in boiling water and stir in
the orange rind and cranberry sauce. Refrigerate the mixture
until it is thickened. Remove from the refrigerator and stir in
the pineapple, celery, and pecans. Pour the mixture into a lightly
oiled 1½-quart mold. Refrigerate the salad until it is firm.
Unmold the salad on the lettuce leaves. Serves 10-12.

Luscious Lime Salad

¼ pound marshmallows
1½ cups milk
I (6 ounce) package lime gelatin
I cup boiling water
I (8 ounce) package cream cheese (at room temperature)
I cup chopped celery
I apple, chopped
I (8 ounce) can crushed pineapple
I cup chopped pecans
Salad greens

In a small saucepan melt the marshmallows in 1 cup of the milk
and allow it to cool. In a measuring cup dissolve the gelatin in
the boiling water. In a large bowl blend the remaining
milk with the cream cheese. To the cream cheese mixture
add the marshmallow and gelatin mixtures. Add the celery,
apple, pineapple, and pecans and mix well. Pour the mixture
into a lightly oiled 3-quart mold. Refrigerate the salad until
it is firm. Unmold the salad on the salad greens. Serves 12.

To make a design in a congealed salad, arrange the fruit
or vegetables on a partially set gelatin layer. Chill
and set before adding the remaining gelatin.

Orange Blossom Salad

1 (6 ounce) package orange gelatin
1 cup boiling water
1 pint orange sherbet
1 (8 ounce) can crushed pineapple, drained
1 cup miniature marshmallows
1 (11 ounce) can mandarin orange slices, drained
1 cup whipped topping or ½ cup whipping cream, whipped
Mint leaves

In a large bowl dissolve the gelatin in the boiling water. Add the orange sherbet and stir until it is melted. Add the remaining ingredients except the mint and mix well. Spoon the mixture into 12 sherbet glasses. Refrigerate the salad until it is firm. Garnish with the mint leaves. Serves 12.

Cheese Lovers' Delight

1 (15¼ ounce) can crushed pineapple (reserve liquid)
1 (3 ounce) package lime gelatin
1 (3 ounce) package lemon gelatin
1 (8 ounce) package cream cheese (at room temperature)
1 cup creamed cottage cheese
4 ounces mild Cheddar cheese, grated
Lettuce leaves
1 (6 ounce) jar maraschino cherries

In a saucepan add enough water to the pineapple liquid to make 2 cups of liquid and bring the mixture to a boil. Add the gelatins, stirring, until it is dissolved and chill the mixture for 30 minutes. Beat the cream cheese with a mixer and stir in the cottage cheese, Cheddar cheese, and pineapple. Combine the gelatin and the cheese mixture. Pour the mixture into a lightly oiled 2-quart ring mold and refrigerate it until it is firm. Unmold the salad on lettuce leaves and garnish it with cherries. Serves 8-10.

Drain frozen or canned fruits thoroughly before adding them to salad molds. Substitute some of the drained liquid for part of the liquid called for in the recipe.

Chicken Salad

2 (3 pound) chickens, cut in pieces
1 rib celery, quartered
1 medium onion, quartered
1 cup finely chopped celery
2 tablespoons finely chopped onion
4 tablespoons sweet pickle relish
3 tablespoons pickle juice
1 cup mayonnaise
3 hard-boiled eggs, chopped
Salt and pepper to taste
1 teaspoon seasoned salt (optional)
Lettuce leaves

In a Dutch oven cover the chicken, celery quarters, and onion quarters with cold water. Bring the water to a boil and reduce the heat to low. Cover and simmer for 1½ hours, or until the chicken is tender. Remove the skin, bone, and cut in bite-size pieces. Transfer the chicken to a large bowl and add the celery, onion, relish, pickle juice, mayonnaise, eggs, salt, and pepper and mix well. Spoon onto the lettuce leaves. Serves 10-12.

Chicken Mousse

2 (2½ pound) chickens
1 teaspoon salt
1 rib celery, quartered
¼ teaspoon pepper
1 onion, quartered
1 bay leaf
1 carrot, sliced
2 envelopes unflavored gelatin
1 (8 ounce) package cream cheese
1 (10½ ounce) can cream of chicken soup
1 cup mayonnaise
2 cups chopped celery
2 tablespoons lemon juice
4 tablespoons chopped olives

In a large pot cover the chicken with cold water and add the next 6 ingredients. Bring the water to a rolling boil, reduce the heat, and simmer for 1½ hours, or until the chicken is tender. Reserve 1 cup of strained broth. When the chicken is cool, skin, bone, and cut it in small pieces. In a large bowl soften the gelatin in the chicken broth. In a saucepan blend the cream cheese with the chicken soup over low heat and add it to the gelatin mixture. To this mixture add the chicken and the remaining ingredients and mix well. Pour the mixture into a 9"x13" pan. Refrigerate the mousse at least 24 hours. Cut the mousse into squares and serve it on lettuce leaves. The mousse may be topped with Homemade Mayonnaise (see Index). Serves 12-16.

Crawfish Days

⅓ cup finely chopped celery
¼ cup minced parsley
2 tablespoons finely chopped pimiento
½ teaspoon white pepper
¼ teaspoon salt
¼ cup mayonnaise
4 cups peeled Boiled Crawfish (see Index)
Crisp salad greens
Cucumber slices
Radish roses
Paprika

In a large bowl mix together thoroughly the celery, parsley, pimiento, pepper, salt, and mayonnaise. To this mixture add the crawfish and mix well. Chill the salad and serve on a bed of greens. Garnish the salad with the slices of cucumber and radish roses. Sprinkle it lightly with the paprika. Serves 4.

Shrimp au Chateau

2 envelopes unflavored gelatin
4 tablespoons hot water
1 (10½ ounce) can cream of mushroom soup
1 (8 ounce) package cream cheese (at room temperature)
¾ cup Hellman's mayonnaise
¼ cup sandwich spread
1 cup finely chopped celery
1 bunch green onions, finely chopped
2-3 pounds Boiled Shrimp (see Index), peeled and deveined
Cayenne to taste

In a saucepan dissolve the gelatin in the hot water. In a separate saucepan warm the soup and add it to the gelatin. Beat the cream cheese with a mixer until it is fluffy. Add the soup and gelatin mixture and continue beating until it is well blended. Fold in the mayonnaise, sandwich spread, celery, green onion, shrimp, and cayenne. Pour the mixture into a lightly oiled 1½-quart mold. Chill the mold for 6 hours. Serves 6-8.

Use as many contrasts of texture and color as possible. Reds, yellows, different shades of green, will make your salad more interesting in taste and appearance.

Shrimp-Stuffed Avocado

2 cups peeled Boiled Shrimp (see Index)
½ cup diced celery
1 tablespoon chopped green onion
1 tablespoon sweet pickle relish
10 stuffed olives, sliced
3 hard-boiled eggs, diced
2 tablespoons lemon juice
½ cup mayonnaise
Salt and pepper to taste
Paprika
3 ripe avocados, halved
Lettuce leaves
Cherry tomatoes
Lemon wedges
Celery sticks

In a large bowl mix together the first 7 ingredients. Add the mayonnaise, salt, pepper, and paprika and toss gently. Chill this mixture thoroughly. Mound the shrimp salad into the avocado halves. Place them on the lettuce leaves. Arrange the cherry tomatoes, lemon wedges, and celery sticks around the avocados. Serves 6.

Spring Fiesta Salad

3 pounds turkey breast, cooked and boned
1 (20 ounce) can water chestnuts, drained and sliced
2 pounds seedless grapes
2 cups sliced celery
2 cups toasted slivered almonds
3 cups mayonnaise
1 tablespoon curry powder
2 tablespoons soy sauce
¼ cup lemon juice
Lettuce leaves
1 (20 ounce) can pineapple chunks, drained
Melons (in season), sliced

Cut the turkey into bite-size pieces and place it in a large bowl. To the turkey add the water chestnuts, grapes, celery, and 1½ cups of the almonds and mix well. In a cup mix the mayonnaise with the curry powder, soy sauce, and lemon juice. Add the mayonnaise mixture to the turkey mixture, tossing gently. Chill the salad for several hours. Spoon it into nests of the lettuce leaves. Top the salad with the remaining almonds and garnish it with the pineapple chunks and melon. Serves 12.

1½ pounds raw shrimp equals 2 cups peeled, cooked shrimp.

Meat Salad au Joseph

1 (3 pound) lean chuck roast
1 bunch celery, quartered
4 carrots, quartered
2 medium onions, quartered
1 clove garlic
1 onion, chopped
1 carton cherry tomatoes, halved
Salad greens
DRESSING:
3 tablespoons olive oil
3 tablespoons wine vinegar

In a large pot simmer the meat and the next 3 ingredients in water to cover for 2½ hours, or until it is very tender. Allow the meat to cool. Shred the meat using a fork. Rub a large wooden salad bowl with the garlic. Place the meat, onion, and tomatoes in the bowl. Pour the dressing ingredients over the meat mixture and toss. Serve the salad on a bed of greens. Serves 12.

Crab Salad Bon Vivant

1⅛ cups Blender Mayonnaise (see Index)
1 tablespoon drained capers
2 tablespoons minced sour pickle
1 tablespoon chopped chives
1 tablespoon minced parsley
¼ teaspoon dried tarragon, crushed
Salt and pepper to taste
½ pound crab meat
2 hearts of lettuce, cut in wedges
2 hard-boiled eggs, quartered
8 asparagus spears
2 tomatoes, sliced
Lemon wedges
Paprika

In a medium bowl combine 1 cup of the mayonnaise, capers, pickle, chives, parsley, tarragon, salt, and pepper. Fold in the crab meat. Mound the crab meat mixture in the center of two serving dishes. Arrange the lettuce, eggs, asparagus, and tomatoes alternately around the mounds of crab meat. Garnish each dish with lemon wedges and a dollop of the remaining mayonnaise. Sprinkle the salad with paprika. Serves 2.

Garden Party Tuna Ring

2 tablespoons unflavored gelatin
4 tablespoons cold water
2 (3 ounce) packages cream cheese (at room temperature)
1 (10½ ounce) can tomato soup
1 (6½ ounce) can tuna, drained
1 cup Miracle Whip salad dressing
1 teaspoon lemon juice
½ cup blanched almonds
1 cup chopped bell pepper
1 cup chopped celery

In a cup dissolve the unflavored gelatin in the cold water.
In a saucepan blend the cream cheese with the soup and warm it.
Stir the gelatin mixture into the cream cheese mixture. Add
the tuna, Miracle Whip, lemon juice, almonds, bell pepper, and
celery and mix well. Pour the mixture into a lightly oiled
ring mold. Refrigerate the mold until it is firm. Serves 8.

Patio Luncheon Salad

1 pound beef stew meat or 1 (2½ pound) chicken
2 avocados, peeled and diced
½ pound onions, diced
⅓ cup olive oil
⅓ cup vinegar
Salt to taste
Salad greens

In a Dutch oven boil the meat or chicken for 1½ hours, or until
it is tender. (If chicken is used, skin and bone.) When the
meat is cool, cut it into thin strips. In a large bowl mix the meat,
avocados, and onion with the oil and vinegar and season with
salt. Serve as a main course salad on the greens. Serves 4.

Canned chicken or beef broth or consommé may be substituted
for basic stocks or broths.

Crab Salad

½ pound crab meat
3 tablespoons olive oil
1 tablespoon wine vinegar
2 ribs celery, finely chopped
1½ tablespoons finely chopped green onion
10 stuffed olives, sliced
1 tablespoon sweet pickle relish
1 tablespoon finely chopped parsley
1 tablespoon lemon juice
3 dashes Worcestershire sauce
Salt and pepper to taste
¼ cup mayonnaise
Lettuce

In a large bowl, using a wire whisk, beat together the oil
and vinegar. Add the remaining ingredients except the
mayonnaise and lettuce and mix gently. Add enough mayonnaise
to bind the ingredients together. Chill thoroughly. Spoon
the crab meat mixture onto the lettuce and serve cold. Serves 4.

Homemade Mayonnaise

2 egg yolks
2 tablespoons white vinegar
1 teaspoon salt
1 teaspoon sugar
1 teaspoon prepared mustard
2 cups Wesson oil

With a fork or whisk mix all of the ingredients except the oil
in the small bowl of an electric mixer. Add a few drops of the
oil and beat on high speed. Add the oil, 1 teaspoon at a time,
until you have used ½ cup. Gradually add the remaining oil
while beating. Refrigerate the mayonnaise. Makes 2 cups.

Blender Mayonnaise

2 eggs
4 tablespoons tarragon vinegar or lemon juice
1 teaspoon dry mustard
1 teaspoon sugar
1 teaspoon salt
¼ teaspoon white pepper
¼ teaspoon cayenne or Tabasco sauce
2 cups salad oil

Place the eggs, vinegar, dry mustard, sugar, salt, pepper, and
cayenne in a blender and blend it a few seconds. Very slowly pour in
the oil, blending at high speed. Store the mayonnaise, covered, in
the refrigerator. Makes 2 cups.

Honey French Dressing

⅓ cup honey
1½ cups salad oil
½ teaspoon salt
1 tablespoon Worcestershire sauce
⅓ cup chili sauce
½ cup vinegar
1 small onion, grated

In a bowl mix all of the ingredients. Transfer the mixture to a quart jar with a lid and refrigerate. Shake well before using. Keeps well. Makes 3 cups.

Celery Seed Salad Dressing

1 cup salad oil
⅔ cup sugar
⅓ cup vinegar
⅓ cup ketchup
1 teaspoon celery seed
1 teaspoon salt
1 teaspoon paprika
1 teaspoon grated onion

In a bowl mix all of the ingredients well. Transfer the mixture to a jar with a lid and refrigerate. Makes 2 cups.

Delicious on fruit salads of any kind
Poppy Seed Dressing

1½ cups sugar
2 teaspoons dry mustard
2 teaspoons salt
⅔ cup vinegar
2½ tablespoons onion juice
2 cups Wesson oil
3 tablespoons poppy seed

In a bowl mix the sugar, mustard, salt, and vinegar. Add the onion juice and stir thoroughly. Add the oil slowly, beating constantly, and continue to beat until it is thick. Add the poppy seed and beat for a few minutes. Transfer the dressing to a jar, cover, and store in a cool place or in the refrigerator. Makes 3½ cups.

Italian Salad Dressing

¾ cup olive oil
2-3 tablespoons red wine vinegar
¾ teaspoon salt
1 clove garlic, minced
1 tablespoon minced onion
½ teaspoon freshly ground pepper
½ teaspoon Italian seasoning (if unavailable, substitute a pinch each of rosemary, savory, sage, oregano, and basil)

Combine all ingredients in a jar and shake well. Cover and refrigerate. Shake well before using. Makes 1 cup.

Thousand Island Dressing

1 cup Blender Mayonnaise (see Index)
1 teaspoon lemon juice
2 tablespoons ketchup
1 teaspoon Worcestershire sauce
2 tablespoons sweet pickle relish
2 tablespoons minced parsley
2 tablespoons minced celery
2 teaspoons minced green onion

In a bowl combine all of the ingredients and mix well. Transfer the dressing to a jar and cover. Store in the refrigerator. Makes 1½ cups.

Add salad dressings just before serving to prevent the greens from becoming limp.

EGGS, RICE, AND PASTA

Some say that, when Marco Polo returned to Venice in 1295, after a quarter-century of travel in medieval Asia, he brought pasta with him. Others say that pasta has been Italian for much longer than that. Whatever the case, pasta, and its Asian counterpart, rice, are excellent vehicles for other good things. Teamed with eggs and cheese, or with meat and a sauce, they provide a good, easy, and inexpensive meal. Both suffer, however, if they are overcooked. They should be firm, and each piece should be separate. Keeping them that way is the practical function of the oil, butter, and sauces which accompany them.

EGGS, RICE, PASTA

Eggs	75
Rice	82
Pasta	86

The Spanish influenced iron grillwork on the balconies of the "French" Quarter are famous the world over — and rightly so! Their beauty is rarely duplicated in such detail, quantity or quality.

Omelet Tips

To insure success in preparing an omelet, the proper pan
must be used. A medium weight, 9″ or 10″ skillet with sloping sides,
a flat bottom, and a smooth surface is ideal. Pans with non-
stick coating are especially desirable, or a pan can be seasoned to
prevent sticking by following these instructions. Cover the bottom
of the pan with vegetable oil, heat slowly, turning the
pan to coat sides. When the pan is hot, remove it from the
heat and cool. Let the pan stand overnight. The next day,
heat the pan again, pour off the oil, and wipe it dry with a paper towel.

Basic Omelet

4 *large eggs*
1 *tablespoon cold water*
¼ *teaspoon salt*
Dash of pepper
2 *tablespoons butter or margarine*

Break the eggs into a medium bowl. Add the water, salt, and pepper
and beat with a fork briskly for 30 seconds or enough to blend the
yolks and whites. In an omelet pan melt the butter over moderate heat
until it begins to sizzle. DO NOT BROWN. Pour in the
eggs. As the edges begin to look set, lift the edges with a fork or
spatula so that the uncooked egg runs under the set portion. Tilt
the pan as necessary to hasten the flow of the egg. Continue lifting the
edges for 3 to 4 minutes, or until all of the uncooked egg has run
under the cooked portion. Smooth the top of the omelet with
a fork. The edges should look firm, the top moist and creamy.
With a metal spatula lift one edge of the omelet;
if it is not brown enough, increase the heat slightly and
continue cooking until golden brown. With the spatula fold ⅓
of the omelet toward the center. Slide the unfolded ⅓ of the
omelet on the center of a serving plate. Invert the pan, folding the
omelet over. Serves 2.

VARIATIONS:

Small amounts of leftover meats or vegetables can be minced and
added to the omelet before cooking.

Small amounts of leftover meats or vegetables can be chopped and
added to a cream or mushroom sauce and served over the omelet.

Sprinkle the nearly done omelet with grated Cheddar or
Parmesan cheese.

For extra flavor a small chopped onion, a few chopped green
onions, or ½ cup of finely chopped mushrooms, sautéed in 2
tablespoons butter, can be added to the eggs.

Eggs will beat to a greater volume if at room temperature.

Filled Omelets

A filled omelet makes a delicious luncheon or supper dish. The filling should always be warm or at room temperature, never chilled. Prepare the filling before starting the omelet, because the omelet demands complete attention. Part of the filling is placed down the center of the omelet before folding it and the remainder poured over and around the omelet after turning it out on the plate.

MUSHROOM OMELET:
Sauté ½ pound sliced mushrooms in 2 tablespoons butter. Season with salt and pepper.

AVOCADO OMELET:
Fill the omelet with diced avocado seasoned with lemon juice, salt, and pepper. Place additional avocado around the omelet on the plate.

FISH OR POULTRY OMELET:
Heat a small amount of cooked fish or poultry in butter and add a little cream, season with salt and pepper, and fill the omelet.

SPINACH OMELET:
Fill the omelet with creamed spinach and serve it with sour cream.

COTTAGE CHEESE OMELET:
Fill the omelet with cottage cheese seasoned with chopped parsley and chives.

Eggs Sardou

4 artichoke bottoms
1 tablespoon chopped green onion
2 tablespoons butter
2 tablespoons flour
1 cup half-and-half cream
1 (10 ounce) package frozen chopped spinach, cooked and drained
2 teaspoons lemon juice
3 tablespoons Parmesan cheese
Salt and pepper to taste
4 eggs, poached
¾ cup Hollandaise Sauce (see Index)
Paprika

In a small saucepan warm the artichoke bottoms in salted water and place them in a greased baking dish. In a separate saucepan sauté the green onion in the butter; blend in the flour, stirring constantly. Gradually pour in the cream and cook until thickened. Combine the spinach, lemon juice, cheese, salt, and pepper, add to the cream sauce, and mix well. Place ¼ of the spinach mixture on each artichoke bottom and keep them warm in the oven. Poach the eggs and place 1 egg on each filled artichoke bottom. Serve the eggs immediately topped with the Hollandaise Sauce and sprinkled with paprika. The Hollandaise Sauce may be kept warm by placing the blender jar in tepid water. Serves 2.

Scotch Eggs

4 hard-boiled eggs
Flour
10 ounces bulk sausage
1 onion, finely chopped
1 egg, beaten
Bread crumbs
Cooking oil

Peel the eggs and dust them with flour. In a bowl combine
the sausage and onion. Cover each whole egg evenly with the
sausage mixture, keeping the shape of the egg. Dip the coated eggs
in the beaten egg and roll them in bread crumbs. Fry the eggs
in deep hot oil for 7 minutes. Transfer the eggs to paper towels
to drain. Serve the eggs sliced in half with a salad. Serves 4.

Deviled Eggs

6 hard-boiled eggs
1/4 teaspoon salt
1/4 teaspoon prepared mustard
1/2 teaspoon vinegar
1/4 teaspoon onion juice
1 tablespoon mayonnaise
Dash of pepper
2-3 drops Worcestershire sauce
12 pimiento strips
Paprika
Parsley, chopped
Chives, chopped

Shell the eggs and cut each in half. Remove the yolks carefully
and force them through a coarse sieve. Add the next 7 ingredients and
mix until smooth and fluffy. Heap the yolk mixture into the
egg whites. Top each half with a strip of pimiento and sprinkle
it with paprika, parsley, and chives. Makes 12 halves.

Eggs à la Gregory

8 slices white bread, crusts removed and cubed
3/4 pound Cheddar cheese, grated
6 eggs
1 pint milk
1 teaspoon salt
1/2 cup butter, melted

In a greased 8″ x 8″ baking dish layer the bread and cheese
ending with a layer of bread. In a bowl beat together the eggs, milk,
and salt. Pour this mixture over the bread and cheese and refrigerate
the dish overnight. Pour the melted butter over the dish and bake
it at 325°F for 45 minutes, or until it is set. Serves 4.

Spinach Bake

3 tablespoons olive oil
½ cup sliced onion
10 eggs
½ pound fresh spinach
⅓ cup Parmesan cheese
1 tablespoon chopped parsley
1 clove garlic, crushed
1 teaspoon salt
¼ teaspoon pepper

In a heavy 10″ skillet with an oven-proof handle heat the oil.
Add the onion and sauté for 5 minutes or until golden.
In a large bowl whisk the eggs until well blended. Add the
remaining ingredients and mix thoroughly. Transfer the mixture to
the skillet and cook over low heat, lifting from the bottom with a
spatula as the eggs set (about 3 minutes). Bake, uncovered, at 350°F
for 10 minutes, or until the top is set. Loosen with a spatula
and slide onto a serving platter. Cut into wedges. Serves 8.

Mardi Gras Brunch Pie

1 pound bulk pork sausage
8 ounces hash brown potatoes, thawed
8-10 eggs
6 ounces half-and-half cream
Salt and pepper to taste

In a skillet brown the sausage breaking it up while stirring. Transfer
it to a plate and set it aside. To the sausage grease add the potatoes
and cook them until they are soft. Using a slotted spatula transfer
the potatoes to a deep-dish pie pan. Mold the potatoes in the pie pan
to form a crust. Arrange the sausage in the bottom of the pie pan. In
a bowl combine the eggs, cream, salt, and pepper and beat the mixture
until frothy. Pour the mixture over the sausage and bake the pie
at 350°F for 25 to 30 minutes, or until set. Serve the pie cut in
wedges. Serves 6.

Quiche Lorraine

1 (9 inch) pie shell
½ pound bacon, fried and crumbled
5 slices Swiss cheese
Green onions to taste, chopped
1½ cups cream
4 eggs, beaten
1 tablespoon flour
Dash of pepper
Garlic salt to taste

Bake the pie shell at 400°F for 5 minutes. In the shell layer the bacon, cheese, and green onion and refrigerate. With a fork mix together the cream, eggs, flour, pepper, and garlic salt. Strain the mixture and pour into the pie shell. Bake the quiche at 400°F for 15 minutes. REDUCE OVEN TEMPERATURE to 325°F and continue baking, for 30 minutes, or until the quiche is set. Serves 6.

Quiche

1 (9 inch) pastry shell
6-8 slices bacon, fried
½ cup grated Swiss cheese
3 eggs
1¼ cups half-and-half cream
¼ teaspoon salt
Pepper to taste
1-2 tablespoons butter, thinly sliced

Bake the pastry shell at 375°F for 10 minutes. In the pastry shell arrange the bacon and sprinkle it with the cheese. In a bowl beat together the eggs, cream, salt, and pepper. Pour the mixture into the shell to within ⅛ inch of the top. Distribute the butter on the top of the quiche. Bake the quiche at 375°F in the top half of the oven for 25 to 30 minutes, or until brown and puffed. A tester should come out clean when inserted in the center.

VARIATION:
To the filling add sliced ham and cheese topped with asparagus, shrimp, mushrooms, or chopped cooked onion. Serves 6.

Crab Quiche

1 (9 inch) pie shell
3 eggs, well beaten
1 cup heavy cream
1 pound lump crab meat
¾ cup grated Gruyère cheese
Dash of salt
6 drops Tabasco sauce
1 tablespoon butter

Using a fork prick the bottom of the pie shell. Bake the pie shell at 400°F for 5 minutes. In a large bowl combine the eggs and cream. Add the crab meat, cheese, salt, and Tabasco sauce and mix gently. Pour the mixture into the pie shell. Bake at 425°F for 40 minutes. Remove the quiche from the oven, dot the top with butter, and allow to cool for 30 minutes. Cut in wedges and serve. Serves 6.

Eggs separate better when they are cold.

Stuffed Eggs

1 dozen eggs
1 teaspoon prepared mustard
2-3 tablespoons pickle relish
3 tablespoons mayonnaise
3 drops Tabasco sauce
Bacon, crisply fried and crumbled (optional)
Minced ham (optional)
Garlic salt to taste
Grated Cheddar cheese to taste
Paprika

In a saucepan cover the eggs with cold salted water. Bring the water to a boil, remove from heat, and let them stand, covered, for 20 minutes. Drain the eggs and place them in cold water. Shell the eggs and cut each in half lengthwise. Transfer the yolks to a medium bowl. Mash the egg yolks and to them add the mustard, pickle relish, mayonnaise, and Tabasco sauce. Add the bacon and ham if desired. Sprinkle the egg whites lightly with garlic salt and fill them with the yolk mixture. Top the stuffed eggs with grated cheese and sprinkle them with paprika. Serve the stuffed eggs chilled. Makes 24.

VARIATIONS:
Force enough cooked asparagus tips through a food mill to make 1 cup. Mash them with the yolks of 6 eggs. Blend in 2 tablespoons mayonnaise, 2 tablespoons lemon juice, salt, and pepper to taste and fill the whites.

Mash ½ cup smoked oysters, ½ teaspoon finely chopped green onion, ½ teaspoon curry powder, salt, and pepper to taste with 2 tablespoons mayonnaise. Combine with mashed egg yolks. Fill the whites and sprinkle the stuffed eggs with paprika.

Mash the yolks of 6 eggs and mix with 1 teaspoon dry mustard, 1 teaspoon Worcestershire sauce, ½ teaspoon pepper, and 2 tablespoons mayonnaise. Add salt to taste and 1 tablespoon chopped parsley. Add more mayonnaise if necessary. Fill the egg whites and garnish them with a sprig of parsley.

Cook eggs at low to moderate heat; high heat will toughen the protein and make them leathery.

Ham Asparagus Quiche

BUTTER PASTRY:
¼ teaspoon salt
1 cup flour
⅓ cup butter or margarine, chilled and sliced
1 egg
1 teaspoon lemon juice
2 teaspoons ice water
FILLING:
¼ pound thinly sliced ham
3 eggs
1 cup half-and-half cream or milk
Salt to taste
Tabasco sauce to taste
1 cup grated Swiss cheese
Pinch of nutmeg
1 (10 ounce) package frozen asparagus, cooked and drained

In a bowl mix together the salt and flour. Add the butter and cut it in with a pastry cutter until the mixture resembles coarse crumbs. In another bowl with a fork beat the egg, lemon juice, and water until blended and pour the mixture over the flour mixture. Toss the mixture with a fork and form into a ball. Wrap the pastry in plastic wrap and place in the freezer for 10 minutes. Transfer the dough to a lightly floured pastry board or cloth. Roll the dough out into a circle 1 to 1½ inches larger than the quiche or pie pan. Line the pan loosely with crust, trim the edges, and crimp them. Prick the pastry with a fork about 12 times and cover with a circle of wax paper. Fill the shell with two cups of dried beans and bake at 425°F for 12 minutes. Cool the crust slightly. Carefully remove the beans and the wax paper.

FILLING:
Arrange the ham in the bottom of the pie shell. In a bowl beat together the eggs, cream, and spices until blended but not frothy. Add the cheese and pour the mixture over the ham. Arrange the asparagus spears spoke fashion over the top. Bake the quiche at 375°F for 30 to 40 minutes. Serves 6.

When beating egg whites the bowl and beaters must be spotlessly clean and dry.

Hawaiian Rice

1½ pounds long grain rice
1 cup butter
3 large onions, chopped
2 large bell peppers, chopped
1 bunch celery, chopped
2 (4 ounce) cans sliced mushrooms
2 (10¾ ounce) cans cream of chicken soup
2 (3 ounce) bottles stuffed olives, sliced
1 (6 ounce) can blanched almonds
1 cup pineapple juice
1 teaspoon vinegar
½ teaspoon salt
½ teaspoon sage
1 teaspoon seasoned salt

In a saucepan boil the rice in water until it is almost tender. Do not overcook. Drain the rice and set it aside. In a large skillet melt the butter over medium heat. Add the onion, bell pepper, and celery and sauté until tender. Add the mushrooms and remove the mixture from the heat. Add 1 can of the soup and 1 can of water. Add 1 bottle of the olives and the almonds. In a large bowl mix together the pineapple juice, vinegar, salt, sage, and seasoned salt. Combine the mixture with the soup mixture and gently fold in the rice. Transfer the mixture to a 4-quart baking dish. Pour the remaining can of soup and 1 soup can of water over the top. Garnish the casserole with the remaining bottle of olives. Bake the dish at 350°F for 45 minutes. Serves 15.

Vermouth Rice

1 cup dry vermouth
1¾ cups water
1½ cups uncooked rice
½ teaspoon salt

In a large saucepan bring the vermouth and water to a boil. Stir in the rice and salt and bring the mixture back to a boil. Cover the rice and cook over low heat for 20 minutes. Serves 6.

Plunge hard-boiled eggs into cold water immediately after cooking for ease in peeling.

Risotto Verde

1 cup rice
4 tablespoons olive oil
1 small onion, finely chopped
1 teaspoon salt
½ teaspoon pepper
½ teaspoon thyme
2½ cups chicken stock
2 tablespoons butter
1 bell pepper, finely chopped
½ cup finely chopped parsley
3 green onions, finely chopped
1 clove garlic, crushed

In a large heavy skillet sauté the rice for 2 to 3 minutes in the olive oil. Add the onion and stir for 1 minute. Add the salt, pepper, thyme, and chicken stock. Bring the mixture to a boil, quickly reduce the heat, and simmer, covered, for 20 to 30 minutes, or until the liquid is absorbed and the rice is tender. Check the mixture after 15 minutes and add water if necessary. Remove the skillet from the heat. In a small saucepan melt the butter and sauté the bell pepper, parsley, green onion, and garlic for 1 minute. Stir the vegetable mixture into the rice mixture, mixing well, and serve. Serves 6.

The French method of braising rice
Rice Pilaf

3 cups converted rice
½ cup butter
3 green onions, minced
2 teaspoons salt
½ teaspoon white pepper
6 cups chicken broth

In a skillet sauté the rice slowly in melted butter for 2 to 3 minutes, or until it appears white and puffy. Add the green onion, salt, pepper, and broth. Transfer the mixture to a 9" x 13" baking dish and bake it, covered, at 350°F for 45 minutes, or until all the liquid is absorbed and the rice is tender. If proportions are to be decreased use 2 cups of liquid to each cup of rice. Serves 12.

Hard water has a tendency to discolor the rice. To correct this add 1 tablespoon vinegar, 1 teaspoon lemon juice, or ½ teaspoon cream of tartar.

Rice

Lemon Rice

2 tablespoons butter
1¼ cups rice
¼ cup dry vermouth
2¼ cups chicken broth
¾ teaspoon salt
Pinch of white pepper
Rind of 1 lemon, grated
2 tablespoons minced parsley

In a skillet melt the butter over medium heat. Add the rice and stir until all grains are coated with butter. Add the vermouth, broth, salt, and pepper. Bring the mixture to a boil. Cover the skillet and lower the heat. Simmer the rice for 20 minutes, or until all of the liquid is absorbed. Toss the rice with the lemon rind and parsley. Serves 6.

Rice Dressing
(Dirty Rice)

½ cup bacon grease
6 pork chops, boned and ground
1 pound chicken livers, ground
1 large onion, ground
1 bell pepper, ground
2 ribs celery, ground
3 cloves garlic, ground
2 cups liquid (combine pan juices from the vegetables with turkey drippings or chicken broth)
1 bay leaf
½ teaspoon ground thyme
Salt and pepper to taste
½ teaspoon red pepper
5 cups cooked rice, chilled
3 green onions with tops, minced
¼ cup minced parsley

In a heavy Dutch oven melt the bacon grease. Add the pork and liver and fry the mixture until very brown. Let the meat stick to the skillet a bit before stirring it. Add the onion, bell pepper, celery, and garlic and cook them until they are wilted. Add the liquid, bay leaf, thyme, salt, pepper, and red pepper. Simmer the mixture for 30 minutes. Remove the bay leaf. Add the rice and toss the mixture until the rice is hot. Stir in the green onion and parsley. Stuff a large turkey with the dressing, or serve as a side dish. Serves 8-10.

Rice almost triples in bulk when cooked; allow ¼ cup uncooked rice per person to provide a generous serving.

Brown Almond Rice

4 tablespoons butter
1 onion, chopped
1 clove garlic, chopped
1 (8 ounce) can beef broth
1 cup brown rice
½ cup sliced almonds
3 tablespoons light raisins
⅛ teaspoon allspice
⅛ teaspoon nutmeg
⅛ teaspoon cinnamon
Salt and pepper to taste

In a large saucepan melt the butter over medium heat. Add the onion and garlic and sauté until transparent. Add the beef broth and 2 cups of water. Add the remaining ingredients and bring the mixture to a boil. Continue boiling until the liquid is reduced to the level of the rice. Lower the heat and steam the rice, covered, for 45 minutes. Serves 4.

Rice with Green Chilies

¾ cup rice, cooked
2 cups sour cream
Salt to taste
½ pound Monterey Jack cheese, cut in strips
1 (6 ounce) can peeled green chilies, cut in strips
Butter
½ cup grated Monterey Jack cheese

In a bowl combine the rice with the sour cream and salt. Arrange ½ of the mixture in the bottom of a 1-quart casserole. Wrap the cheese strips in the strips of green chili and arrange them on top of the rice in the casserole. Add the remaining rice mixture and dot the top with butter and the grated cheese. Bake the casserole at 350°F for 20 minutes, or until the cheese is melted and bubbly. Serves 4.

To vary the rice flavor add 3 chicken or beef bouillon cubes to 3 cups of water.

Pancit

3 tablespoons butter
3 cloves garlic, pressed
4 carrots, cut in thin strips
6 green onions, diagonally sliced in 1-inch pieces
1 package rice sticks (approximately 1 pound)
8 cups shrimp stock or chicken stock
2 ½ cups peeled boiled shrimp (mildly seasoned)
Lemon wedges or sweet limes
Soy sauce to taste

In a skillet melt the butter. Add the garlic and sauté until soft. Add the carrots and a small amount of water and simmer for 5 minutes. Add the green onion and simmer for 5 minutes, adding more water if necessary. Soak the rice sticks for 3 minutes in cold water and drain. In a Dutch oven or kettle bring the stock to a boil. Add the rice sticks, boil for 5 minutes, or until the sticks are tender, and drain. In a large bowl combine the rice sticks, shrimp, and vegetables. Serve the Pancit on a platter or in a casserole garnished with lemon and sprinkled with soy sauce. Serves 6-8.

Fettuccine

1 (16 ounce) package fettuccine or thin noodles
1 cup butter
½ cup chopped parsley (optional)
½ teaspoon salt
Freshly ground pepper to taste
1 egg, slightly beaten
½ cup heavy cream, heated
2 cups grated Parmesan cheese

Cook the noodles according to the package directions. Slice ½ of the butter into a warm bowl or chafing dish. Add the parsley, salt, and pepper. Drain the noodles and pour into the warmed bowl. Slice in the remaining butter and toss the mixture gently, turning the noodles. While tossing the mixture, add the egg and small amounts of the cream until the noodles are well coated. Add the cheese and toss lightly until the noodles are thoroughly coated. Serves 8.

Add 1 tablespoon of cooking oil to boiling water to prevent pasta from sticking.

BREADS

If you think about it, bread is one of the world's most wonderful inventions. In fact, it depends upon a series of discoveries—a kind of grain that can be threshed without heating it, the process of grinding it into flour, leavening, and the oven. The result was to turn the soggy grain pastes our distant ancestors ate into one of the most satisfying and varied foods we have. It smells good and tastes better, and supplements more expensive foods.

BREADS

The spires of St. Louis Cathedral loom over the trees of Jackson Square. This sight is beautiful at any time but particularly inspiring when seen at dawn.

Kaplan Coffee Cake

¾ cup butter (at room temperature)
2 cups sugar
4 eggs
2¾ cups flour
2½ teaspoons baking powder
1 cup milk
2 teaspoons vanilla
TOPPING:
1 cup chopped nuts
1 tablespoon cinnamon
3 tablespoons sugar
6 tablespoons butter

In the bowl of an electric mixer cream the butter, sugar, and eggs. Into another bowl sift the flour and baking powder 3 times. Add to the creamed butter alternately with the milk and vanilla. Pour the batter into a well-greased and floured bundt pan or 9" x 13" baking pan. In a small bowl combine the nuts, cinnamon, and sugar. Dot the batter with the butter and sprinkle topping over the entire surface. Bake at 300°F for 35 to 45 minutes. If a bundt pan was used, let cool 5 minutes and invert to a wire rack to cool completely. Serves 24.

Grandmother's Sour Cream Coffee Cake

1 cup margarine
2 cups sugar
3 large eggs
2 cups sifted flour
1 teaspoon baking powder
½ teaspoon salt
1 (8 ounce) carton sour cream
1 teaspoon each vanilla, lemon, and almond extract
½ cup brown sugar
4 teaspoons cinnamon
1 cup ground pecans

In the large bowl of an electric mixer cream the margarine and sugar at high speed for 10 minutes, or until it is fluffy. Add the eggs, 1 at a time, to the margarine mixture. Into another bowl sift together the flour, baking powder, and salt. Add the sour cream, vanilla, and dry ingredients alternately to the margarine mixture, beginning and ending with the dry ingredients. Pour ½ of the batter into a greased and floured tube or bundt pan. In a separate bowl mix together the brown sugar, cinnamon, and pecans. Liberally sprinkle ½ of the pecan mixture over the batter in the pan. Add the remaining batter and sprinkle or gently press the remaining pecan mixture into the top. Bake at 325°F for 1 hour. Cool the cake in the pan for 5 minutes. Transfer the cake to a wire rack to continue cooling. Serves 14.

Kolachy

1 package dry yeast
2 tablespoons warm water
4 cups flour
¼ cup sugar
1 teaspoon salt
1 teaspoon grated lemon rind
¾ cup butter (at room temperature)
3 egg yolks
1 cup heavy cream
FILLING:
1½ cups prunes or dates
½ cup water
¼ cup sugar
½ teaspoon cinnamon

In a small bowl soften the yeast in warm water. In a large bowl
combine the flour, sugar, and salt. Add the lemon rind and
yeast and cut in the butter. In another bowl beat the egg yolks
into the cream, add to the flour mixture, and stir until blended.
Cover the dough with a damp cloth and store in the refrigerator
overnight. Punch the dough down as often as possible as it
doubles in bulk. An hour and a half before serving, roll the dough
on a lightly floured surface to ¼ inch thickness. Cut the dough with
a 2-inch biscuit cutter. Place the dough rounds on ungreased
baking sheets. Cover the dough and let it rise for 1 hour. While
the dough is rising, prepare the filling. In a saucepan cook the
prunes in water until tender. Stir in the sugar and cinnamon.
Let the filling cool before placing it on the dough. Depress the
center of the dough rounds and fill each with ¾ teaspoon filling.
Bake at 375°F for 12 minutes. Top with a pat of butter and
sprinkle with confectioners' sugar immediately. Serve hot.
Makes 48.

Old South Coffee Cake

1 package dry yeast
¼ cup warm water
1 cup sugar
1 teaspoon salt
¾ cup milk
1 egg
¼ cup shortening
3½-3¾ cups flour
½ cup butter, melted
1 teaspoon cinnamon
½ cup chopped nuts
Raisins

In a large bowl dissolve the yeast in water. In a saucepan combine ¼ cup of the sugar, salt, and milk and scald. When cool add the milk mixture, egg, shortening, and about ½ of the flour to dissolved yeast. Beat with a spoon until smooth. Gradually add more flour until it handles easily, and pulls away from the side of bowl. Transfer the dough to a floured board and knead until smooth. Put in a greased bowl and turn to grease the top. Cover with a damp cloth and let rise in a warm place about 90 minutes or until double in bulk. Punch the dough down. In a small bowl prepare the coating mixture by combing the remaining sugar, cinnamon, and nuts. Form the dough in walnut-size balls. Roll the balls in melted butter and in the sugar mixture. Place 1 layer of balls in greased tube pan so they barely touch. Sprinkle with raisins. Add another layer of balls and sprinkle with more raisins, pressing in a bit. Cover the coffee cake and let it rise about 45 minutes until double in bulk. Bake at 375°F for 35 to 40 minutes. Loosen the cake from the pan and invert it so the butter runs down the cake. Break apart to serve. Serves 16-20.

Beignets

(French Market Doughnuts)

½ cup boiling water
2 tablespoons shortening
¼ cup sugar
½ teaspoon salt
½ cup evaporated milk
½ package dry yeast
¼ cup warm water
1 egg, beaten
3¾ cups sifted flour
Confectioners' sugar

In a large mixing bowl pour the boiling water over the shortening, sugar, and salt. Add the milk and let stand until warm. In a small bowl dissolve the yeast in the warm water and add to the milk mixture with the egg. Stir in 2 cups flour and beat. Add enough flour to make a soft dough. Place the dough in a greased bowl turning to grease the top. Cover with wax paper and a cloth and chill until ready to use. On a lightly floured surface roll the dough to ⅛ inch thickness. Do not let dough rise before frying. Cut into 2-inch squares and fry, a few at a time, in deep hot fat (360°F). Brown on 1 side, turn and brown on the other side. Drain on paper towels. Sprinkle with the confectioners' sugar and serve hot. Makes 30 doughnuts.

One package of dry yeast equals 1 package cake yeast.

Doughnuts

1 cup butter (at room temperature)
2 cups sugar
2 cups milk
2 packages dry yeast
4 tablespoons warm water
4 cups flour

In the bowl of an electric mixer cream together the butter, sugar, and milk. Dissolve the yeast in the water, add the flour, and add this mixture to the sugar mixture. Set the sponge aside. Continue the dough after the sponge has been set aside overnight or for at least 9 hours, covered, in a warm place.

2 eggs
1 teaspoon cinnamon (optional)
½ teaspoon mace (optional)
3 cups flour (approximately)
Oil for deep frying

In the bowl of an electric mixer beat the eggs until light and add them with the spices to the sponge. With a wooden spoon beat in enough flour to form a dough that can be easily rolled. Set aside in a warm place to rise until doubled in bulk or about 30 to 90 minutes. Roll out to ⅓ inch thickness, cut into rounds, and remove centers. (Reserve the centers for fried doughnut holes.) Let the doughnuts rise until doubled in bulk. Heat the oil in a deep fat fryer to a rolling boil (375°F). Fry the doughnuts until golden brown on both sides. Transfer the doughnuts with a slotted spoon to paper towels to drain. While the doughnuts are still hot, place them on a wire rack and drizzle with Glaze. Makes 36 doughnuts.

HEAVY GLAZE:
½ cup honey
⅔ cup confectioners' sugar, sifted

Thoroughly blend the honey and sugar.

SUGAR GLAZE:
4½ cups sugar
1 cup water

In a medium saucepan combine the sugar and water. Stir the mixture well. Cook over medium heat until the sugar dissolves and a candy thermometer registers 228°F. DO NOT STIR. Gently remove the syrup from the heat with as little agitation as possible to prevent crystallization and let cool slightly.

An old New Orleans delicacy sold by street vendors on Sunday mornings carrying them in baskets on their heads

Calas

½ cup uncooked rice
½ tablespoon dry yeast
½ cup lukewarm water
3 eggs, well beaten
½ cup sugar
1½ cups sifted flour
½ teaspoon salt
½ teaspoon ground cinnamon
Oil for frying
Confectioners' sugar

In a saucepan cook the rice until it is mush and cool. In a bowl dissolve the yeast in the water. Add the rice to the yeast and mix well. Cover the dish and let the rice mixture rise overnight. In the morning add the eggs, sugar, flour, salt, and cinnamon and beat well making a thick batter. Let rise in a warm place for 30 minutes. Drop by tablespoonfuls in hot deep oil (365°F) and cook for 3 minutes or until golden brown. Drain on paper towels and dust with sugar. Makes 24.

Pain Perdu
(Lost Bread)

5 eggs
2 tablespoons orange flower water or orange juice
3 tablespoons brandy
½ cup sugar
1 lemon, juiced
Twist of lemon peel
6-8 slices stale bread
3 tablespoons butter
Confectioners' sugar
Grated nutmeg

In a bowl beat the eggs until they are light and fluffy. Stir in the orange flower water, brandy, and sugar and mix thoroughly. Add the lemon juice and lemon peel. Cut the bread into triangles or rounds and soak them in the egg mixture for about ½ hour. In a medium skillet melt the butter. Remove the bread from the egg mixture and fry it until lightly browned on both sides. Sprinkle the bread with the confectioners' sugar and nutmeg.

To proof yeast combine 1 teaspoon sugar with the yeast and warm water called for in the recipe. If the mixture bubbles up quickly, the yeast is good.

Buttermilk Griddle Cakes

2 cups flour
¼ cup sugar
1 teaspoon baking soda
1 teaspoon salt
2 tablespoons cornmeal
1 cup buttermilk
1½ cups milk
1 egg
1 tablespoon oil

Into a large mixing bowl sift together the flour, sugar, baking soda, and salt. Add the cornmeal. In another mixing bowl combine the buttermilk, milk, egg, and oil. Add the liquid mixture to the dry ingredients and stir just enough to moisten the dry ingredients. Do not beat. Heat a griddle or skillet and grease if necessary. Drop the batter onto the hot griddle by spoonfuls. The cakes are ready to turn when air bubbles form on the surface of the cake. Turn them only once. Serve hot with melted butter and syrup. Serves 3-6.

Date Bread

1 cup chopped dates
1 teaspoon baking soda
¾ cup boiling water
½ cup sugar
1 egg
4 tablespoons butter, melted
1¾ cups flour
1 teaspoon baking powder
½ teaspoon salt
½ cup chopped nuts

Place dates and soda in a small bowl; cover with boiling water and let stand until cool. In the bowl of an electric mixer cream together the sugar, egg, and butter. Into the creamed mixture sift the flour, baking powder, and salt and continue to beat until thoroughly blended. Stir in the nuts and soaked dates. Pour the batter into a greased and floured 9″ x 5″ x 3″ loaf pan. Bake at 350°F for 50 to 60 minutes. Cool the loaf in the pan for 5 minutes. Transfer to a wire rack to continue cooling. Makes 1 loaf.

Sour cream may be substituted for buttermilk.

Banana Bread

½ cup butter
1 cup sugar
2 eggs
2 cups flour
½ teaspoon salt
1 teaspoon baking soda
1 cup mashed banana
1 cup coarsely chopped pecans

In the large bowl of an electric mixer cream together the butter and sugar. Add the eggs, 1 at a time, beating after each addition. In another bowl combine the flour, salt, and soda. Add this mixture to the butter mixture, alternating with the mashed banana. Stir in the pecans. Pour the batter into a greased and floured 9″ x 5″ x 3″ loaf pan. Bake at 350°F for 55 minutes, or until a cake tester inserted in the center comes out clean. Remove the bread from the oven and cool for 5 minutes in the pan. Remove the loaf from the pan and transfer it to a rack to complete cooling. Makes 1 loaf.

Raisin Walnut Bread

¾ cup flour
2½ teaspoons baking powder
1 teaspoon baking soda
¾ teaspoon salt
1½ cups whole wheat flour
¾ cup brown sugar
¾ cup walnuts
¾ cup raisins
1½ cups buttermilk

Into a large bowl sift together the flour, baking powder, soda, and salt. Stir into this mixture the whole wheat flour, brown sugar, walnuts, and raisins. Pour the buttermilk into the dry ingredients and mix until well blended. Pour the batter into a greased and floured 9″ x 5″ x 3″ baking pan and bake the bread at 350°F for 1 to 1½ hours. Remove the bread from the oven. Cool in the pan for 10 minutes. Remove the bread from the pan and transfer to a wire rack to cool. Makes 1 loaf.

To test yeast loaf for doneness, tap it; it will sound hollow when done.

Pumpkin Bread

4 eggs
3 cups sugar
1 (16 ounce) can pumpkin
3½ cups flour
1¼ teaspoons salt
1 teaspoon baking powder
1 teaspoon baking soda
1 teaspoon cinnamon
1 teaspoon nutmeg
1 cup vegetable oil
¾ cup water
½ cup raisins or nuts

In the large bowl of an electric mixer cream together the eggs, sugar, and pumpkin. Into another large bowl sift the flour, salt, baking powder, baking soda, cinnamon, and nutmeg. Combine the oil and water in a small bowl. To the creamed mixture add the flour mixture alternately with the oil and water, ⅓ at a time. Beat well after each addition. Stir in the raisins and pour the batter into 3 greased and floured 9″ x 5″ x 3″ loaf pans. Bake at 350°F for 70 minutes. Remove the loaves from the oven and cool in pans 5 to 10 minutes. Remove to wire racks to cool completely. Makes 3 loaves.

Orange Grape-Nut Bread

2 cups flour
1 cup sugar
3½ teaspoons baking powder
1 teaspoon salt
1 cup whole wheat flour
¾ cup grape-nuts cereal
1 egg
¾ cup orange juice
4 teaspoons grated orange rind
¼ cup butter, melted
¾ cup milk

Into a large mixing bowl sift the flour, sugar, baking powder, and salt. Stir in the whole wheat flour and cereal. In a small bowl beat the egg lightly. Stir in the orange juice, orange rind, butter, and milk. Pour the liquid into the flour mixture and stir until it is blended. Pour the batter into a greased and floured 9″ x 5″ x 3″ pan. Bake at 350°F for 50 to 60 minutes. Cool the bread in the pan for 10 minutes. Remove it from the pan and cool completely on a wire rack. Makes 1 loaf.

Flours rich in gluten make the best bread. Bread flour is richest in gluten, but all-purpose flour works satisfactorily.

Whole Wheat Banana Bread

2 cups sugar
4 tablespoons margarine
2 eggs
1½ cups milk
1½ cups sifted flour
1½ cups sifted whole wheat flour
7 teaspoons baking powder
1 teaspoon salt
1½ cups chopped nuts
2 cups mashed banana

In the large bowl of an electric mixer cream together the sugar, margarine, and eggs. Stir in the milk. In another bowl combine the dry ingredients and stir into the egg mixture until well blended. Stir in the nuts and banana. Pour the batter into 2 greased and floured 9" x 5" x 3" loaf pans. Bake at 325°F for 1 hour and 10 minutes. The tops will crack during baking. Remove the loaves from the oven and cool in the pans for 5 minutes. Turn out onto wire racks. The bread may be wrapped and frozen. Makes 2 loaves.

Gingerbread

½ cup sugar
1 cup black molasses
½ cup butter
1 teaspoon ginger
1 teaspoon cinnamon
1 teaspoon ground cloves
2½ cups flour
2 teaspoons baking soda
2 eggs, well beaten

In the bowl of an electric mixer cream the sugar, molasses, and butter together. In another bowl sift together the ginger, cinnamon, cloves, and flour. Add this combination to the sugar mixture and continue beating. Dissolve the soda in 1 cup hot water and add the mixture with the eggs to the batter mixing until it is well blended. Pour the batter into a 9" x 13" pan that has been greased and floured. Bake at 350°F for 30 to 35 minutes. Remove the gingerbread from the oven and serve it sprinkled with confectioners' sugar, with a dollop of whipped cream, or in the traditional manner with applesauce. Serves 18.

Freezing: Bread should be thoroughly cooled and wrapped in an air-tight package.

Blueberry Muffins

1½ cups flour, sifted
½ cup sugar
3 teaspoons baking powder
½ teaspoon salt
1 egg, well beaten
½ cup milk
¼ cup oil
1 cup blueberries, drained

Into a mixing bowl sift the dry ingredients together. In another
bowl mix the egg and milk together and add to the dry ingredients.
Before this mixture is completely blended, add the oil and
blueberries. Grease a 12-cup muffin tin well and fill each cup
⅔ full. Bake at 400°F for 20 to 25 minutes. The muffins
may be frozen after baking. Makes 12 muffins.

Keep Awhile Muffins

2 cups All-Bran cereal
2 cups crumbled Shredded Wheat cereal
½ cup boiling water
3 cups sugar
1 cup margarine
4 eggs, slightly beaten
½ teaspoon baking powder
4½ teaspoons baking soda
2 teaspoons salt
5 cups flour
1 quart buttermilk

In a large bowl combine the cereals. Stir in the boiling water.
In a separate large bowl cream the sugar and margarine. Stir
in the eggs and cereal mixture. In another bowl combine the
baking powder, soda, salt, and flour. Add the flour mixture
to the cereal mixture alternately with the buttermilk. Pour the
batter into well-greased muffin tins. Bake at 400°F for 20 to 25
minutes.

For perfect bread it is important to let the dough rise exactly
the right amount. To test, press your finger into the dough. If
the imprint remains, the dough is ready.

The King Cake saga begins on the 6th of January, Twelfth Night as it is known in New Orleans, and ends on Ash Wednesday. The old tradition of a bean or china doll baked inside has been replaced with a plastic baby doll, but the excitement of finding it has not changed. The person who gets the slice containing the baby is king or queen for a week and must also provide a new King Cake to be served the next week. This opens up endless party possibilities in a party-oriented city and the ritual is a popular custom in family groups, offices, schools and Mardi Gras organizations. One of the carnival organizations in past days actually chose their king and queen with the bean found in the King Cake.

Mardi Gras King Cake

½ cup milk
½ cup sugar
1½ teaspoons salt
½ cup shortening
⅓ cup warm water (110°-115°F)
2 packages dry yeast
3 eggs
1 teaspoon grated lemon rind
½ teaspoon nutmeg
4½-5 cups bread flour, sifted
1 (1 inch) china baby doll

In a saucepan combine the milk, sugar, salt, and shortening. Scald and cool to lukewarm. In a large bowl dissolve the yeast in the warm water. DO NOT PUT YEAST IN HOT WATER AS IT WILL KILL THE YEAST AND YOUR DOUGH WON'T RISE. Add the milk mixture, eggs, lemon rind, nutmeg, and 2 cups of the flour. Beat until smooth. Add the remaining flour, 1 cup at a time. Transfer the dough to a floured board. Knead 5 minutes or until smooth and elastic. Place the dough in a greased bowl, turn over, and cover with a damp cloth. Let the dough rise in a warm place free from draft 90 minutes to 2 hours. When the dough is double in bulk, punch it down and knead it about 5 minutes. Divide the dough into thirds. Roll each portion into a strip 28-30 inches long. Braid the strips and shape the braid into an oval on a greased baking sheet. Secure ends. Carefully insert baby doll into the dough. Cover and let rise until the dough is double in bulk, about 1 hour. Bake the King Cake at 375°F for 20 minutes or until golden brown. Watch carefully. Cool the cake completely, frost it with Lemon Glaze, and sprinkle it with alternating stripes of purple, gold, and green sugars.

LEMON GLAZE:
1½ cups confectioners' sugar
1 teaspoon lemon juice
2 tablespoons water
Yellow food coloring

In a bowl combine the sugar, lemon juice, water, and tint with the food coloring and blend well.

Breads

Whole Wheat Crackers

¼ cup butter
1¾ cups whole wheat flour
1 cup flour
½ teaspoon baking soda
½ teaspoon salt
1 cup buttermilk
¼ cup honey

In a large mixing bowl cut the butter into the dry ingredients.
Pour the buttermilk and honey into the flour mixture and mix
well with a fork. Roll the dough flat into rounds on a well-floured
surface and place on baking sheets. Bake at 400°F for 5 to
8 minutes. Transfer to wire racks to cool. Makes 6-8 rounds.

Scandinavian Crisp Bread

1½ cups flour
1 cup rye flour
2 tablespoons brown sugar
2 teaspoons caraway seed
1 teaspoon baking powder
¼ teaspoon salt
¼ cup butter or margarine
½ cup water

In a large mixing bowl stir together the flour, rye flour, brown
sugar, caraway seed, baking powder, and salt until thoroughly
blended. Using a pastry blender cut the butter into the flour
mixture until the mixture resembles coarse crumbs. Add the water
all at once and stir until the mixture can be gathered in a ball.
Transfer the dough to a lightly floured surface. Knead the dough
gently 8 or 9 strokes. Divide the dough into 6 portions and
shape these into balls. On a floured surface roll each ball into
an 8-inch round. Using an index finger, make a 1-inch hole in
the center of each. With a fork prick the entire surface of each
round. Using a wide spatula, place 2 or 3 rounds on a lightly
greased baking sheet. Bake at 325°F for 15 minutes. Turn the
bread over and bake for 7 to 8 minutes more, or until the bread
is crisp. Remove the rounds from the oven. Cool on a rack.
Repeat rolling and baking the remaining dough. Makes 6 breads
rounds.

Zucchini Bread

3 eggs
1 cup oil
2 cups sugar
2 cups grated zucchini
2 teaspoons vanilla
3 cups flour, sifted
1 teaspoon baking soda
¼ teaspoon baking powder
1 teaspoon salt
3 teaspoons cinnamon
½ cup nuts

In the bowl of an electric mixer beat the eggs until light and creamy.
Add the oil, sugar, zucchini, and vanilla and mix lightly, but
well. In a separate bowl mix the flour, baking soda, baking
powder, salt, and cinnamon. Add the dry ingredients to the liquid
mixture with the nuts and blend well. Pour the batter into 2
well-greased and floured 9" x 5" x 3" loaf pans. Bake at 325°F
for 1 hour. Remove the loaves from the pans and transfer them to
wire racks to cool. Makes 2 loaves.

Oatmeal Bread

1 package dry yeast
1¾ cups warm water
¼ cup light molasses
4½ cups flour
1½ cups uncooked quick cooking oatmeal
2 eggs, beaten
2 tablespoons butter, melted
1 teaspoon salt
2 teaspoons milk

In a small bowl dissolve yeast in warm water and add the molasses.
In a large mixing bowl combine 2 cups of the flour, oats, 1 egg,
butter, and salt. Add the yeast mixture. Stir in enough additional
flour to make soft dough. Transfer the dough to a lightly floured
surface. Cover the dough with bowl for 10 minutes. Knead dough
until smooth and elastic, about 8 to 10 minutes. Place in a liberally
greased bowl and oil the surface of the dough. Cover with plastic
wrap and a damp cloth and let rise in a warm place about 1 hour,
or until double in bulk. Punch down the dough. Divide the
dough into 4 equal portions and shape into 4 round loaves.
Place on a large greased baking sheet. In a small bowl beat
1 egg and the milk. Brush the loaves lightly with the egg mixture.
Let rise, uncovered, in a warm place until double in bulk, about
45 minutes. Before baking brush with the egg mixture again. Bake
at 400°F for 18 to 20 minutes or until browned and loaves
sound hollow when tapped. Makes 4 loaves.

Dill Cottage Cheese Bread

1 package dry yeast
¼ cup warm water
1 cup creamed cottage cheese
2 tablespoons sugar
1 tablespoon minced onion
1 teaspoon dill seed
1 teaspoon salt
¼ teaspoon baking soda
1 egg, beaten
2¼-2½ cups flour
¼ cup shortening

In a large bowl dissolve the yeast in warm water. In a saucepan heat the cottage cheese, sugar, onion, dill seed, salt, and baking soda to lukewarm. Add this mixture to dissolved yeast and beat in the egg. Gradually stir in flour to form a soft dough. Transfer the dough to a floured surface and knead until smooth, about 5 minutes. Place the dough in a greased bowl, turning to grease the surface. Cover with a damp cloth and let rise in a warm place for 1 to 1½ hours or until double in bulk. Punch down and cover. Let the dough rest 10 minutes. Shape into a loaf and place in greased 9" x 5" x 3" loaf pan. Let rise, covered, in a warm place for 1 hour or until double in bulk. Bake at 350°F for 40 minutes. Remove the bread from the pan and brush with butter. Slice with serrated knife when cool. Makes 1 loaf.

Waynoka's Rye Bread

1 package dry yeast
1½ cups warm water
1 tablespoon sugar or molasses
1½ teaspoons salt
2 cups rye flour
1 cup milk
1 tablespoon shortening
½ teaspoon caraway seed (optional)
3 cups flour
3-4 cups additional flour for kneading

In a large mixing bowl dissolve the yeast in warm water. Add sugar, salt, and rye flour. Stir and set yeast sponge aside to rest, about 15 minutes. In a small saucepan scald the milk over medium heat. As it bubbles, remove from heat and cool. Add the milk to the yeast sponge. Beat with a heavy wooden spoon, adding in shortening and caraway seed and 3 cups flour. Beat until smooth. Turn out onto a floured cloth and begin kneading in the remaining flour until dough is elastic. Enough flour has been added when a depression has been made in dough and remains when hand is removed. The dough will not stick to hand at this point. Place dough in a well-greased bowl. Spread oil on surface and cover with a damp cloth. Let rise until double in bulk, about 1½ hours.

Roll out on bread board. Divide dough in 2 portions. Let dough
rest 15 minutes. Shape and place in buttered 9" x 5" x 3" loaf pans.
Let rise until double in bulk, about 1½ hours. Bake the bread
at 375°F for 40 minutes, or until it draws away from
sides of the pans. Let cool in pan 5 minutes. Transfer to a wire
rack to cool. Makes 2 loaves.

Easy Salt-Rising Bread

STARTER:
1 medium Irish potato, peeled and thinly sliced
1 teaspoon salt
2 tablespoons cornmeal
1 teaspoon sugar
1 teaspoon baking soda
1 pint boiling water

In a large bowl place the potato and sprinkle with the salt,
cornmeal, sugar, and soda. Cover with boiling water. Place a
loosely woven cloth over the bowl and set in a warm place for
at least 24 hours. Stir the starter several times during the 24 hour
period. If the potato ferment is not really frothy and foaming,
discard and begin again.

DOUGH:
6 cups flour
2 teaspoons salt
2 tablespoons sugar
2 tablespoons shortening

Remove and discard potato from starter. Into a large bowl pour
the liquid from the starter, discarding cornmeal. To the liquid
add 3 cups of the flour. Beat with a heavy wooden spoon until
thoroughly blended. Cover the bowl and set in a warm place for
1½ to 2 hours. Add the remaining ingredients to the sponge
and stir well. Transfer the dough to a floured surface and knead
the dough for about 10 minutes. Shape into a loaf and transfer
to a 9" x 5" x 3" loaf pan. Set the bread aside in a warm place
until double in bulk, about 1½ hours. Bake at 375°F for 40
minutes. Remove the loaf from the oven and let stand in the pan for
5 minutes. Remove the bread from the pan. Cool on rack or
serve hot. Makes 1 loaf.

To knead dough, press it flat using the heels of hands folding
it to the center. Repeat the process of pressing and folding
for about 15 minutes.

New Orleans French Bread

1 package dry yeast
1 tablespoon salt
1 tablespoon sugar
2 cups warm water
5-5½ cups flour
2 tablespoons butter, melted
2 tablespoons cornmeal

In a large bowl dissolve the yeast, salt, and sugar in the warm water. Gradually stir in the flour, adding only until the mixture refuses to absorb more. On a floured board knead the dough for 3 to 4 minutes. Transfer the dough to a greased bowl and brush the top lightly with butter. Cover with a damp cloth. Set the dough aside in a warm place to rise for 1½ hours, or until it is double in bulk. Butter a baking sheet and sprinkle it with cornmeal, shaking off the excess. Punch down the dough. Transfer the dough to a floured board and divide it into thirds. Roll each portion into a 8" x 13" rectangle. Roll each rectangle up from the long side, seal, and shape ends. Place the loaves on the prepared baking sheet and with a sharp knife make several diagonal cuts across the tops. Brush lightly with melted butter. Let rise in a warm place about 45 minutes. Place the bread on the middle rack in the oven. Place a pan of hot water on the bottom of the oven. Bake at 450°F for 5 minutes. REDUCE OVEN TEMPERATURE to 350°F and continue baking for 30 minutes. Makes 3 loaves.

Crescent Rolls

2 packages dry yeast
½ cup warm water
½ cup milk
½ cup sugar
½ cup shortening
2 teaspoons salt
4½-5 cups flour
3 eggs
½ cup melted butter

In a small bowl soften the yeast in the water. In a saucepan bring the milk to a boil and add the sugar, shortening, and salt. Transfer the mixture to a large bowl and cool to lukewarm. Stir 1½ cups of the flour into the milk mixture and beat well. Add the yeast and eggs. Beat thoroughly until smooth. Stir in enough of the remaining flour to make a moderately stiff dough. Transfer the dough to a lightly floured surface and knead 5 to 8 minutes until smooth and elastic. Shape the dough into a ball. Place in a lightly greased bowl and turn once. Cover and let rise in a warm place until double in bulk, about 1 to 1½ hours.

Punch the dough down and transfer it to a lightly floured surface. Cover and let rest 10 minutes. Divide the dough into 3 balls. Roll each ball into a 12-inch circle. Brush the dough with the melted butter. Cut into 12 pie-shaped wedges. To shape crescents, begin at the wide end of the wedge and roll toward the point. Place the rolls point side down on greased baking sheets about 2-3 inches apart. Cover the rolls with plastic wrap or a damp cloth and let rise in a warm place until double in bulk, about 30 to 45 minutes. Brush the rolls with melted butter. Bake at 400°F for 10 to 12 minutes. Makes 36 rolls.

Basic Refrigerator Rolls

2 packages dry yeast
2 cups warm water
2 teaspoons salt
½ cup sugar
6-8 cups flour
¼ cup shortening
1 egg

In a large bowl soften the yeast with the water. Add the salt, sugar, and about ½ cup of the flour. Stir and let rest for 15 minutes. To the yeast mixture stir in about 2-3 cups of the flour. Add the shortening and egg and with a wooden spoon beat the dough briskly for about 5 minutes. Add in another 2 cups flour and work until smooth. Transfer the dough to a well-floured board or cloth. Begin kneading in the remaining flour and continue until the bread is very elastic. This takes about 15 minutes. The bread has been sufficiently kneaded and added to when the hand does not come away sticky when held on the dough for 30 seconds. Place the dough in a well-oiled bowl, brushing oil over the surface, and cover it with a damp cloth. It is important to keep this cloth damp until all the dough has been used. Let the dough rise in a warm place away from draft for 1 hour or until double in bulk. Punch the dough down kneading it back into a small ball. Oil the surface of the dough and cover. At this point either prepare the dinner rolls or refrigerate the dough for as long as 3 days. If refrigerating, keep the cloth damp, repeatedly knead the dough down as it rises to double in bulk, and oil the surface as needed. Makes 48 dinner rolls.

PREPARATION OF BASIC DINNER ROLL:
Basic white roll dough
3 tablespoons oil

For a simple roll remove the needed portion of basic white roll dough. Pinch a ball of dough about 3 inches in diameter for each roll. In a 9″ x 13″ baking pan place 3 tablespoons oil. Drag the ball of dough through the oil and place the balls about 1 inch apart in the pan. When the pan is filled, cover with a damp cloth. Let rise in a warm place until double in bulk, about 1 hour. Bake at 350°F for 30 minutes.

Caraway Puffs

1 package dry yeast
2⅓ cups flour, sifted
¼ teaspoon baking soda
1 cup creamed cottage cheese
¼ cup water
2 tablespoons sugar
1 tablespoon butter or margarine
1 teaspoon salt
1 egg
2 teaspoons caraway seed
2 teaspoons grated onion

In the large bowl of an electric mixer combine the yeast, 1⅓ cups of the flour, and baking soda. In a medium saucepan over medium heat combine the cottage cheese, water, sugar, butter, and salt, stirring, until the butter melts. Add to the dry ingredients. Add the egg, seed, and onion and beat with an electric mixer on low speed for ½ minute, then on high speed for 3 minutes. Stir in the remaining flour. Place the dough in a greased bowl, turning once. Cover and let rise in a warm place until double in bulk, about 1½ hours. Divide the dough into 12 portions and place each portion in a 2½-inch cup of a well-greased muffin tin. Cover the rolls and let them rise for 40 minutes or double in bulk. Bake at 400°F for 12 to 15 minutes. Makes 12 rolls.

Eggdrop Dumplings

1 cup flour
¼ teaspoon salt
1 teaspoon baking powder
1 egg
3 tablespoons milk

Into a mixing bowl sift together the flour, salt, and baking powder. Quickly mix in the egg and milk. Drop the dough by tablespoonfuls into any hot broth, cover, and cook 12 to 15 minutes without removing the lid from the saucepan. Serve immediately. For a more "noodle like" dumpling combine the ingredients as shown above. On a liberally floured surface roll out the dough, turning several times, and flattening out with the palm of the hand to about ½ inch thick. With a knife cut the dough into 2-inch wide strips and drop the dumplings into broth. This will make a slightly tougher dough. Serves 4.

Cheese Lovers' Spoon Bread

4 tablespoons butter
2 cups milk
½ cup yellow cornmeal
3 eggs, separated
½ cup sharp Cheddar cheese
½ teaspoon salt
¼ teaspoon baking powder

Melt 2 tablespoons of the butter in a 1-quart casserole by placing it in the oven. In a saucepan scald the milk and add the cornmeal slowly (so as not to form lumps). Cook over low heat, stirring constantly, until thick. Remove the mixture from the heat and add the remaining butter, stirring, until it is melted and thoroughly blended. In a small bowl beat the egg yolks well. Take a small amount of cornmeal mixture from the pan and blend well with the egg yolks. Return this mixture to the saucepan and add the cheese, mixing well. Put the egg whites in the bowl of an electric mixer and sprinkle the salt and baking powder on top. Beat the whites until soft peaks form and fold them into the cornmeal mixture. Pour the spoon bread into the buttered casserole and bake at 375°F for 30 to 35 minutes. Serve immediately.
NOTE: Spoon bread looks like a soufflé and takes the place of grits or other starch. It is excellent served with Creole Daube or Grillades (see Index). Serves 8-10.

Dumpling Batter

1½ cups flour
2 teaspoons baking powder
¾ teaspoon salt
3 tablespoons shortening
1 teaspoon minced onion (optional)
3 tablespoons minced parsley or chives (optional)
¾ cup milk

In a mixing bowl combine the dry ingredients. Cut in the shortening with a pastry blender or 2 knives until the mixture resembles coarse meal. Add the minced onion and parsley. Blend in the milk, using a large mixing spoon. Mix only until well moistened. Drop by spoonfulls into gently boiling stew, gravy, or broth. Cook slowly for 10 minutes, uncovered, and 10 minutes, covered. A domed cover will help prevent soggy dumplings.

Raised Corn Bread Loaves or Rolls

1 package dry yeast
¼ cup warm water
2 cups milk, scalded
½ cup yellow cornmeal
2 teaspoons salt
2 tablespoons sugar
3 tablespoons shortening
2 eggs, beaten
6¾-8 cups flour
¼ cup salad oil

In a large bowl dissolve the yeast in the warm water. To the
scalded milk add the cornmeal, salt, sugar, and shortening and
stir until all lumps are removed. Add the cornmeal mixture to
the dissolved yeast. Vigorously stir in the eggs and ¾ cup of
the flour. Cover and set aside for 2½ hours. With a wooden
spoon vigorously beat in enough remaining flour (about 4 cups)
to form a dough which pulls away from the bowl. This will make
the dough manageable. Turn the dough out onto a liberally floured
surface. Knead in the remaining flour as needed until smooth
and elastic. Knead at least 15 minutes. If preparing rolls, pour
salad oil into a 9″ x 13″ pan. Form the dough into large balls.
Place the balls in the oiled pan; turn the balls to coat them with oil.
Let rise until double in bulk, about 60 to 90 minutes, and bake
at 350°F for 30 minutes. If preparing loaves, shape the dough into
2 rectangles and place in 2 liberally oiled 9″ x 5″ x 3″ pans. Let rise
until double in bulk. Bake at 425°F for 15 minutes. REDUCE
OVEN TEMPERATURE to 375°F and continue baking 20
minutes, or until the bread pulls away from the sides of the pans.
Let cool in pans for 5 minutes. Makes 2 loaves.

Spoon Bread

3 eggs, separated
4 cups milk
1 cup white cornmeal
1 teaspoon salt
1 teaspoon baking powder
2 tablespoons butter

In the bowl of an electric mixer beat the egg whites until stiff.
Set these aside. In a large saucepan scald 3 cups of the milk.
In a bowl mix the white cornmeal with the remaining milk and
stir this mixture into the saucepan containing the scalded milk.
Continue to heat. Stir the yolks into the cornmeal mixture. Continue
stirring and when the mixture thickens, remove it from the
heat and add the salt, baking powder, and butter. Fold in the
egg whites. Pour the mixture into a greased 2-quart casserole
and bake at 350°F for 45 to 55 minutes or until browned on top.
Serve immediately. Serves 6-8.

PICKLES AND JELLIES

Frequently, necessity does us a good turn. This is the
case with pickles, jellies, and jams. They originated
in the need to preserve summer vegetables and fruits
for winter use. We continue to make them because
they're easy and satisfying, a joy to look at and to eat.
They bring a vivid reminder of summer to the dank
days of winter, and there's something special about
adorning your table with things you made yourself.

PICKLES AND JELLIES

Tranquility and traditional beauty in a scene typical of many famous French Quarter Restaurants in New Orleans. Note the tiled floor and ceiling fans used with elegant chandeliers.

Sweet and Sour Mirliton Pickles

6 quarts sliced mirliton (12-14)
6 onions
1 cup salt
1½ quarts white vinegar
¼ teaspoon red pepper
6 cups sugar
½ cup mustard seed
1½ tablespoons celery seed

Soak the mirliton and onions in salted water to cover for 3 to
5 hours. Drain and taste them. If they are too salty, rinse and
drain them. Combine the vinegar, pepper, sugar, mustard seed, and
celery seed and bring the mixture to a boil. Reduce the heat
and simmer for 10 minutes. Add the mirliton and onions and bring
the mixture back to a boil and boil it for 10 minutes. Pack
the pickles in hot, sterilized jars and seal them. Makes 5 quarts.

Dill Pickled Onions

1½ pounds small onions
1 head fresh dill or 1 tablespoon dill seed per jar
¼ teaspoon crushed dried red pepper per jar
2 cups water
2 cups white vinegar
5 teaspoons pickling salt

Slice the onions into ¼-inch slices and separate the slices into
rings. Pack the onion rings into 3 hot, sterilized jars. Add the dill
and red pepper to each jar. In a saucepan combine the water,
vinegar, and salt and bring the mixture to a boil. Pour the mixture
over the onions in the jars to within ½ inch of the top. Adjust
the lids and process the jars of onions in a boiling water bath for
5 minutes. (Start timing when the water returns to a boil.) Store
the pickled onions for three weeks before serving them. Makes
3 pints.

Pickled Carrots

3 cups vinegar
9 cups water
1 cup salt
4 pounds carrots
1 clove garlic per jar
Sprig of dill per jar
½ teaspoon red pepper per jar

Mix the vinegar, water, and salt together. Boil the mixture for
5 minutes and let it to cool. Scrape the carrots and pack them into
jars. Add the garlic, dill, and red pepper to each jar. Pour the
cooled liquid over the carrots. Seal the jars. Let the pickled
carrots age for 2 weeks before serving.

Watermelon Rind Pickles

1 watermelon rind
1 gallon water
¼ cup slaked lime
3 cups white distilled vinegar
7 cups sugar
Red food coloring
1 cup red cinnamon candies (red hots)

Pare the rind, removing the green skin and all of the red meat. Cut the rind in 1-inch cubes. Combine the water and lime. Add the rind and soak it overnight in the refrigerator. Drain the rind cubes and rinse them well in cold water. Cover the rind with water, cook it for 30 minutes, and drain thoroughly. Combine the vinegar, sugar, several drops of the red food coloring, and candies. Pour the mixture over the rind and boil slowly for 1 hour, or until the rind looks clear. Be sure that the syrup covers the rind throughout cooking. Pack the pickles in hot, sterilized jars. Cover them with the syrup, seal the jars, and process them for 5 minutes in boiling water. Makes about 7 pints.

14 Day Sweet Pickles

2 gallons sliced cucumbers
2 cups salt (not iodized)
1 gallon boiling water
1 tablespoon powdered alum
PICKLING MIXTURE:
5 pints vinegar
6 cups sugar
5 teaspoons celery seed
3 tablespoons broken cinnamon stick
3 cups sugar

Into a clean stone jar put the cucumbers. Dissolve the salt in the boiling water and pour it, while hot, over the cucumbers. Cover the cucumbers with a non-metallic cover and weight them down, making sure they are totally submerged for 1 week. On the eighth day drain them, pour 1 gallon of boiling water over them, and let them stand for 24 hours. On the ninth day drain them, pour 1 gallon of boiling water with the alum over them, and let them stand for 24 hours. On the following day drain them again, pour 1 gallon boiling water over them, let them stand for 24 hours, and drain them. To pickle the cucumbers heat the vinegar to boiling and add the 6 cups sugar, celery seed, and broken cinnamon stick. Pour the mixture over the pickles. Drain the pickles each morning for 3 mornings, reserving the drained liquid. To the drained liquid add 1 cup sugar each morning, reheat the mixture, and pour it back over the pickles. The third and last morning, pack the pickles into hot, sterilized jars, pour the hot liquid over them, and seal the jars. Makes 16 pints.

Green Tomato Pickles

---

7 pounds green tomatoes, thickly sliced

2 gallons water

3 cups lime juice

Soak the tomatoes in the water and lime juice for 24 hours. Rinse the tomatoes and soak them in clear water for 6 hours.

SYRUP:

5 pounds sugar

3 quarts white vinegar

1 teaspoon celery seed

1 teaspoon whole ginger

1 teaspoon whole allspice

1 teaspoon whole cloves

Combine the syrup ingredients and let the mixture come to a boil. Drain the tomatoes and put them in a large granite pot, enameled pot, or a large crock. Pour the hot syrup over the tomatoes and let them stand overnight. Drain the syrup and cook it for 1 hour. Put the tomatoes in hot, sterilized jars, pour the hot syrup over them, and seal the jars. Makes 6 pints.

Bread and Butter Pickles

---

6 medium cucumbers, washed and sliced

2 large white onions, chopped

1 bell pepper, chopped

⅛ cup salt

1 cup cider vinegar

1 cup sugar

½ tablespoon white mustard seed

¼ teaspoon turmeric

In a non-metallic pot combine the cucumbers, onion, bell pepper, and salt and let the mixture stand for 3 hours, stirring often. In a large kettle combine the vinegar, sugar, mustard seed, and turmeric and bring the mixture to a boil. Drain the vegetables and add them to the vinegar mixture. Heat the mixture thoroughly, stirring often, but DO NOT BOIL. Pack the pickles into hot, sterilized jars and seal the jars immediately. Let the pickles age for 2 to 3 weeks before serving them. Makes 3 pints.

Select only unwaxed cucumbers for pickles.

Bread and Butter Pickles II

3 quarts cucumbers, washed
¼ teaspoon alum
1 tablespoon salt
1 quart water
1 quart vinegar
1 cup sugar
1 tablespoon mustard seed
¼ teaspoon turmeric

Cut the cucumbers in thin slices and soak them overnight in a brine made of the alum, salt, and water. In a non-metallic pot combine the vinegar, sugar, mustard seed, and turmeric and bring the mixture to a boil. Drain the brine from the cucumbers and add them to the vinegar mixture. Boil the mixture for 5 to 6 minutes. Pack the pickles into hot, sterilized jars and seal the jars. Makes 4 pints.

Dill Pickles

24 (3-4 inch) garden fresh cucumbers
1 cup vinegar
2 cups water
1 tablespoon granulated pickling salt per quart
Fresh dill
1 teaspoon mustard seed per jar
1 teaspoon celery seed per jar

Scrub the cucumbers with a brush. In a non-metallic pot combine the vinegar, water, and pickling salt and bring the mixture to a boil. Pack the cucumbers loosely in hot, sterilized quart jars. Add the dill, mustard seed, and celery seed to each jar. Pour the hot brine over the cucumbers within 1 inch from the top of the jar and seal the jar. Place the jars in a large pot with a cover. Add water to the pot up to the neck of the jars and boil, covered, for 20 minutes. Store the pickles for 1 month before serving them. Makes 6-8 quarts.

Dill Pickle Strips

3 quarts water
1 quart vinegar
1 cup salt
12-16 medium cucumbers, washed and cut in strips
1 teaspoon dill seed

Combine the water, vinegar, and salt and bring the mixture to a boil. Pack the cucumber into hot, sterilized jars and add the dill seed. Pour the boiling mixture into the jars and seal them. Let the pickles age for at least 2 months before serving them. Makes 4 pints.

Rosy Pickled Eggs

12 hard-boiled eggs, peeled
1 small white onion, sliced in rings
1-2 wide-neck canning jars
1 cup beet juice
1 cup vinegar
4 cups water
1 clove garlic
1 medium bay leaf
2 teaspoons mixed pickling spices
½ teaspoon salt

Divide the eggs and onion rings into sterilized jars. Mix the
remaining ingredients and pour the mixture over the eggs and
onions. Refrigerate the eggs for several days before serving them.
The eggs will keep for several weeks. Makes 2 quarts.

Summer Vegetable Relish

2 cups sliced cucumber
2 cups chopped bell pepper
2 cups chopped cabbage
2 cups chopped onion
2 cups chopped green tomato
2 quarts water
½ cup salt
2 cups cut fresh string beans
2 cups chopped celery
2 cups chopped mirliton
2 cups chopped carrot
2 cups chopped cauliflower

Soak the cucumber, bell pepper, cabbage, onion, and tomato
overnight in the water and salt. Cook the remaining vegetables
for 15 minutes or until tender. Drain both vegetable mixtures
well.

SYRUP:
1 quart cider vinegar
2 cups water
4 cups sugar
2 tablespoons celery seed
4 tablespoons mustard seed
2 tablespoons turmeric

Combine the syrup ingredients and bring the mixture to a boil.
Add the vegetables to the syrup and boil for 10 minutes. Place
the relish in hot, sterilized jars and seal them.

Select sound, firm, unbruised foods to avoid spoilage.

Cranberry Relish

2 quarts fresh cranberries, washed
1 cup vinegar
2 orange rinds, grated
2 oranges, juiced
6 cups sugar
1 pound raisins
2 tablespoons ground cinnamon
1 tablespoon ground cloves

In a large pot combine the cranberries and vinegar and let
them stand for 10 minutes. Add the remaining ingredients. Cook
the mixture over medium heat until the cranberries pop open.
Cool the relish, transfer it to jars, and seal the jars or freeze
them. The relish keeps, refrigerated, for 4 weeks. Makes 3-4 pints.

Garden Corn Relish

20 large ears sweet corn or 6 cups frozen whole kernel corn
1 small head cabbage, finely chopped
4 cups finely chopped celery
1 cup finely chopped green bell pepper
½ cup finely chopped red bell pepper
1 cup finely chopped onion
2 cups sugar
2 cups white vinegar
2 ¼ cups water
¼ cup flour
2 tablespoons salt
2 teaspoons celery seed
2 tablespoons dry mustard
1 teaspoon turmeric
¼ teaspoon cayenne

If using fresh corn, place it in a saucepan of boiling water and boil
it for 5 minutes. Plunge the corn into cold water to cool. Remove
all the kernels and place them in a large stainless steel or enameled
cooking pot. Add the cabbage, celery, bell pepper, onion, and
sugar. In a bowl mix together the vinegar, water, flour, and
spices and add the mixture to the vegetables. Bring the relish
to a boil and simmer for 5 minutes, uncovered. Pour the relish
into hot, sterilized jars and seal them. Makes 4 quarts.

Fill 1 jar at a time and wipe the top free of all food particles
before sealing.

Never double a preserve or jelly recipe.

Chutney

4 cups chopped papaya
2 cups chopped apple
1 cup packed brown sugar
¾ cup white vinegar
½ cup raisins
½ cup water
½ cup chopped bell pepper
¼ cup chopped onion
3 tablespoons lime juice
2 tablespoons canned, seeded green chilies
1 tablespoon chopped candied ginger
1 teaspoon salt
2 cloves garlic, crushed
¼ cup slivered almonds

In a Dutch oven combine all the ingredients except the almonds. Cook the mixture, covered, for 30 minutes, stirring frequently. Add the almonds and cook, uncovered, for 30 minutes. Mash the fruit and nuts slightly with a potato masher. Cool the chutney and transfer it to sterilized jars. Seal the jars with wax, or store them in the refrigerator.

Pickled Peaches

10 pounds peaches, peeled
4 pounds sugar
1 quart dark apple cider vinegar
1 cheesecloth bag, double thickness
2 tablespoons ground cinnamon
2 tablespoons ground cloves
2 tablespoons ground allspice

Place the peaches in cold water to cover. In a non-metallic pot combine the sugar and vinegar and bring the mixture to a boil. Add the cheesecloth bag containing the cinnamon, cloves, and allspice and boil the mixture for 10 minutes. Drain the peaches and transfer them to a crock. Pour the vinegar mixture over the peaches, cover the crock, and let them stand overnight. On the second day drain the syrup from the crock, bring it to a boil, pour it back over the peaches, and let them stand, covered, overnight. On the third day drain the syrup from the crock, bring it to a boil, and add the peaches to it, a few at a time. Cook the peaches in the syrup until a broom straw can be easily stuck into them. Transfer the peaches to hot, sterilized jars, fill the jars with the syrup, and seal them immediately. Makes 5-6 quarts.

Always store preserves and jellies in a cool, dark, dry place.

Brandied Peaches

Peaches
1 cup sugar
3 cups water
2 fifths bourbon

Blanch peaches in boiling water, 2 minute maximum. Remove at once and peel. Combine sugar and water; boil for 5 minutes to make a simple syrup. Place 4-5 peaches in each sterilized jar. Fill jars 1/2 full of bourbon. Add boiling simple syrup up to 1/4 inch of the jar tops. Screw on hot, sterilized lids until resistence is felt, then turn back a quarter turn. Place rack in a large pot with a cover. Fill pot with water to within 1 inch of jar tops and bring to a slow boil. (Measure height of jars to calculate water needed.) Slowly, leaving 2 inches space between jars, lower jars (metal canning tongs implement this process) into boiling water. Add sufficient water to bring it 1 inch above lid tops. Bring again to a slow boil. Boil, covered, for 30 minutes. Remove from water bath; immediately tighten lids and cool jars on clean towels in a draft free location. Store jars upside down for at least 8 weeks. Serve peaches, chilled, alone or with ice cream. Serve remaining brandy as an after-dinner drink.

Fig Preserves

5 pounds figs, cleaned
2 quarts water, boiling
½ cup baking soda
5 pounds sugar
1 cup thin lemon slices

Soak the figs in the boiling water, to which the baking soda has been added, for 15 minutes. Drain and rinse them in cool water. Combine the sugar and 3 cups of water and boil it to make a thick syrup. Place the figs in the syrup and cook over low heat for 45 minutes to 1 hour. Remove from the heat and cover the pot. Let the figs stand in the syrup overnight. The next day, bring the figs back to a boil, add the lemon, and cook for 1 hour. Transfer the figs to sterilized jars and seal them. Makes 16 half pints.

Frozen Figs

Fresh figs
Sugar

Many people in Southern Louisiana have fig trees and freezers and may not be aware that figs may be frozen easily and successfully. Peel the figs, layer them in containers, and sprinkle each layer generously with sugar. They should be frozen in small quantities. The figs must be used as soon as they are thawed.

Delicious on hot or cold meats or on cream cheese served with crackers

Hot Pepper Jelly

¾ cup bell pepper
3-4 hot peppers, seeds removed
1½ cups cider vinegar
6½ cups sugar
1 bottle liquid fruit pectin
Red or green food coloring

In a blender grind together the bell pepper and hot peppers with a little of the vinegar. In a pot combine the remaining vinegar, peppers, and sugar. Add the pectin, bring the mixture to a boil, and boil for 1 minute, stirring constantly. Remove from the heat and skim off the foam. Add the food coloring. Pour the mixture into hot, sterilized jars and seal them. Makes 6 half pints.
PRECAUTION: Wear rubber gloves to cut and clean the peppers. Do not touch your face while preparing the peppers. Rinse the blender with vinegar.

Basil Jelly

6½ cups sugar
1 cup white vinegar
6-8 drops green food coloring
2 cups water
1 cup fresh basil leaves, lightly packed
Cheesecloth bag
1 (6 ounce) bottle liquid fruit pectin

In a large saucepan or Dutch oven combine the sugar, vinegar, food coloring, and water. Tie the basil leaves in a cheesecloth bag and with a rolling pin bruise the basil and add to the mixture. Bring the mixture to a boil, stir in the pectin, and return it to a full rolling boil. Boil vigorously for 1 minute, stirring constantly. Remove from the heat, discard the basil bag, and skim the froth. Pour the jelly into hot, sterilized jars, and seal them. Makes 7 (½ pint) jars.

ROSEMARY JELLY:

Prepare Basil Jelly except substitute rosemary leaves for the basil and yellow food coloring for the green.

Use utensils made of enamelware, stainless steel, glass, or aluminum. Other metals will react with acids or salts and produce undesirable results.

Cranberry Claret Jelly

3½ cups sugar
1 cup bottled cranberry juice
1 cup claret wine
3 ounces liquid fruit pectin

In the top of a double boiler combine the sugar, cranberry juice, and wine. Place it over rapidly boiling water and cook, stirring, for 2 minutes, or until the sugar is dissolved. Remove from the heat, add the fruit pectin, and bring the mixture to a rolling boil. Boil the mixture for 1 minute, stirring constantly. Remove from the heat and remove the foam with a metal spoon. Pour the mixture into hot, sterilized jars and seal them. Makes 6 half pints.

Excellent served with meat

Parsley Jelly

2 large bunches parsley, washed
3 quarts water
½ cup lime juice
5 cups sugar
2 teaspoons grated lime rind
½ bottle liquid fruit pectin
Green food coloring
4 tablespoons finely chopped parsley

In a kettle place the parsley and water, bring the water to a boil, and simmer, covered, for 20 minutes. Strain the parsley and discard it, reserving the liquid. Return the liquid to the kettle and boil it rapidly until it is reduced to 3 cups. To the parsley liquid add the lime juice, sugar, and lime rind. Cook the mixture over moderate heat, stirring, until the sugar dissolves. Bring the mixture to a boil. Add the pectin and boil vigorously for 1 minute. Remove the mixture from the heat. Stir in the food coloring to the desired shade and blend in the parsley. Skim off the foam. Quickly ladle the mixture into hot, sterilized jelly glasses to ½ inch from the top and seal them. Makes 5 (8 ounce) glasses.

Jar Preparation: Use only standard jars that are free from cracks, nicks, or sharp edges. Wash the jars and covers in hot soapy water and rinse well. Place the jars and rims in a large pot filled with water and boil, covered, for 15 minutes. Add the lids and let them stand in the hot water until ready to use.

POULTRY

It is difficult to think of any food with more varied possibilities than poultry. It can be fried, boiled, stewed, or roasted, stuffed and garnished, or plain. It can be made into a soup or a salad, or eaten hot or cold. It is good by itself, with rice or pasta, or in a sandwich. No wonder it is everybody's favorite.

POULTRY

Seldom in any other city in the world will the observer find such elaborate and unique costumes used by band members or "second-liners." This unique style of dress adds another dimension to the pleasure of becoming a part of "New Orleans Style" music and entertainment.

Sherried Artichoke Chicken

1 frying chicken, cut up
Salt and pepper to taste
Paprika
6 tablespoons butter or margarine
1 (16 ounce) can artichoke hearts, drained
¼ pound fresh mushrooms, sliced
3 tablespoons chopped green onion
2 tablespoons flour
⅔ cup chicken broth
¼ cup sherry
½ teaspoon crushed rosemary

Season the chicken generously with the salt, pepper, and paprika.
In a skillet melt half of the butter over moderately high heat.
Add the chicken pieces and fry them until they are brown
on all sides. Transfer the chicken to a 2-quart casserole. Arrange the
artichoke hearts between the chicken pieces. Add the
remaining butter to the drippings in the skillet. Add the mushrooms
and green onion and sauté until tender. Sprinkle the flour
over the mushrooms and green onion. Stir in the chicken broth,
sherry, and rosemary. Cook the mixture, stirring constantly,
for 3 to 5 minutes. Pour the sauce over the chicken. Bake, covered, at
375°F for 40 minutes, or until the chicken is tender. Serves 4.

Spicy Baked Chicken

2 chickens, cut up and skinned
2 teaspoons salt
2 teaspoons curry powder
1 teaspoon dry mustard
1 teaspoon paprika
2 teaspoons oregano
4 bouillon cubes
1 cup boiling water
4-6 dashes Tabasco sauce
2 cloves garlic, pressed
4 teaspoons Worcestershire sauce

Remove any excess fat from the chicken. In a shallow baking pan
place the chicken pieces meaty side down. Mix together the
dry ingredients. Dissolve the bouillon cubes in boiling water. To
the bouillon add the Tabasco sauce, garlic, and Worcestershire
sauce. Gradually stir the liquid mixture into the dry mixture
and mix well. Spoon the mixture over the chicken and bake
the dish at 350°F for 30 minutes. Turn the chicken
over and baste it thoroughly. Continue baking the dish for
20 minutes. INCREASE OVEN TEMPERATURE to 400°F and
continue baking for 10 minutes, or until the chicken is brown. Serves
8-10.

Chicken Paprika

1 (2½ pound) frying chicken, cut up
1 cup flour
½ cup margarine
1 small onion, finely chopped
2 tablespoons chopped bell pepper
1 tablespoon finely chopped celery
1 (10½ ounce) can chicken broth
1 (4 ounce) can chopped mushrooms
1 (2 ounce) jar pimiento, chopped
Salt and pepper to taste
1 teaspoon paprika
1 (12 ounce) package egg noodles, cooked

Roll the chicken pieces in the flour to coat them. In a large
skillet melt the margarine over medium heat. Add the chicken and fry
it until it is golden brown. Transfer the chicken to a plate. To
the skillet add the onion, bell pepper, and celery and sauté until
tender. Add the chicken pieces, chicken broth, mushrooms,
pimiento, salt, pepper, and paprika. Cook the mixture for
45 minutes, or until the chicken is fork tender. Serve
the chicken and gravy over the noodles. Serves 6.

Poulet et Champignon

6 chicken breast quarters
Salt and pepper to taste
6 tablespoons margarine
6 bay leaves
1 bell pepper, cut in 12 rings
½ pound mushrooms, sliced
1 (10¾ ounce) can golden mushroom soup

Season the chicken quarters with salt and pepper and arrange
them in a 9″ x 13″ baking pan, wing side up. Top each breast
with 1 tablespoon of the margarine, 1 bay leaf, and 2 slices
of bell pepper. Arrange the mushrooms evenly over the chicken.
Spoon the soup on top of the chicken and mushroom combination.
Bake, covered with foil, at 350°F for 1¼ hours, basting often. Stir
in a small amount of water, if it is needed, to prevent the
sauce from burning. Transfer the chicken breasts to a heated
platter and serve them covered with the sauce. Serves 6.

Look for a bird that is plump and round-breasted with
short legs. The skin should be clean, soft, and
without bruises.

Chicken and Fresh Fruit Casserole

½ cup margarine
1 medium onion, sliced
1 pound tomatoes, sliced
3 peaches, cut in wedges
2 apples, cut in wedges
¼ cup raisins
¼ cup almonds
1 Boiled Chicken (see Index)

In a deep skillet melt the margarine over medium heat. Add the onion and sauté until tender. Stir in the tomatoes, peaches, apples, raisins, and almonds and simmer for 15 minutes. Skin, bone, and dice the chicken. Add the chicken to the fruit mixture. Simmer the mixture, covered, for 10 minutes. Serves 4-6.

Chicken Chablis

6 tablespoons flour
1½ teaspoons salt
¼ teaspoon pepper
6 chicken breasts, boned, skinned, and halved
3 tablespoons oil
8 tablespoons butter or margarine
1 cup chopped onion
1 (10¾ ounce) can golden mushroom soup
¾ cup water
¾ cup Chablis wine
½ teaspoon lemon juice
1 pound fresh mushrooms, halved
1 (10 ounce) package frozen green peas
3 cups rice, cooked

On wax paper combine the flour, 1 teaspoon of the salt, and pepper. Coat each piece of chicken with this mixture. In a large skillet heat the oil and 2 tablespoons of the butter. Add the chicken, a few pieces at a time, and sauté over moderately high heat for 2 to 3 minutes on each side or until they are golden. Remove the chicken breasts and set aside. In the same skillet sauté the onion. Add the soup, water, ½ cup of the wine, lemon juice, and the remaining salt and bring the mixture to a boil. Return the chicken to the skillet. Reduce the heat and simmer, covered, for 10 minutes, or until the chicken is tender. In another skillet melt the remaining butter. Add the mushrooms and sauté for 5 minutes or until golden. Stir the peas into the skillet with the chicken. Cook, covered, for 5 minutes. Stir in the sautéed mushrooms and the remaining wine and heat thoroughly. Serve over rice. Serves 12.

3½ pounds of cooked chicken will yield 3 cups diced chicken.

Curried Chicken

1 frying chicken, boiled, boned, and cubed (reserve fat)
2 tablespoons flour
2 cups chicken stock
1 rib celery, chopped
1 large onion, chopped
Salt to taste
1 tablespoon curry powder
2-2½ cups rice, cooked
Condiments: unsweetened toasted coconut, toasted sliced almonds, crisp bacon pieces, boiled egg whites, chopped boiled egg yolks, chutney

In a large skillet melt 2 tablespoons of the chicken fat. Add the flour, stirring constantly. Remove the pan from the heat, add the stock in a stream, whisking, and whisk the mixture until the sauce is thickened and smooth. Add the celery and onion to the sauce and simmer for 1½ hours. Add the salt, chicken, and curry powder. Simmer the mixture for 5 minutes. Serve over hot rice with condiments. Serves 8-10.

Orange Chicken

1 lemon, juiced
1 frying chicken, cut up
1½ teaspoons garlic salt
¼ teaspoon pepper
½ teaspoon cinnamon
2 tablespoons butter
2 tablespoons olive oil
1½-2 cups orange juice
¼ teaspoon oregano
1 cup rice, cooked

Pour the lemon juice over the chicken pieces. Sprinkle them with the garlic salt, pepper, and cinnamon. Let stand for 30 minutes. In a 10-inch skillet, over medium heat, heat the butter and olive oil. Add the chicken pieces and brown them, skin side down. Turn the pieces over, add the orange juice, and sprinkle with the oregano. Cook, over low heat, for 45 minutes to 1 hour or until tender and gravy forms. If the gravy gets too thick, add more orange juice and stir well. Serve with rice. Serves 4.

To bone chicken breasts, turn skin side down. Push against ribs of the breast until joints holding breastbone break. Push away flesh until it is just attached at the top. Pull out the breastbone and cartilage. Using a sharp pointed knife, carefully cut meat away from rib bones. Continue cutting until wishbone is reached. Remove wishbone and remainder of rib section.

Dilled Chicken

2 tablespoons butter

1 frying chicken, cut up

1 (16 ounce) can tomatoes, chopped

1 tablespoon snipped fresh dill

2 tablespoons lemon juice

1 teaspoon sugar

2 cloves garlic, crushed

Salt and lemon pepper to taste

In a Dutch oven melt the butter over medium heat. Add the chicken and brown. Stir in the tomatoes, dill, lemon juice, sugar, garlic, salt, and lemon pepper. Bring the mixture to a boil. Reduce the heat to low and simmer, covered, for 35 to 40 minutes, or until the chicken is tender. Serves 4.

Tropical Chicken

1 chicken, cut in serving pieces

½ cup flour

½ cup salad oil

1 teaspoon salt

¼ teaspoon pepper

SAUCE:

1 (1 pound, 4 ounce) can sliced pineapple (reserve liquid)

1 cup sugar

2 tablespoons cornstarch

¾ cup cider vinegar

2 tablespoons soy sauce

¼ teaspoon ginger

1 chicken bouillon cube

1 large bell pepper, cut in ¼-inch circles

1 cup rice, cooked

Wash the chicken and pat it dry. Coat the chicken with the flour. In a large skillet heat the oil over medium heat. Brown the chicken and transfer it to a 9″ x 13″ baking dish, arranging the pieces skin side up. Sprinkle the chicken with the salt and pepper. In a 2-cup measuring cup add water to the pineapple liquid until it measures 1¼ cups. In a medium saucepan over medium heat combine the pineapple liquid, sugar, cornstarch, vinegar, soy sauce, ginger, and bouillon cube. Bring the sauce to a boil, stirring constantly, and boil for 2 minutes. Pour the sauce over the chicken. Bake the dish, uncovered, at 350°F for 30 minutes. Remove from the oven and arrange the pineapple slices and green pepper on top of the chicken. Continue baking for 30 minutes, or until the chicken is tender. Serve the chicken with rice. Serves 4.

Refreezing defrosted poultry is not recommended.

Chicken Clemenceau

1 small chicken, cut in serving pieces
Salt and pepper to taste
¼ cup butter
1 cup cubed potatoes
¼ cup cooking oil
½ cup sliced fresh mushrooms
1 teaspoon minced garlic
1 cup small green peas, drained
1 teaspoon minced parsley

Season the chicken with salt and pepper. In a 9-inch skillet
melt the butter and sauté the chicken until it is tender and
golden brown. Transfer the chicken to paper towels to drain.
In a separate skillet heat the oil. Add the potatoes and fry
them until they are golden brown. Season the potatoes with
salt and pepper and drain them on paper towels. In the skillet
used to cook the chicken sauté the mushrooms, garlic, and fried
potatoes for 5 minutes. Add the peas and parsley and heat the
mixture thoroughly. Arrange the chicken pieces on a platter
and cover them with the vegetable mixture. Serves 2.

Chicken Sauterne

¾ cup sauterne wine
½ cup Wishbone Italian salad dressing
3 cloves garlic, halved
1 tablespoon Worcestershire sauce
8 chicken breasts, boned
2 tablespoons butter
½ pound mushrooms, sliced
½ lemon
1 cup flour
Salt and pepper to taste
Paprika
3 tablespoons bacon grease or butter
7 green onions, chopped
½ cup chopped parsley
1½ cups chicken broth
½ teaspoon each rosemary, thyme, and basil
¼ teaspoon oregano

In a large bowl combine the wine, salad dressing, garlic, and
Worcestershire sauce. Add the chicken and allow it to marinate
for at least 1 to 2 hours. In a saucepan melt the butter over
medium heat. Add the mushrooms and sauté for 3 to 5 minutes.
Squeeze the lemon over the mushrooms and reserve them. Remove
the chicken from the marinade and reserve the marinade. Combine
the flour, salt, pepper, and paprika and roll the chicken in
the mixture to coat it. In a large skillet melt the grease
over medium heat. Add the chicken and fry it until it is light

brown. Transfer the chicken to a 9″ x 13″ baking pan. Remove
any excess grease from the skillet and discard it, allowing
the brown scrapings to remain. Add the green onion, and ¼ cup
of the parsley to the skillet and sauté until limp. Add the
broth and herbs and simmer the mixture for 10 minutes. Strain
the marinade, discard the garlic, and add the marinade to the
broth mixture. Simmer the mixture for 5 minutes and pour it
over the chicken. Arrange the mushrooms on the top and sprinkle
the chicken with the remaining parsley. Bake the dish at
350°F for 40 minutes. Serves 8.

Chicken Pie Supreme

1 large frying chicken
⅓ cup butter
½ cup chopped onion
¼ cup chopped celery
⅓ cup flour
1½ teaspoons salt
3 cups chicken broth
¼ cup chopped pimiento
1 cup frozen peas, cooked
1 (6 ounce) can mushrooms
BISCUITS:
2 cups flour
4 teaspoons baking powder
½ teaspoon salt
½ teaspoon cream of tartar
2 teaspoons sugar
½ cup shortening
⅔ cup milk

Prepare the chicken in accordance with the instructions for
Boiled Chicken (see Index). When the chicken is tender remove
it from the pot and allow it to cool. Strain the broth and
reserve it. Skin and bone the chicken and coarsely chop the
meat. In a large heavy saucepan melt the butter over medium
heat. Add the onion and celery and sauté until tender. Blend
in the flour and salt. Gradually stir in the broth and continue
cooking, stirring constantly, until it is thick. Add the
chicken, pimiento, peas, and mushrooms and heat until the mixture
is bubbly. Transfer the mixture to a shallow 2-quart casserole
and keep it warm while preparing the biscuits. Into a bowl
sift together the flour, baking powder, salt, cream of tartar,
and sugar. Add the shortening and cut it into the dry mixture
until the mixture resembles coarse crumbs. With a fork stir
in the milk and continue stirring, until the dough follows the
fork around the bowl. Transfer the mixture to a floured
surface and knead it for 30 seconds. Pat the dough out to a ½-inch
thickness. Using a biscuit cutter cut it into 16 biscuits.
Bake the biscuits on an ungreased cookie sheet at 400°F
for 10 to 12 minutes. Place the hot biscuits on top of the
casserole and serve. Serves 6-8.

Teriyaki Chicken

1 pint soy sauce

3 pints water

½ cup sugar

½ cup white wine

1 onion, finely chopped

3-4 cloves garlic, chopped

3-4 slices fresh ginger root or 1 tablespoon ground ginger

3 frying chickens, cut up

Combine all the ingredients except the chicken in a large
container and mix well. Add the chicken pieces to the
mixture and marinate them 8 to 12 hours in the refrigerator.
Remove the chicken pieces and barbecue them slowly for
30 to 45 minutes, or bake them at 350°F for 1 hour. Serves 10-12.

Chicken Sauce Piquant

4 chicken breasts, boned

4 chicken thighs, boned

Salt and pepper to taste

Red pepper to taste

Garlic powder to taste

¼ cup olive oil

4 tablespoons flour

1 large onion, finely chopped

1 (14 ounce) can tomato sauce

2 bay leaves

6 cloves garlic

¼ teaspoon red pepper

1 teaspoon sugar

¼ cup red wine

8 ounces fresh mushrooms, sliced

1 medium bell pepper, chopped

2 cups rice, cooked

Season the chicken liberally with salt, pepper, red pepper, and
garlic powder. In a large pot heat the oil. Add the chicken
and brown both sides over medium heat. Transfer the browned
chicken pieces to a plate. DO NOT DRAIN AS ALL JUICES
THAT COLLECT WILL BE RETURNED TO THE POT. When all
pieces are browned, pour off all but 2 tablespoons of the oil. Stir
in the flour until lightly browned. Add the onion and cook
until tender. Add the tomato sauce, 3½ cups water, bay leaves, garlic,
red pepper, sugar, and wine. Simmer the mixture for
1 hour. Add the chicken, mushrooms, and bell pepper. Simmer,
covered, over low heat for 45 minutes. Serve over rice. Serves 8.

When using wine in cooking, remember the better the wine
the better the dish.

Chicken Valencia

1 ⅓ cups raisins
4 tablespoons sherry
4 tablespoons butter or margarine
1 ¼ cups orange juice
½ cup ham, chopped
2 tablespoons chopped fresh parsley
½ teaspoon grated orange rind
½ cup stale bread crumbs
12 large chicken breasts, boned
2 cups chicken broth
2 tablespoons instant minced onion
Salt and pepper to taste
1 cinnamon stick
1 tablespoon cornstarch

Marinate the raisins in the sherry for 30 minutes. Chop ½ cup
of the raisins and combine them with the butter, ¼ cup of the
orange juice, ham, parsley, orange rind, and bread crumbs. With
a wooden mallet flatten the chicken, skin side down, between
sheets of wax paper. Place the stuffing in the center of each
breast. Fold each chicken breast over to enclose the stuffing
and secure them with wooden picks. Wrap the chicken breasts in
foil and bake them at 350°F for 1½ hours, basting frequently, with
the sauce. Prepare the sauce by combining the remaining orange
juice, broth, onion, salt, pepper, and cinnamon stick and simmer
for 5 minutes. Remove and discard the cinnamon stick from the
sauce. Add the remaining raisins and simmer for 3 to 4 minutes.
Thicken the sauce with the cornstarch mixed with cold water. To
serve, remove the foil, place each chicken breast on an orange
slice, and pour the sauce over the chicken. Serves 12.

Boiled Chicken

1 chicken
1 carrot, quartered
1 rib celery, quartered
1 onion, quartered
2 parsley sprigs, chopped
Salt and pepper to taste

In a large pot place the chicken in water to cover.
Add the remaining ingredients and boil it for 1½ hours,
or until it is tender. Reserve and freeze any leftover
stock for later use.

Wash fresh poultry with cold running water and pat it
dry before storing or cooking. Loosely wrap it in wax
paper or foil. May be kept refrigerated for 1 or 2 days.

Chicken Verde

1 (4 pound) hen
½ cup margarine
½ cup chopped bell pepper
1 cup chopped celery
1 cup chopped onion
½ pound processed cheese
1 (6 ounce) jar stuffed olives, drained
1 (6 ounce) can sliced mushrooms, drained
1 (10 ounce) package spinach noodles
1 (10¾ ounce) can mushroom soup

In a stock pot boil the hen, in enough salted water to reduce to 4 cups, for 2 hours or until it is tender. Transfer the hen to a plate to cool and reserve the stock. Bone the chicken and cut it in large pieces. In a skillet melt the margarine. Add the bell pepper, celery, and onion and sauté until tender. Stir in the cheese, olives, and mushrooms and continue stirring until the cheese is melted. Add the chicken. Remove from the heat. In a medium saucepan cook the noodles, according to package directions, in 3 cups of the chicken stock. To this mixture add the soup and mix well. Combine both the mixtures over medium heat, adding chicken stock as needed to moisten the mixture, and serve hot. Serves 6-8.

Jalapeño Chicken

1 large frying chicken, cut up or 6 breasts
¾ cup chicken broth
¼ cup white wine
Salt and pepper to taste
Lemon juice to taste
Butter or margarine
2 cloves garlic, chopped
2 cups chopped onion
1½ cups chopped celery
1 pound Velveeta cheese, sliced
Jalapeño peppers, sliced
1 (2 ounce) jar pimientos, sliced
1½ cups rice, cooked

Place the chicken in a greased 7" x 11" baking dish. Add the broth, wine, salt, pepper, and lemon juice. Dot with the butter. Bake, uncovered, at 350°F for 30 minutes. Remove the chicken from the oven and add the garlic, onion, and celery. Return it to the oven and bake for 1 hour or until browned. Remove the dish from the oven, add the cheese, and top with the Jalapeño peppers and pimiento. (The more peppers, the hotter the dish.) Return the dish to the oven and bake, basting occasionally, for 15 minutes, or until the cheese is melted. Serve the chicken over the rice. Serves 6.

Croquettes

3 tablespoons butter
4 tablespoons flour
1 cup milk
Salt and pepper to taste
1 teaspoon Tony Chachere's Creole seasoning (optional)
2 eggs, separated
Parsley to taste, chopped
1½ cups finely chopped chicken
1 cup finely chopped ham
2 tablespoons Parmesan cheese
1 egg, beaten
Seasoned bread crumbs, finely crushed
Cooking oil

In a large deep skillet melt the butter over medium heat. Add the flour and milk, stirring constantly, until the sauce is smooth. Remove the mixture from the heat and add the salt, pepper, Creole seasoning, egg yolks, and parsley. Return the mixture to the heat, stirring, for 1 to 2 minutes, or until the mixture is smooth. Add the meat and cheese to the sauce and mix well. Transfer the mixture to a platter and allow it to cool. Shape the mixture into 8-10 croquettes. Mix the egg with 1 teaspoon water. Dip each croquette in the egg mixture and roll it in the bread crumbs. Refrigerate the croquettes for 2 hours. Deep fry the croquettes in hot oil until they are golden brown and crisp. Serve hot. Serves 4.

Fiesta Chicken

1 frying chicken
Salt and pepper to taste
1 (7½ ounce) package Doritos
1 (10¾ ounce) can cream of mushroom soup
1 pound Cheddar cheese, grated
½ small onion, chopped
1 (4 ounce) can green chili peppers

Place the chicken in a Dutch oven with water to cover, salt, and pepper. Over high heat allow the water to come to a rolling boil. Reduce the heat and simmer until the chicken is fork tender. Remove the chicken and reserve the broth. Skin and bone the chicken. Pour the Doritos into the bottom of a 4-quart casserole. Arrange the chicken meat on top of the Doritos. Combine the soup and 3 cups of the reserved broth and pour the mixture over the chicken. Top the casserole with the cheese, onion, and chili peppers. Bake, covered, at 325°F for 30 minutes. Serves 6.

When frying chicken add 1 teaspoon ground ginger to the seasoned flour for variation.

Chicken Amandine

6 chicken breasts, skinned and boned
Salt and pepper to taste
5 tablespoons flour
½ cup butter or margarine
½ cup blanched chopped almonds
1 cup chicken broth
1 cup half-and-half cream
½ cup sherry
1½ cups saffron rice, cooked

Season the chicken with salt and pepper. Pat the chicken with
1 tablespoon of the flour. In a large skillet over medium heat
melt ¼ cup of the butter. Add the chicken and sauté for 20
minutes or until tender and golden brown. Remove the chicken
from the skillet and transfer to a warm oven while making the sauce.
Reduce the heat to low and add the remaining butter. Add the
remaining flour and stir the mixture until smooth and bubbly.
Add the almonds and sauté until golden. Stir in the chicken
broth, half-and-half cream, sherry, salt, and pepper. Place
the chicken on a hot platter, cover with the sauce, and serve
with the saffron rice. Serves 6.

Chicken and Snow Peas

2 tablespoons soy sauce
2 tablespoons dry sherry
1 teaspoon ground ginger
1 clove garlic, crushed
2 large whole chicken breasts, skinned, boned, and cut in bite-size pieces
¼ cup margarine
2 cups sliced fresh mushrooms
1 cup thinly sliced celery
½ cup chopped green onion
1 (7 ounce) package frozen snow peas, thawed
1 (8 ounce) can water chestnuts, sliced
1 tablespoon cornstarch
1 cup chicken broth
1-1½ cups rice, cooked

In a bowl blend together the soy sauce, dry sherry, ginger, and
garlic. Marinate the chicken pieces in this mixture for 30 minutes.
In a wok or large skillet melt the margarine over medium heat.
Add the chicken, mushrooms, celery, green onion, and snow peas and
sauté for 10 to 15 minutes, stirring constantly, until
the chicken is tender and the vegetables are still crisp.
Stir in the water chestnuts. Combine the cornstarch and
chicken broth. Stir it into the chicken mixture and cook
until thick. Serve over hot rice. Serves 4-6.

Inexpensive, easy to make, delicious, different

Keo Paht

¼ cup peanut oil
2 cloves garlic, mashed
1 medium onion, minced
1 cup diced chicken breast
3-5 cups cooked, day-old rice
1 egg, slightly beaten
Freshly ground pepper to taste
Crushed red pepper to taste
Salt to taste
1 tomato, cut in wedges

In a wok or large skillet heat the oil over medium heat.
Add the garlic, onion, and chicken and sauté, stirring constantly,
until the onion is limp and the meat is white. Add the rice,
stirring frequently, until it is hot and coated with the oil.
Add the egg and scramble it. Stir the mixture until it is full of
yellow specks of egg. Stir in the pepper and red pepper.
Add the salt and tomato wedges and cook, covered, for 3 minutes.
Serves 2-3.

Lafitte Chicken Spaghetti

1 hen
Salt and pepper to taste
2 cloves
3 medium onions, chopped
3 cloves garlic, chopped
3 ribs celery, chopped
½ cup chopped parsley
1 bell pepper, chopped
2 (16 ounce) cans tomatoes
2 (8 ounce) cans mushrooms
3 hard-boiled eggs, chopped
1 (16 ounce) package spaghetti

In a Dutch oven parboil the hen in water to cover, salt, pepper,
and cloves. Transfer the hen to a platter. Allow the stock to
cool. Skim and reserve fat and reserve the stock. Bone the hen
and cut it in pieces. In a Dutch oven melt the chicken fat.
Add the onion, garlic, and celery and sauté until tender.
Stir in the parsley, bell pepper, and tomatoes. Add the chicken,
mushrooms, and eggs. Cook the spaghetti in the chicken stock
and combine it with the chicken mixture. Use the stock for
moistening the mixture. Serves 14-16.

Do not stuff poultry before freezing it. Bacteria may
develop during the time it takes to heat stuffed poultry.

Parisian Cutlets

1 (3 pound) chicken
1 cup fresh bread crumbs
1 cup heavy cream
1 teaspoon salt
White pepper to taste
1 tablespoon dry vermouth
½ cup butter (at room temperature)
1 egg yolk, lightly beaten
Flour
Dry bread crumbs
½ pound fresh mushrooms, sliced
¼ cup Chablis wine
Chopped parsley

Remove the skin, bone, and tendons from the chicken. In a food
processor fitted with the chopping blade process the chicken
until it is thoroughly chopped. Soak the crumbs in ½ cup of the
cream and squeeze them dry. In a bowl combine the chicken, bread
crumbs, salt, pepper, vermouth, and 2 tablespoons of the butter.
Mix well and add the egg yolk. In a skillet melt 2 tablespoons
of the butter. Add the mushrooms and sauté them until they are
coated with butter. Season with salt and pepper and steam,
covered, for 5 minutes. With a slotted spoon transfer the
mushrooms to a dish and reserve the juices. Transfer the chicken
mixture to a wet wooden surface. Shape the mixture in a rectangle
and divide it into 6 equal sections. Surface and hands should be
damp for easy handling. Form each section in a cutlet shape.
Sprinkle the flour on the cutlets and coat them with the
bread crumbs. Sauté in the remaining butter for 5 minutes on each
side. Arrange them on a heated platter. Add the wine, mushroom
juices, and cream and simmer for 2 to 3 minutes. Add the mushrooms
and pour the sauce over the cutlets. Serve garnished with parsley.
Serves 6.

Never overcook chicken livers. They are delicate and can be
easily toughened by overcooking.

Oven-Fried Chicken

1 (2½ pound) frying chicken, cut up
¼ cup flour
2 eggs
1½ teaspoons salt
1 tablespoon paprika
½ teaspoon onion salt·
2 tablespoons lemon juice
¼ cup butter or margarine
1 cup Italian seasoned bread crumbs

Shake the chicken pieces in a bag with the flour. Beat together the eggs with the salt, paprika, onion salt, and lemon juice until well blended. Melt the butter in a small saucepan. Dip the floured chicken, one piece at a time, in the egg mixture, then in the crumbs, turning to coat evenly, and then in the butter. Arrange the chicken, skin side down, in a 9″ x 13″ baking dish. Bake the dish at 350°F for 45 minutes, turning once, or until fork tender. Serves 4.

Chicken Medley

1 frying chicken, cut up
Garlic salt to taste
Salt and pepper to taste
4 slices bacon, cut in small pieces
2 medium onions, chopped
1-2 cloves garlic, minced
1-2 tomatoes, cut in eighths
1 cup uncooked rice
1 pound pepperoni sausage, sliced (optional)
12-14 cabbage leaves
2½ cups water

Rub the chicken pieces with a mixture of garlic salt, salt, and pepper. In a large skillet fry the bacon until it is crisp. If the bacon grease is not sufficient to brown the chicken, add a small amount of cooking oil. Add the chicken and cook it until it is brown on all sides. Transfer the chicken pieces to a Dutch oven. To the skillet add the onion, garlic, tomato, rice, and sausage and sauté until the onion is soft. Cover the skillet and simmer the mixture for 10 to 15 minutes. In the Dutch oven cover the chicken with the cabbage leaves. Pour the rice mixture over the chicken and cabbage combination. Add the water. Cook, covered, over low heat for 1 hour, or until all the liquid is absorbed. Serves 4.

A good fat covering is an indication of tender meat.

Herbed Chicken in Foil

1 tablespoon butter
1 onion, sliced
½ cup rice, cooked
1 (2½-3 pound) chicken, cut up
Kitchen Bouquet
1 (10¾ ounce) can cream of mushroom soup
3 tablespoons chopped parsley
2 teaspoons marjoram
1 teaspoon salt
Dash of pepper
½ cup white wine

Cut 4 squares of foil and lightly butter each square. On each
piece of foil place a slice of onion and sprinkle with 4
tablespoons of the cooked rice. Top with a serving size portion
of the chicken. Brush the chicken lightly with Kitchen Bouquet.
Mix the soup, parsley, marjoram, salt, and pepper. Spoon the
mixture over the chicken. Pour 2 tablespoons of the wine over
each serving. Close the foil and place on a baking sheet. Bake
at 450°F for 1 hour or until done. Serves 4.

Ruth's Chicken

½ cup butter or margarine
3 cloves garlic, pressed
1 teaspoon Worcestershire sauce
1 lemon, juiced
½ cup cracker crumbs
½ cup Parmesan cheese
1 frying chicken, cut up
Salt and pepper to taste
1 (12 ounce) package noodles, cooked and buttered

In a saucepan over low heat combine the butter, garlic,
Worcestershire sauce, and lemon juice and remove from the heat.
On wax paper mix the cracker crumbs and Parmesan cheese.
Season the chicken with the salt and pepper. Dip each piece
of chicken in the butter sauce and roll it in the crumb mixture.
Arrange the chicken in a 9" x 13" casserole and pour the remaining
butter mixture over it. Sprinkle the dish with the remaining
crumb mixture. Bake, covered, at 350°F for 30 minutes. Uncover
and continue baking for 20 to 30 minutes. Serve the chicken
with the buttered noodles. Serves 4.

Larger birds have more meat in proportion to bone
than smaller birds.

Turkey Hash

2 medium potatoes, peeled and diced
2 tablespoons margarine
½ cup chopped onion
¼ cup chopped celery
1 cup diced cooked turkey
½ cup chicken stock
1 cup turkey gravy
3 tablespoons chopped parsley

In a small saucepan cook the potato in salted water to cover
for 15 minutes and drain well. In a skillet melt the margarine.
Add the onion and celery and sauté until soft. Add the turkey,
stock, potatoes, and gravy and mix well. Add the parsley.
Remove the mixture from the heat and allow it to stand,
uncovered. Transfer the hash to a baking dish and bake at 350°F
for 15 to 20 minutes. Serves 2.

Turkey Poulette

4 tablespoons flour
11 tablespoons butter, melted
2 cups milk, heated
3 green onions, white only, chopped
8 large mushroom caps, sliced
½ cup white wine
Salt and pepper to taste
2 slices toast, crusts removed
6 strips bacon, crisply fried
6 slices cooked turkey breast
¼ cup grated Parmesan cheese

In a heavy skillet blend the flour and ½ cup of the butter,
cooking the roux over low heat for several minutes. Gradually
add the milk and cook the sauce, stirring constantly, until it
is smooth and thick. In a separate skillet sauté the green
onion and mushrooms in 3 tablespoons butter until tender. Stir
in the white sauce and add the wine, salt, and pepper. In the
bottom of a shallow casserole place the slices of toast. Cover
the toast with the bacon and turkey. Pour the sauce over the
mixture and sprinkle the top with Parmesan cheese. Bake the
dish at 425°F for 6 minutes, or until the top is golden brown.
Serves 2.

To carve roast turkey, chicken, or duck cut off the legs
and wings. Slice the breast meat at right angles to the
cutting surface.

Mom's Oyster Dressing

½ cup cooking oil
6 large onions, chopped
4 large cloves garlic, chopped
6 dozen oysters, drained (reserve liquor)
2 (8 ounce) packages Pepperidge Farm herb seasoned stuffing mix
1 cup chopped celery
1 cup chopped bell pepper
½ cup chopped parsley
2 eggs, beaten
½ cup butter or margarine
Salt and pepper to taste

In a Dutch oven heat the oil. Add the onions and garlic and sauté over medium heat until browned. Add the drained oysters and cook until the edges curl. Add the stuffing mix and oyster liquor. The mixture should be moist. If there is not sufficient oyster liquor, add a small amount of water. Add the celery, bell pepper, parsley, eggs, butter, salt, and pepper. Cook, stirring occasionally, for 20 minutes, adding water as necessary to maintain a moist consistency. Loosely stuff an 18-22 pound turkey with the dressing, truss, and roast it. Proportions may be decreased for stuffing a smaller fowl.

Sausage Corn Bread Dressing

1 cup yellow corn meal
1 cup flour
4 teaspoons baking powder
½ teaspoon salt
1 cup milk
1 egg
¼ cup vegetable oil
½ cup butter
1 cup finely chopped celery
2 cups finely chopped green onion
2 cups finely chopped mushrooms
2 (8 ounce) packages Pepperidge Farm herb seasoned stuffing mix
3 (10 ounce) cans chicken broth
1 (16 ounce) package country sausage

In a large bowl mix together the corn meal, flour, baking powder, salt, milk, egg, and vegetable oil and pour the mixture into a greased iron skillet. Bake at 400°F for 20 minutes. Remove the corn bread from the oven and allow it to cool. In a skillet melt the butter. Add the celery, green onion, and mushrooms and sauté until just tender. Crumble the corn bread into a large bowl, stir in the vegetables, stuffing mix, chicken broth, and sausage and mix well. Transfer the mixture to a greased baking dish and bake, covered, at 350°F for 1 hour. Serves 8-10.

Deviled Turkey Gougère

½ cup milk
½ cup water
4 tablespoons margarine
Salt and pepper to taste
1 cup flour
4 large eggs, beaten
½ pound Cheddar cheese, diced
SAUCE:
2 tablespoons margarine
1 small onion, chopped
¼ cup flour
1¼ cups turkey stock
1 tablespoon curry powder
2 tablespoons chopped sweet pickle
1 tablespoon cranberry sauce or jelly
1 teaspoon lemon juice
½ pound cooked turkey meat, chopped

In a large saucepan over medium heat combine the milk, water,
margarine, salt, and pepper, stirring, until the margarine is
melted. Remove the pan from heat, whisk in the flour, and beat
well until the mixture leaves the sides of the pan. Allow to
cool slightly. Gradually add the eggs to the mixture, beating
well, to produce a smooth shiny paste. Stir in the cheese.
Spoon the mixture into a greased baking dish, leaving a hole
in the center. Bake at 375°F for 35 to 40 minutes or until
golden brown and crisp. DO NOT OPEN DOOR while baking
or the gougère will collapse. In a large saucepan over
medium heat melt the margarine. Add the onion and cook until
softened. Stir in the flour and cook for 3 minutes. Add the stock,
stirring constantly, until boiling. Reduce the heat and simmer for
2 minutes. Add the remaining ingredients except the turkey.
Stir well and cook over low heat for 5 minutes. Add the turkey and
heat the sauce thoroughly. Pour the sauce into the center of the
gougère. Serves 6.

Allow 1 to 1½ pounds of pigeon, squab, or Cornish game hen
per person.

Traditional Corn Bread Dressing

2 cups crumbled day-old corn bread
2 cups toasted bread crumbs
¾ cup chopped onion
¾ cup chopped celery
⅓ cup chopped bell pepper
3 tablespoons chopped parsley
6 eggs, beaten
6 cups chicken broth
Salt and pepper to taste

In a large mixing bowl combine all of the ingredients together. Pour the mixture into a greased 9" x 13" baking dish. Bake, uncovered, at 350°F for 1½ hours or until golden brown. Serves 12.

Glazed Cornish Hens

SAUCE:
¼ cup lemon juice
1½ cups orange juice
3 tablespoons lemon peel
3 tablespoons orange peel
2 cups currant jelly
1 cup Madeira wine
2 teaspoons dry mustard
1 teaspoon ginger
½ teaspoon salt
⅛ teaspoon Tabasco sauce

In a medium saucepan over medium heat combine the lemon juice, orange juice, lemon peel, and orange peel and bring the mixture to a boil. Reduce the heat and simmer for 20 minutes. Add the remaining sauce ingredients and cook over low heat for 2 hours, stirring occasionally, or until the sauce is thickened.

8 (1 pound) Cornish hens
Salt and pepper to taste
⅓ cup butter, melted

Sprinkle the body cavity of each hen with salt and pepper and tie the legs together. Arrange the hens, breast side up, in a roasting pan and brush them with the butter. Bake, uncovered, at 500°F for 15 minutes. Remove the hens from the oven and REDUCE OVEN TEMPERATURE to 400°F. Turn them breast side down and pour ½ cup water over the hens. Bake, covered, for 30 minutes. Turn the hens breast side up and baste them with the pan juices. Bake the hens, uncovered, for 25 minutes. Brush them with the sauce and continue baking for 5 minutes. Transfer the hens to a heated platter and serve them accompanied by the remaining sauce in a heated sauceboat. Serves 8.

Stuffed Rock Cornish Hens

4 rock Cornish hens, thawed
Salt to taste
1½ cups herb stuffing mix
½ cup white raisins
1 cup orange juice
½ cup sherry
1 tablespoon butter

Rinse and pat dry the hens and sprinkle them inside and outside with salt. Prepare the stuffing mix according to the package directions, keeping it on the dry side, and stir in the raisins. Pack the cavities loosely with the stuffing and truss the hens. Wrap any leftover stuffing in foil and add it to the roasting pan. Arrange the hens on the rack of a roasting pan. Roast the hens at 400°F for 45 minutes or until a light golden brown. In a small saucepan combine the orange juice, sherry, and butter and cook over medium heat until the butter is melted. REDUCE OVEN TEMPERATURE TO 300°F. Pour the sauce over the hens and continue baking, basting frequently, for 30 minutes. Remove the hens with a slotted spoon and transfer them to a heated platter.
Serve the sauce in a heated sauceboat to be served over the dressing. Serves 4.

Wild Duck with Brandy

2 wild ducks
Salt and pepper to taste
4 ounces brandy
1 cup dry wine
2 large onions, finely chopped
1 tablespoon chopped parsley
½ teaspoon thyme
½ teaspoon marjoram
¼ teaspoon allspice
1 bay leaf
1 tablespoon butter
⅓ cup olive oil
1 clove garlic, crushed
½ pound fresh mushrooms, sliced

Disjoint the ducks and place the pieces in a crock or large bowl. Sprinkle them with salt and pepper and add the brandy, wine, onion, parsley, thyme, marjoram, allspice, and bay leaf. Allow to stand for 5 hours at room temperature, turning the pieces of duck occasionally. In a heavy skillet or Dutch oven heat the butter, olive oil, and garlic. Add the duck pieces and brown well over medium heat, on all sides, for 15 to 20 minutes. Add the mushrooms and the strained marinade. Cook, covered, for 1½ hours or until the duck is tender. Transfer the duck to a hot platter, thicken the sauce slightly by vigorous boiling, and pour the sauce over the duck. Serves 4.

Wild Duck à la Jus Orange

¼ cup brandy

1¼ cups orange juice

2 wild ducks (reserve and chop giblets)

4 cups boiling water

1 teaspoon salt

1 cup uncooked wild rice, washed

1 cup boiling chicken broth

4 tablespoons unsalted butter

1½ tablespoons minced chives

1½ tablespoons minced parsley

2 tablespoons minced green onion

2 tablespoons minced celery tops

1½ tablespoons minced sweet basil

2 juniper berries, crushed

Salt to taste

Freshly ground pepper to taste

Pinch nutmeg

1 teaspoon grated orange rind

2 teaspoons lemon juice

2 cups dry red wine

3 tablespoons orange-flavored liqueur

Mix the brandy with ¼ cup of the orange juice. Rub the ducks, inside and out, with this mixture and set them aside. Into the top of a double boiler pour the boiling water. Immediately add 1 teaspoon salt and the wild rice. Place the top of the double boiler directly over medium heat and cook for 5 minutes. Fill the bottom portion of the double boiler with boiling water and cover it with the top containing the rice. Add the chicken broth to the rice mixture and steam, tightly covered, for 30 to 45 minutes, or until the rice is tender. In a bowl cream the butter with the chives, parsley, green onion, celery tops, and basil. Season the mixture with the juniper berries, salt, pepper, and nutmeg. In a large saucepan melt the butter mixture. Add the wild rice and giblets and cook briefly, tossing the mixture until the rice is coated with the butter. Stuff the ducks with this mixture and truss them. Place the ducks in an open roasting pan and pour the remaining orange juice into the pan. Add the orange rind, lemon juice, and 1 cup of the wine. Roast at 400°F for 3 to 4 hours, depending on the size and age of the ducks, basting often. Transfer the ducks to a hot platter. To the juices in the bottom of the roasting pan, add the remainder of the wine and scrape the pan while stirring. Add the orange liqueur and bring the mixture to a boil on the top of the stove. Serve the ducks with the sauce poured over them. Serves 4.

Refrigerate poultry and gravy in separate containers.

MEATS
Preparing meat may seem like the simplest kind of cooking. However, there's an art to selecting the proper cut, cooking it correctly, and seasoning it temptingly. If mastered, it enables us to use cheaper cuts and unpopular parts of the animal with results which will be pleasing, rather than disappointing.

MEATS

Beef	147
Veal	160
Game	162
Pork	164
Sauces	169

In a city famed for its beautiful and stately old homes, it is a rare treat indeed to be able to observe another fast-disappearing tradition; the antique St. Charles Avenue Streetcars. A ride on the charming and efficient streetcar is the ideal way to view this most beautiful of all cities.

Creole Daube

1 (3-5 pound) boneless chuck roast
Seasoning salt, pepper, red pepper, and paprika
2-3 cloves garlic, halved
½ cup vegetable oil
¼ cup flour
1 cup chopped onion
¼ cup chopped bell pepper
1 rib celery, chopped
2-3 green onions, chopped
1 (8 ounce) can tomato sauce
¼ cup red wine
1 cup water
¼ cup chopped parsley
1-2 bay leaves
¼ teaspoon sugar
½ teaspoon salt
Red pepper to taste

Season the roast with seasoning salt, peppers, and paprika.
Make slits in the roast and insert the garlic. In a 5-quart
Dutch oven heat ¼ cup of the oil. Over medium heat brown
the roast on all sides. Reduce the heat to low and continue
to cook, covered, while preparing the roux. (If roast sticks
add ½ cup of water.) In a separate heavy pot heat the
remaining oil. Add the flour, stirring constantly, over
medium heat until the roux is the color of chocolate.
Reduce the heat to low and add the onion, bell pepper, celery,
and green onion and cook until they are limp. Stir in the
tomato sauce and cook for 10 minutes. Add the wine and 1 cup
water slowly to the roux. Add the parsley, bay leaves, sugar,
salt, and pepper to the tomato sauce mixture. Pour the sauce
over the roast. Simmer slowly on top of the stove for 2 to 3
hours, or until the roast is very tender. Add more water if
needed. Serves 8-10.

Quick and Easy Beef Stew

1 (1¼ ounce) package dry onion soup mix
1 (10¾ ounce) can cream of mushroom soup
10-11 ounces Burgundy wine
1½ pounds stew meat

In a bowl mix together the soup mix, mushroom soup,
and wine. Place the meat in a deep baking dish or electric
skillet and pour the sauce over it. Bake, covered, at 350°F
or simmer in an electric skillet at 250°F for 1½ hours.
Serves 4.

Spread hamburger patties with Roquefort cheese before broiling.

Inside-Out Ravioli Casserole

1 (10 ounce) package shell macaroni
1 (10 ounce) package frozen chopped spinach
5 tablespoons olive oil
1 medium onion, chopped
1-2 cloves garlic, minced
1 pound ground beef
1 (16 ounce) jar spaghetti sauce with mushrooms
1 (8 ounce) can tomato sauce
1 (6 ounce) can tomato paste
2 eggs
1 cup grated sharp cheese
½ cup soft bread crumbs

Cook the macaroni and spinach, separately, according to
package directions reserving the spinach liquid. In a large skillet
heat 1 tablespoon of the oil. Add the onion and garlic and
sauté until soft. Add the meat and brown it. Add the spaghetti sauce,
tomato sauce, and tomato paste to the meat mixture. Add
water to the spinach liquid to equal 1 cup. Add the liquid to the
meat sauce. In a large bowl mix together the spinach, eggs,
and remaining oil. To this mixture whip in rapidly the macaroni so
that the spinach mixture goes into the shells. Transfer the
shell mixture to a greased 9″ x 13″ baking dish. Cover with grated
cheese, pour in the meat sauce, and top with bread crumbs. Bake
at 350°F for 30 minutes. Serves 8.

Beef Stroganoff

3 tablespoons olive oil or cooking oil
2 pounds round steak, cut in strips ¼″ wide x 1″ long
1 onion, finely chopped
½ pound mushrooms, sliced
1 tablespoon tomato paste
1 tablespoon flour
½ cup sherry
Salt and white pepper to taste
1 pint sour cream
Noodles, cooked and drained

In a heavy skillet heat the oil. Add the meat and brown it.
Push the meat to one side of the skillet and add the onion
and mushrooms. Sauté over medium-high heat until the onion
is soft and mix with the meat. Stir in the tomato paste.
Sprinkle the flour over all and blend well. Add the sherry
and stir until a gravy is formed. Season with salt and pepper.
Cook, covered, until the meat is tender. Blend in the sour
cream and heat, but do not boil. Serve the Stroganoff over
the noodles. Serves 6.

Lasagne

¼ cup olive oil
2 cloves garlic, minced
½ bell pepper, chopped
½ cup finely chopped celery
1 medium onion, finely chopped
1½ pounds lean ground beef
2½ teaspoons salt
¼ teaspoon pepper
½ teaspoon basil
1 teaspoon oregano
1 tablespoon parsley
2 (6 ounce) cans tomato paste
1 (8 ounce) can tomato sauce
¾ cup hot water
1 tablespoon olive oil
1 tablespoon salt
8-10 lasagne noodles
2 eggs, beaten
1 pint cottage cheese
½ pound mozzarella cheese, cut in strips
Parmesan cheese, grated

In a Dutch oven heat the oil. Add the garlic, bell pepper, celery, and onion and sauté until soft. Add the beef, salt, pepper, basil, oregano, and parsley and cook until crumbly. Add the tomato paste, tomato sauce, and water and simmer for 1 hour. Fill a large pot with water, bring it to a rapid boil, and add 1 tablespoon each olive oil and salt. Gently lower the noodles, 1 at a time, into the boiling water. Cook the noodles for 15 minutes. Add cold water to stop cooking. Remove the noodles gently with tongs to a colander to drain. In a bowl blend the egg with the cottage cheese. In a 9" x 13" baking pan spread a thin layer of meat sauce. Top with ½ of the noodles, all of the cottage cheese mixture, followed by ½ of the mozzarella cheese. Spread another thin layer of meat sauce (using ½ of remaining sauce), then the remaining noodles. Top this 2nd layer of noodles with remaining meat sauce, then with remaining mozzarella cheese. Sprinkle with Parmesan cheese. Bake, covered, at 350° for 15 minutes. Uncover and continue baking for 15 minutes longer. Serves 8-10.

Marinate less tender cuts of steak in Italian or French dressing overnight. Use the sauce for basting the meat while cooking.

Meat cooked in beer

Carbonades à la Flamande

½ cup cooking oil
4 pounds lean beef, cut in ½-inch cubes
½ cup flour
2 pounds large onions, thickly sliced
6 cloves garlic, crushed
3 tablespoons dark brown sugar
¼ cup red wine vinegar
½ cup chopped parsley
2 small bay leaves
2 tablespoons thyme leaves
1 tablespoon salt
Freshly ground pepper to taste
2 (10½ ounce) cans beef consommé
2 (12 ounce) cans beer
Dumpling Batter (see Index)

Heat the oil in a large skillet. Dredge the meat in
flour and brown, a few pieces at a time, over medium heat.
Place the browned meat in an 8-quart baking dish. To the
skillet add the onion and garlic and brown lightly. Add
more oil if necessary. Transfer the mixture to the baking
dish and stir in the sugar, 2 tablespoons of the vinegar,
parsley, bay leaves, thyme, salt, and pepper. Pour off any
oil in the skillet. In the skillet heat the consommé,
stirring, to loosen the brown bits. Pour the consommé and
beer over the meat mixture. Bake, covered, at 325°F for
2 hours. Transfer the casserole to the top of the stove.
Stir in the remaining vinegar and cook over medium heat
until the sauce bubbles. Drop dumplings in and cook for
15 minutes. Serves 10.

Spaghetti Pie

6 ounces thin spaghetti, cooked and drained
2 tablespoons butter or margarine
⅓ cup grated Parmesan cheese
2 eggs, beaten
1 pound lean ground beef
½ cup chopped onion
¼ cup chopped bell pepper
1 (8 ounce) can tomato sauce
1 (6 ounce) can tomato paste
1 teaspoon sugar
1 teaspoon dried oregano, crushed
1 clove garlic, grated
½ cup water
½ cup sliced mushrooms
1 cup grated mozzarella cheese

Into the cooked spaghetti stir the butter, Parmesan cheese, and eggs and set aside. In a skillet sauté the ground beef, onion, and bell pepper until the vegetables are tender and the meat is browned. Drain off the excess grease. Stir in the tomato sauce, tomato paste, sugar, oregano, garlic, water, and mushrooms and simmer the mixture for 15 minutes. Line a buttered 10″ baking dish or pie pan with the spaghetti mixture. Ladle the meat mixture onto the spaghetti. Bake the dish, uncovered, at 350°F for 20 minutes. Sprinkle the mozzarella cheese over the top and continue baking for 5 minutes, or until the cheese melts. Serves 6.

Beef Bourguignon

¼ cup diced bacon
¼ cup flour
1 teaspoon paprika
2 teaspoons salt
3 pounds lean beef chuck, cut in 1½-inch cubes
6 tablespoons margarine
⅓ cup chopped carrot
1 medium onion, chopped
1 clove garlic, crushed
¼ teaspoon thyme
¼ cup chopped parsley
1 bay leaf
½ teaspoon Tabasco sauce
2 cups beef bouillon
1 cup dry red wine
8 small white onions, peeled
8 small carrots, cut in pieces
8 small new potatoes, scrubbed
½ pound mushrooms, sliced

In a Dutch oven cook the bacon until crisp, remove, and reserve it. In a bowl combine the flour, paprika, and 1½ teaspoons of the salt. Roll the beef cubes in the flour mixture. To the bacon grease in the Dutch oven add 4 tablespoons of the margarine and melt it over medium-high heat. Add the beef cubes and fry them until they are browned on all sides. Add the chopped carrot, chopped onion, and garlic and sauté until the onion is limp. Add the thyme, ½ of the parsley, bay leaf, Tabasco sauce, bacon, bouillon, and wine. Simmer the mixture, covered, for 2 hours, or until the meat is nearly tender. Add more bouillon and wine if the liquid does not cover the meat. Add the small onions, carrot pieces, and the remaining salt. Continue cooking for 15 to 20 minutes. Add the potatoes and continue cooking for 30 minutes. In a small pan sauté the mushrooms in the remaining margarine. Add the mushrooms to the beef mixture and continue cooking until the vegetables are tender. If a thicker consistency is desired, stir in 1 tablespoon flour dissolved in 2 tablespoons water and cook until the mixture is thickened. Serve the dish sprinkled with the remaining parsley. Serves 8.

Dolma
(Stuffed Grape Leaves)

½ cup uncooked long grain rice
6 tablespoons olive oil
½ cup finely chopped onion
½ pound lean ground beef
½ cup finely chopped green onion
½ cup finely chopped parsley
2 tablespoons dried dill
2 teaspoons finely snipped fresh mint (optional)
3 tablespoons lemon juice
½ teaspoon turmeric
½ teaspoon oregano
1 teaspoon salt
Pepper to taste
40 preserved grape leaves
Lemon wedges

Boil the rice in 1½ cups briskly boiling water for 10 minutes, drain, and reserve it. In a heavy skillet heat the olive oil over moderate heat until a haze forms. Add the onion and cook, stirring, until golden brown. Stir in the ground beef, breaking up lumps, and cook until browned. Drain off the excess grease. Reduce the heat and add the rice, green onion, parsley, dill, mint, lemon juice, turmeric, oregano, salt, and pepper. Cook the stuffing for 3 to 4 minutes and reserve it. In a large pot bring 2 quarts water to a boil. Drop in the grape leaves and remove from the heat. Soak the leaves for 1 minute and transfer them to cold water. Separate the leaves and drain them on paper towels. To stuff the leaves spread 30 leaves dull side up, flat on a plate. Place 1 tablespoon of the stuffing on the center of each leaf. Turn up the stem end and fold the leaf over the stuffing. Layer the bottom of a 2-3 quart casserole, with a tight fitting cover, with the 10 unstuffed leaves. Arrange the stuffed leaves, with the seam side down, in the casserole. Sprinkle the dish with the remaining 2 tablespoons of the oil and 2 tablespoons water. Simmer, tightly covered, for 50 minutes. Serve the Dolma hot or at room temperature garnished with lemon wedges. Serves 6-8

Moussaka Romano

1 pound ground beef
1 large onion, chopped
2 cloves garlic, minced
2 (12 ounce) cans tomato paste
5½ teaspoons salt
1 teaspoon sugar
½ teaspoon pepper
1 teaspoon oregano, crushed
1 teaspoon sweet basil, crushed
4 cups water
2 medium eggplants, peeled and sliced ⅜ inch thick
¼ cup butter
¼ cup flour
2 cups milk
1 (15 ounce) carton cottage cheese
3 eggs
1 pound lasagne noodles
5 tablespoons cooking oil
½ cup grated Parmesan cheese

In a large skillet brown the ground beef. Add the onion
and garlic and cook until soft. Add the tomato paste, 2
teaspoons of the salt, sugar, pepper, oregano, and basil.
Stir in the water and simmer, uncovered, for 1 hour. Place
the eggplant slices on a large surface and sprinkle them
with 1 tablespoon of the salt. Let them stand for 15
minutes. In a medium saucepan melt the butter. Add the flour
and ½ teaspoon of the salt to make a paste. Slowly stir in
the milk and continue cooking, stirring constantly, until
the sauce is thick and smooth. In a small bowl combine
the white sauce, cottage cheese, and eggs. Cook the
lasagne noodles in boiling salted water with 1 tablespoon
of the oil and cook for 12 minutes or until not quite tender.
Transfer the noodles to a colander, rinse them with cold water,
and drain them. Pat off all excess moisture. While the lasagne
noodles are cooking, rinse and pat dry the eggplant slices. In
another skillet heat the remaining oil. Add the eggplant slices and
fry them until light golden brown. In a 9″ x 13″ baking pan
layer ⅓ of the meat mixture, ½ of the eggplant, ⅓ of the
cottage cheese mixture, and ½ of the noodles. Repeat the
layers, reserving ⅓ of the meat mixture and ⅓ of the
cottage cheese mixture. Dot the top of the dish with the
reserved cottage cheese mixture. Spoon the reserved meat
mixture onto the cottage cheese dots and swirl the 2
mixtures together with a spoon. Sprinkle the top of the
dish with Parmesan cheese. Bake at 350°F for 45 minutes.
Remove the dish from the oven and let it stand for 10
minutes before cutting it into squares to serve. Serves 6-8.

Salt should be added after the beef is browned. Adding
it before cooking draws out the juices and retards browning.

Grillades

4 pounds veal or beef rounds, trimmed of fat
½ cup bacon grease
½ cup flour
1 cup chopped onion
1 cup chopped green onion
¾ cup chopped celery
1 cup chopped bell pepper
3 cloves garlic, minced
1 (16 ounce) can tomatoes
1 teaspoon thyme
1 cup water
1 cup Burgundy wine
¼ pound fresh mushrooms, chopped
3 teaspoons salt
½ teaspoon pepper
2 bay leaves
½ teaspoon Tabasco sauce
2 tablespoons Worcestershire sauce
¼ cup chopped parsley
2-2½ cups rice, cooked or 1½-2 cups grits, cooked

Cut the meat into serving-size pieces. Using a mallet
flatten the meat to a thickness of ¼ inch. In a Dutch
oven heat ¼ cup of the bacon grease over medium heat.
Add the meat and fry it until it is browned. Transfer the
meat to a plate and set it aside. To the Dutch oven add the
remaining bacon grease and the flour, stirring constantly,
until the roux is dark brown. To the roux add the onion,
green onion, celery, bell pepper, and garlic and sauté until
soft. Add the tomatoes and thyme and cook for 3 minutes.
Add the water, wine, and mushrooms, and stir well. Return
the meat to the pot. Add the salt, pepper, bay leaves,
Tabasco sauce, and Worcestershire sauce. Lower the heat
and continue cooking, stirring. If veal rounds are used simmer
for 1 hour, but for beef rounds simmer 2 hours. Remove the
bay leaves and stir in the parsley. The dish is best
refrigerated for 8 hours and reheated before serving.
Serve with the rice or grits. Serves 8-10.

Marinate steaks in Italian dressing for 1 hour before broiling.

Enchiladas with Chili Sauce

CHILI SAUCE:

½ pound bulk pork sausage

1½ pounds lean ground beef

1 large onion, chopped

½ small bell pepper, chopped

2-3 cloves garlic, crushed

4 tablespoons flour

¼ cup chili powder

½ teaspoon oregano

½ teaspoon ground cumin

1½ teaspoons salt

1 (16 ounce) can tomato purée

2½ cups water

½ ounce sweet chocolate (optional)

1-2 green chilies, chopped (optional)

In a large heavy Dutch oven cook most of the fat from the
sausage. Pour off the fat, add the beef, and cook for a
few minutes. Add the onion, bell pepper, and garlic. When
the onion is clear and the meat is thoroughly cooked, blend
together the flour, chili powder, oregano, cumin, and salt
and add to the meat mixture. Stir constantly for 3 minutes
to allow the flour to coat the meat and brown slightly. Add
the tomato purée and cook for 5 minutes, or until it is
thoroughly mixed with the meat. Add the water and chocolate
and continue cooking the mixture for 1 hour. Adjust the
seasoning and add the chilies.

ENCHILADAS:

1 pound mild Cheddar cheese, grated

1 large onion, chopped

1 cup cooking oil

16 tortillas

In a bowl combine the cheese and onion. In a skillet heat
the oil over moderately high heat until very hot. Using
tongs dip the tortillas, 1 at a time, into the hot oil
to soften them so they will roll easily. Place them between
layers of absorbent paper toweling to drain. Place a
heaping tablespoon of the cheese and onion mixture in the
center of each tortilla. With a slotted spoon dip a little
meat from the chili sauce and place it on top of the cheese
and onion. Roll the tortilla tightly, tucking the edge under
the filling. Place the enchiladas close together in a
shallow baking dish. Pour the chili sauce generously over
the enchiladas and sprinkle any remaining cheese and onion
on top. Bake the enchiladas at 350°F for 15 to 20 minutes,
or until the cheese is melted. Serves 8.

Prepare the day before serving
Enchilada Casserole

2 pounds ground chuck
1 large onion, finely chopped
1 (16 ounce) can whole tomatoes, drained
1 (10 ounce) can Ro-Tel tomatoes, drained
1 (10 ounce) package frozen chopped spinach, cooked and drained
Salt and pepper to taste
1 (10 ¾ ounce) can cream of mushroom soup
1 (8 ounce) carton sour cream
¼ cup milk
¼ teaspoon garlic powder
12-16 tortillas
½ cup margarine, melted
1 (4 ounce) can green chilies, chopped
½ pound Cheddar cheese, grated

Brown the meat in a large skillet. Pour off the grease.
Stir in the onion and sauté slightly. Add the tomatoes,
spinach, salt, and pepper. In a bowl combine the soup, sour
cream, milk, and garlic powder. Cut the tortillas into strips
and dip them in melted margarine. Cover the bottom and sides
of a baking dish with tortilla strips. Spoon in the meat
mixture. Scatter chopped chilies on top of the meat mixture.
Add ½ of the grated cheese and the remaining tortillas. Pour
the soup mixture on top of the casserole and add the remaining
cheese. Refrigerate overnight. Bake, uncovered, at 325°F
for 35 to 45 minutes or until bubbly. Serves 8.

Accompaniment for roast beef
Yorkshire Pudding

1 cup flour
¾ teaspoon salt
2 eggs, well beaten
1½ cups milk
¼ cup hot beef drippings

Sift the flour and salt together. In a large bowl
combine the eggs and milk. Gradually add the flour
mixture to the egg mixture and beat well with an egg
beater. Pour the hot drippings into an 8″x8″x2″
baking dish and add the egg mixture. Bake at 450°F for
25 to 30 minutes. Cut in squares to serve. Serves 6.

For ease in cutting raw meats have the meat partially
frozen and cut with an electric knife.

Orange-Glazed Grilled Chuck

1½ cups pineapple juice
1 (4/5 ounce) envelope instant meat marinade
1 teaspoon ground ginger
¼ teaspoon ground cloves
¼ teaspoon salt
Coarsely ground pepper to taste
1 (3-4 pound) beef arm roast
¾ cup orange marmalade
¼ cup cooking oil

In a bowl combine 1 cup of the pineapple juice, marinade, ginger, cloves, salt, and pepper. Pour the mixture over the meat in a shallow dish. Marinate the meat for 15 minutes, turning the meat several times. Remove the meat from the marinade and place it on a grill. Stir the remaining pineapple juice, marmalade, and oil into the marinade. Cook the meat over medium coals for 45 minutes to 1 hour, turning several times, and brushing it with the marinade mixture. Serves 6-8.

Oven Barbecued Meat Balls

1 cup bread crumbs
¾ cup milk
1½-2 pounds lean ground beef
1 teaspoon salt
Pepper to taste
3 tablespoons Worcestershire sauce
⅓ cup vinegar
4½ tablespoons sugar
¾ cup ketchup
¾ cup water
¾ cup chopped onion
¾ cup chopped bell pepper

In a bowl moisten the bread crumbs with the milk and combine them with the meat, salt, and pepper. Shape the mixture into 24 meat balls and place them in a 9″ x 13″ baking dish. In another bowl combine the remaining ingredients to make the barbecue sauce. Pour the sauce over the meat balls and bake them, covered, at 375°F for 1 to 1½ hours. Serves 8-10.

Italian Meat Balls

2 pounds ground beef
1½ cups Italian seasoned bread crumbs
¾ cup grated Italian cheese
Salt and pepper to taste
4 eggs
1 large onion, grated
1 clove garlic, grated
¼ cup water
Chopped parsley
Italian Sauce (see Index)

In a large bowl mix all the ingredients except the Italian Sauce
and form the mixture into small balls. Place the meat balls
in an oiled baking dish. Bake them at 375°F, turning once to brown
them evenly, for 15 to 20 minutes. When the meat balls are
browned, pour the Italian Sauce over them and continue baking
for 2 hours. Makes 26-30 meat balls.

Braised Beef Burgundy

3 pounds round steak, cut in 2-inch cubes
Flour
Salt and pepper to taste
¼ cup butter
½ cup coarsely chopped onion
½ cup coarsely chopped green onion
½ cup coarsely chopped carrot
1 clove garlic, crushed
1 tablespoon chopped parsley
1 tablespoon chopped chives
2 tablespoons brandy
1 bouquet garni (2 bay leaves, 8 sprigs parsley, 1 sprig thyme, 2 celery leaves, all tied together with string)
2 whole cloves
Dash of crushed marjoram
8 peppercorns, crushed
1 teaspoon salt
Red Burgundy wine

Dredge the meat cubes in seasoned flour. Melt the butter in
a large heavy skillet and sear the cubes on very high heat.
Transfer the meat to a 4-quart casserole. Reduce the heat
to low and add the onion, green onion, carrot, garlic, parsley,
and chives, stirring, until browned. Put the brandy in a
soup ladle, ignite it, and drip it over the beef cubes in
the casserole. Add the browned vegetables to the meat. Add
the bouquet garni, cloves, marjoram, peppercorns, and salt.
Pour enough wine over the meat to cover it. Bake, covered
tightly, at 350°F for 3½ hours. To serve remove the bouquet
garni. Serves 6.

Beef Brisket with Savory Marinade

1 brisket of beef
MARINADE:
1 cup salad oil
¾ cup soy sauce
½ cup lemon juice
¼ cup Worcestershire sauce
¼ cup prepared yellow mustard
2 tablespoons salt
1½ teaspoons pepper
1½ teaspoons red pepper
2 cloves garlic, minced
4 ounces Italian salad dressing
Dry red wine

In a quart jar combine the marinade ingredients except the wine. Fill the jar to the top with the wine. Place the meat in a large shallow dish. Pour the marinade over the meat to cover. Marinate the brisket in the refrigerator, turning and basting occasionally, for 24 to 48 hours. In a barbecue pit or a smoker place a pan on ashen coals. Place the brisket on the grill centered over the pan. Close the lid and adjust the vents to almost closed. Smoke the brisket, uncovered, for 4 to 6 hours, or until a meat thermometer registers 200°F, basting with pan juices. Serve the brisket thinly sliced.

Savory Pepper Steak

1 (½ inch thick) beef round steak, cut in strips
¼ cup flour
½ teaspoon salt
⅛ teaspoon pepper
¼ cup oil
1 (16 ounce) can tomatoes (reserve liquid)
1 (8 ounce) can tomato sauce
¾ cup water
½ cup chopped onion
1½ teaspoons basil
⅛ teaspoon garlic powder
1½ teaspoons Worcestershire sauce
2 large bell peppers, cut in strips
1 cup rice, cooked

Dredge the meat in flour, salt, and pepper. In a heavy skillet with a lid heat the oil. Add the meat and brown it. Combine the tomato sauce, tomato liquid, and water and pour it over the meat. Stir in the onion, basil, and garlic powder. Simmer the mixture, covered, for 1¼ hours, or until the meat is tender. Add the Worcestershire sauce and bell pepper and simmer for 5 minutes. If the gravy is too thin, blend together about 3 tablespoons flour and water and add to the sauce. Cook, stirring, until the mixture is bubbly. Add the tomatoes and cook for 5 minutes. Serve over hot rice. Serves 6.

Veau à la Citrone

6 veal cutlets, ¼ inch thick
Salt and pepper to taste
½ cup butter
2 tablespoons finely chopped green onion
1 tablespoon finely chopped parsley
2 tablespoons fresh lemon juice
¼ cup fresh orange juice
¼ cup Grand Marnier
2 teaspoons grated lemon rind
2 teaspoons grated orange rind
1 cup milk
2 tablespoons flour
1 cup chicken stock
8 ounces fresh mushrooms, sliced
½ cup sour cream

With a wooden mallet pound the cutlets until they are very thin and season them with salt and pepper. In a heavy skillet sauté the cutlets in butter over high heat, turning them several times, until they are lightly browned. (Do not let the butter burn.) Arrange the cutlets in a shallow baking dish and bake, covered, at 300°F for 20 minutes. Add the green onion to the juices in the skillet and sauté until they are soft. Stir in the lemon juice, orange juice, Grand Marnier, lemon rind, and orange rind. Simmer the mixture over low heat, stirring, to loosen all the brown bits from the bottom of the skillet. In a cup mix the milk and flour well and add the mixture to the skillet. Cook the sauce, stirring, over low heat until it is smooth and thick. (It may appear to curdle at first, but this will disappear as it thickens.) Add the chicken stock and mushrooms and mix well. Remove from heat and carefully stir in the sour cream. Season the sauce with salt and pepper. Pour the sauce over the veal just before serving. Serves 4.

Veal Italiano

2 pounds veal round steak
3 tablespoons olive oil
1 tablespoon crumbled dry bread
12 cloves garlic
2 ripe tomatoes, peeled, seeded, and chopped
1 teaspoon sweet basil
Salt and pepper to taste
¾ cup white wine
Risotto (see Index)

Cut the veal in serving-size pieces. In a heavy skillet heat the oil. Add the veal pieces and brown them. Stir in the bread, garlic, tomatoes, basil, salt, and pepper. Add the wine and simmer the veal for 1 hour, or until it is tender. Serve with the Risotto. Serves 4.

Veal Cordon Bleu

12 veal cutlets
6 slices provolone cheese
6 slices boiled ham
Flour
2 eggs, beaten
Bread crumbs
Butter
1 lemon, sliced

Place the cutlets between 2 sheets of wax paper and using a mallet or the flat side of a heavy knife pound them until they are thin. Place a slice of provolone cheese on each of 6 veal slices, cover each with a slice of ham, and top them with the remaining 6 slices of veal. Pound the edges together to seal them. Dredge the packets in flour, dip them in the egg, and coat them with bread crumbs. Melt the butter in a heavy skillet to a depth of ¼ inch. Add the veal packets and sauté them for 8 minutes, turning them once, or until the meat is browned and the cheese is melted. Serve the veal with a slice of lemon. Serves 6.

Veal with Wine Sauce

2 tablespoons butter
2 pounds veal, cut in bite-size pieces
1 pound fresh mushrooms, sliced
6 green onions, minced
2 cloves garlic, finely chopped
1 teaspoon dried rosemary leaves, crushed
1 teaspoon dried tarragon leaves, crushed
1 tablespoon flour
1 cup Madeira wine
1 cube chicken bouillon
Salt and pepper to taste
1-1½ cups saffron rice, cooked

In a large skillet melt 1 tablespoon of the butter. Add the veal and sauté it slowly. Add the mushrooms, green onion, garlic, rosemary, and tarragon. Be careful not to burn the herbs while the veal is browning. In a saucepan melt the remaining butter. Add the flour, stirring constantly, over medium heat until it is brown. Stir in the wine and bouillon cube. Add the veal and cook over low heat, covered, for 30 minutes, adding more wine if liquid is needed. Serve over the rice. Serves 4-6.

Basting Sauce for Veal: Combine ½ cup melted butter, 1 tablespoon grated lime rind, ¼ cup lime juice, ½ teaspoon marjoram, and ½ teaspoon thyme.

Black Forest Venison Stew

MARINADE:

2 white onions, chopped

3 green onions, chopped

2 ribs celery, chopped

2 whole cloves

½ teaspoon each of rosemary, thyme, and oregano

2 bay leaves, crushed

12 juniper berries

2 cloves garlic, crushed

10 black peppercorns

2 tablespoons dried parsley

1 teaspoon salt

1 fifth red wine

1 cup olive oil

¼ cup wine vinegar

In a large pot combine all marinade ingredients, simmer for
10 minutes, and cool.

5 pounds venison stew meat

6 slices bacon

¼ cup butter

2 onions, chopped

4 tablespoons flour

2 cups beef broth

Salt and pepper to taste

1 teaspoon dried marjoram

10 juniper berries

1 cup sour cream

1 (16 ounce) package egg noodles, cooked and drained

Marinate the venison for 24 hours. Remove the venison
from the marinade, reserving the marinade. Pat the venison
completely dry. Strain the marinade, reserving 2 cups.
Place the bacon in a large roasting pan and brown it
thoroughly. Add the butter and melt it. Add the meat and
brown it quickly on all sides. Transfer the meat to a dish.
Add the onion and sauté until it is brown. Stir in the flour,
browning it for about 3 minutes. Return the meat to the pan.
Add the broth and reserved marinade and simmer, stirring,
until it is slightly thickened. Season the dish with salt
and pepper and add the marjoram and juniper berries.
Simmer for 1½ hours, or until the meat is tender. Skim
off all the grease and stir in the sour cream. Serve the
stew over the noodles. Serves 8.

Venison contains very little fat and should be cooked by
a moist-heat method with some grease or fat added.

Fried Rabbit

1 rabbit, cut up
Salt and pepper to taste
½ cup flour
½ cup shortening
½ cup butter
Parsley
Lemon slices
GRAVY:
1 tablespoon flour
1 cup evaporated milk

Season the rabbit liberally with salt and pepper and dredge it in the flour. In a large skillet melt the shortening and butter. Add the rabbit and fry over medium heat. Reduce the heat to low and cook, covered, for 45 minutes or until tender. Remove the rabbit and keep it warm. Pour off all grease except about 1 kitchen spoonful. Add the flour, stirring, until it is a light golden color. Gradually add the milk, stirring constantly, until the desired consistency is reached. Serve the dish garnished with parsley and lemon slices. Serves 4.

Game Marinade

3 cloves garlic, pressed
¼ teaspoon pepper
½ teaspoon salt
1 whole clove
½ teaspoon chopped celery
1 onion, chopped
½ cup chopped parsley
1 carrot, grated
2 cups white wine
1 cup vinegar

In a bowl mix the garlic, pepper, salt, and clove together. Add the celery, onion, parsley, carrot, wine, and vinegar. Stir the marinade well. Marinate the meat overnight. When cooking the meat, add the marinade to the pot. Makes 3½ cups.

Soak venison in milk overnight in the refrigerator to help remove the wild taste.

Sweet and Sour Spareribs

2/3 cup water
½ cup vinegar
¼ cup ketchup
1 tablespoon Worcestershire sauce
3 dashes hot pepper sauce
¼ teaspoon paprika
2 cups brown sugar
¼ cup margarine
2 Bermuda onions, chopped
2 cloves garlic, chopped
5 pounds spareribs, separated into ribs

In a large saucepan combine the water, vinegar, ketchup, Worcestershire sauce, hot pepper sauce, paprika, and brown sugar and mix well. In a medium saucepan melt the margarine. Add the onion and garlic and sauté until tender and add to the brown sugar mixture. Bring it to a boil and simmer for 20 minutes. Place the spareribs and sauce in a shallow pan. Bake at 400°F for 1 to 1¼ hours or until fork tender. Serves 6.

Sweet and Sour Pork

1½ pounds boneless pork, cut in 1-inch cubes
Flour
Salt and pepper to taste
2 tablespoons cooking oil
½ cup barbecue sauce
¼ cup vinegar
½ cup water
1 bell pepper, cut in strips
1 (12 ounce) jar pineapple preserves

Coat the meat with the flour seasoned with salt and pepper. In a skillet heat the oil. Add the pork and brown it. Add the barbecue sauce, vinegar, and water. Simmer, covered, for 45 minutes. Add the bell pepper and preserves and simmer for 15 minutes. Serves 6.

Home-cured, Smithfield, or Virginia ham should be scrubbed well under running water and soaked in cold water for 12 to 24 hours before cooking.

Natchitoches Meat Pies

FILLING:
2 tablespoons shortening
2 tablespoons flour
1 cup finely chopped onion
1 pound lean ground pork
½ pound ground beef
1½ teaspoons pepper
1½ teaspoons red pepper
1 cup finely chopped celery
½ cup finely chopped fresh parsley
½ cup finely chopped bell pepper
2 cloves garlic, minced
1 bay leaf
1-2 tablespoons flour
DOUGH:
4 cups flour
3 teaspoons baking powder
1 teaspoon salt
1 tablespoon shortening
1 egg
1⅓ cups milk

In a heavy skillet heat the shortening. Add the flour and brown it. Add the onion and cook until wilted but not brown. Stir in the pork, beef, pepper, and red pepper. Brown the meat and simmer the mixture for 15 minutes. Skim off any excess grease. Add the remaining ingredients except the flour and simmer over low heat for 20 minutes. If needed, add a little water. Sprinkle the flour over the mixture and stir until well blended over low heat. Cool the filling and refrigerate it for at least 1 hour, but preferably overnight. In a large bowl mix the dry ingredients together. Cut the shortening into the flour mixture. Add the egg. Stir in enough milk to make a soft dough. Chill the dough at least 1 hour, but preferably overnight. Divide the dough in 2-inch balls. Place each ball of dough on a floured board and roll it flat into a circle about 5 inches in diameter. Place a heaping tablespoon of filling on ½ of the circle. Fold the dough over the filling, moisten the edges with water, and crimp them together with a fork. The pies may be frozen at this stage. In a deep fryer fry the pies in deep hot fat at 350°F until light golden brown. Makes 30-40 pies.

Ham Loaf

1 pound ground ham
1 pound ground pork
¾ cup bread crumbs
1 teaspoon horseradish
1 cup milk
⅓ cup chopped onion
2 eggs
1 tablespoon chopped parsley
¼ cup finely chopped celery
Pepper to taste
GLAZE:
½ cup brown sugar
½ cup cider vinegar
1 teaspoon prepared mustard

In a large bowl mix all the loaf ingredients together and form the
mixture into a loaf. Transfer the loaf to a baking pan. Bake
the loaf, covered, at 350°F for 30 minutes. Remove the loaf from
the oven and pour off the drippings. In a saucepan combine
the glaze ingredients and bring the mixture to a boil, reduce the
heat, and simmer for 1 minute. Remove the saucepan from
the heat, baste the loaf with the glaze, and continue baking,
uncovered, for 1 hour. Serve the ham loaf with the Tangy Sauce.
Serves 6-8.

TANGY SAUCE:
¼ cup mayonnaise
¼ cup sour cream
3 tablespoons prepared mustard
1 tablespoon minced olives
3 tablespoons horseradish
Salt to taste
1 lemon, juiced

In a bowl thoroughly blend all of the ingredients.

Pork Chops and Scalloped Potatoes

3 tablespoons bacon grease
6 pork chops
1 medium onion, chopped
1 clove garlic, finely chopped
2 tablespoons flour
1¼ cups milk
6 medium potatoes, peeled and sliced
1 cup grated Daisy cheese
½ cup sliced mushrooms
Salt and pepper to taste

In a heavy skillet heat the grease over medium heat. Add
the pork chops and brown them. Transfer the chops to a plate
and set aside. To the skillet add the onion and garlic and sauté
until soft. Stir in the flour and add 1 cup of the milk, stirring constantly, until the sauce is thick. In a casserole alternate layers
of the potatoes, cheese, mushrooms, and sauce. Place the
chops on top and add the remaining milk. Bake at 350°F for 1 hour.
Serves 6.

Sausage and Ham Jambalaya

2 tablespoons cooking oil
1 cup chopped onion
1 bell pepper, chopped
3 ribs celery, chopped
5 green onions, chopped
1 (10 ounce) can tomatoes (reserve liquid), chopped
1 (10 ounce) can Ro-Tel tomatoes (reserve liquid), chopped
2 cups diced ham
4 tablespoons tomato paste
¼ cup minced parsley
2 cloves garlic, minced
1 bay leaf
1 teaspoon thyme leaves
1 teaspoon basil
Salt and pepper to taste
¼ cup Worcestershire sauce
3 cups water
12 pork sausages, halved
1 pound smoked sausage, cut in 1-inch slices
2 cups uncooked Uncle Ben's Converted Rice

In a Dutch oven heat the oil. Add the onion and bell pepper
and sauté until tender. Add the celery, green onion, and
tomatoes and cook until soft. Add the ham and tomato paste
and fry the mixture until it begins to brown. Add the
parsley, garlic, seasonings, Worcestershire sauce, reserved
tomato liquids, and 2 cups water. Cook this gravy for 1 hour.
In a separate large skillet fry the pork sausages and smoked
sausage and discard the grease. Add the sausage to the gravy
and rinse out the skillet with 1 cup water and add to the gravy.
Place the rice in the gravy mixture and cover tightly. When
it starts to bubble, lower the heat and cook until the rice
is done. Several times during cooking, lift the mixture gently
with a spoon to keep it from sticking. If the water is gone
before the rice is cooked, add a little more hot water to the
gravy. Serves 8-10.

Always cook pork well done for best flavor; the meat
should be firm, juicy, and tender, not dry or crumbly.

Oven Pork Chops

1 cup rice
2 cups beef bouillon
2 tablespoons cooking oil
8 pork chops
1 medium onion, finely chopped
2 cloves garlic, finely chopped
½ teaspoon sage
Salt and pepper to taste

In a saucepan combine the rice and beef bouillon and cook, covered, for 20 minutes. Do not stir. In a large skillet heat the oil over medium heat. Add the chops and fry them until they are browned. Transfer the chops to a plate and set aside. To the skillet add the onion and garlic and sauté until tender. Add the cooked rice to the onion and garlic mixture. Mix in the sage, salt, and pepper. In a baking dish, spread the rice mixture and top it with the pork chops. Bake, covered, at 350°F for 30 minutes. Uncover and continue baking for 10 minutes. Serves 4.

Ham-Spaghetti Skillet Meal

4 slices bacon
1 cup chopped onion
½ bell pepper, chopped
2 cups cubed ham
2 cloves garlic, chopped
1 (16 ounce) can tomatoes
1 (8 ounce) can tomato sauce
⅛ teaspoon oregano
¼ teaspoon basil
Salt and white pepper to taste
1½ cups uncooked spaghetti, broken in 1½-inch pieces
1 cup grated Cheddar cheese

In a deep skillet fry the bacon until it is crisp. Transfer it to paper towels to drain. To the bacon grease add the onion, bell pepper, and ham and brown slightly over medium heat. Stir in the remaining ingredients, except the cheese. Add ½ cup water if needed. Simmer, covered, for 30 minutes. Add the cheese and continue cooking for 10 minutes. Serves 4-6.

Glaze ham with a syrup made by combining 1 cup honey and 1 cup brown sugar, cooked until the sugar is dissolved.

Italian Sauce

1 tablespoon olive oil
4 large cloves garlic, crushed
1 (12 ounce) can tomato paste
1 (16 ounce) can tomato purée
3 teaspoons sugar
1 bay leaf
1 teaspoon sweet basil leaves
⅓ cup dry red wine
1 teaspoon Tony Chachere's Creole seasoning or salt
1 pork chop, browned (optional)
4 cups water (approximately)
1 tablespoon fresh parsley
2 tablespoons grated Romano cheese
½ teaspoon oregano leaves
Pepper to taste
Mushrooms (optional)

In a large Dutch oven heat the oil. Add the garlic and
sauté until soft, do not brown. Add the tomato paste and cook,
stirring frequently, for 15 minutes, or until it loses some
of its red color. Thoroughly stir in the purée, sugar, bay
leaf, sweet basil, wine, Creole seasoning, pork, and water.
Simmer, covered, for at least 3 hours. Extended cooking
tends to enhance the flavor, but may require additional water.
Add the parsley, cheese, oregano, and pepper 30 minutes
before serving. Adjust salt and add the mushrooms. Makes
1 quart.

Mushroom Steak Sauce

¼ cup butter
½ teaspoon salt
Dash of pepper
6 tablespoons flour
½ cup light cream
1 (10½ ounce) can condensed beef or chicken broth
¾ cup water
3 tablespoons Burgundy wine
12 fresh mushrooms, sliced

In a saucepan melt the butter over low heat. Stir in the salt,
pepper, and flour and cook for 5 minutes, but do not brown.
Stir in cream, gradually, until the sauce is smooth. Stir in the broth,
water, and wine. Cook, stirring, over low heat until the
sauce bubbles and thickens. Add the mushrooms and simmer
for 5 minutes, or until the mushrooms are cooked. Makes 3½ cups.

Steak Butters: Combine ½ cup butter with 2 tablespoons
mustard, 2 tablespoons horseradish, 2 tablespoons lemon juice,
or 2 tablespoons chopped parsley.

Bearnaise Sauce

¾ cup Hollandaise Sauce (see Index)

3 tablespoons tarragon vinegar

2 teaspoons chopped onion

¼ teaspoon pepper

Place all ingredients in a blender and process on low speed
for 5 minutes.

Barbeque Sauce

1 cup vinegar

1 cup water

½ cup ketchup

2 tablespoons Worcestershire sauce

1 lemon, juiced

1 tablespoon dry mustard

2 tablespoons chili powder

¼ teaspoon cayenne

1 teaspoon pepper

1 teaspoon salt

¼ cup sugar

2 bay leaves

2 cloves garlic, minced

1 medium onion, grated

In a saucepan combine all the ingredients. Simmer the mixture
for 10 minutes. Refrigerate the unused mixture. Makes 2 cups.

Jezebel Sauce

1 (18 ounce) jar pineapple preserves

1 (18 ounce) jar apple jelly

1 (2 ounce) can dry mustard

1 (5 ounce) jar horseradish

In a large bowl mix all the ingredients together well.
Divide the sauce in jars and refrigerate. Serve the sauce
on pork, roast beef, or as an appetizer over Philadelphia
cream cheese. Makes about 1 quart.

Roquefort Steak Sauce

4 ounces Roquefort cheese (at room temperature)

¼ cup olive oil

1 clove garlic, crushed

1 tablespoon brandy

In a small bowl blend all ingredients thoroughly.
Using a knife spread the sauce on 1 side of sizzling
broiled steaks and serve immediately on heated steak plates.

SEAFOOD

People who live near the coast are fortunate in the variety of good things to eat that seafood offers—many kinds of fish, crabs, shrimp, crawfish, oysters, frogs, turtles, eels, and squid. Now that frozen seafood of good quality is widely available, formerly local dishes can be made anywhere with only minor sacrifices of taste and texture. However, seafood must be fresh or freshly frozen, and it must be carefully cooked. Seasoning is important, too. It should enhance, rather than disguise, the flavor of the seafood.

SEAFOOD

Steamboat races on the Mississippi — leisurely strolls along the riverbank watching steamboats ply their trade — through the legacy of Mark Twain, all Americans share this heritage! Here in New Orleans it is a living legacy, complete with calliopes and a chance to take a ride yourself on the greatest of the world's rivers.

Stuffed Crabs

1 cup butter or margarine
1 cup finely chopped bell pepper
1 cup finely chopped green onion
½ cup finely chopped white onion
2 cloves garlic, minced
¼ teaspoon thyme
1 bay leaf
1 cup finely chopped celery
1 loaf French bread
2 cups milk
4 teaspoons salt
1 teaspoon pepper
¼ teaspoon cayenne
3 pounds crab meat
Paprika
Buttered bread crumbs

In a Dutch oven melt ¾ cup of the butter. Add the bell pepper, green onion, and onion and sauté for 5 minutes. Add the garlic, thyme, and bay leaf. Continue cooking over low heat until the onions are soft. Add the remaining ¼ cup butter and celery and continue cooking for 5 minutes. Remove the mixture from the heat. Break the French bread into small pieces and soak in the milk until the bread is saturated and squeeze it. Add the bread to the seasoning mixture and mix well. Return to medium heat for 5 minutes. Add the salt, pepper, cayenne, and crab meat and mix thoroughly. Remove the bay leaf. Arrange the crab mixture in individual shells. Top with the buttered bread crumbs, a sprinkle of paprika, and a dot of butter. Bake at 400°F for 10 minutes. Serves 8.

Boiled Crabs

1 bag crab boil, or 1½ tablespoons liquid crab boil (see page 203)
1 cup salt
2 tablespoons cayenne
3 onions, halved
1 small head garlic, cloves peeled and halved
3 lemons, halved
4 ribs celery, halved
12 live crabs

Into a large soup kettle pour enough water to measure 10 inches, or enough to cover the crabs when they are added. Add the crab boil, salt, cayenne, onions, garlic, lemons, and celery. Bring the mixture to a boil and continue boiling, covered, for 20 minutes. Remove the cover and lower the crabs into the boiling water. Allow the water to return to a boil and continue cooking for 15 to 20 minutes. Remove the kettle from the heat. Allow the crabs to remain in the seasoned water for 30 minutes in order to absorb the seasonings. Transfer the crabs to a large platter and serve.

Crab and Artichoke Casserole

3 tablespoons butter or margarine
3 tablespoons flour
1½ cups milk
¼ teaspoon Worcestershire sauce
1 teaspoon salt
⅛ teaspoon pepper
⅔ cup grated Parmesan or Romano cheese
4 hard-boiled eggs, peeled and quartered
1 (14 ounce) can artichoke hearts, drained
2 cups crab meat

In a medium saucepan melt the butter over medium-low heat.
Add the flour, stirring constantly, until the mixture is smooth.
Add the milk and cook the sauce, stirring constantly, until it is
smooth and bubbly. Season the sauce with the Worcestershire sauce,
salt, pepper, and ⅓ cup of the cheese. Add the eggs, artichoke
hearts, and crab meat to the cream sauce. Transfer the mixture
to a 1½-quart casserole. Sprinkle the top of the casserole
with the remaining cheese and bake it at 350°F for 30 minutes.
Serves 6.

Crab Meat au Gratin

5 tablespoons butter
3 tablespoons flour
1 cup milk
1 cup chicken bouillon
1 egg, well beaten
3 tablespoons sherry
Dash of Tabasco sauce
1 tablespoon Worcestershire sauce
1 teaspoon salt
1 teaspoon pepper
1 pound lump white crab meat
1 cup grated Cheddar cheese

In a large skillet make a white sauce with the butter, flour,
and milk. Add the bouillon and egg. Cook 1 minute, stirring
constantly. Remove from heat. Add the wine, Tabasco sauce,
Worcestershire sauce, salt, and pepper. Add the crab meat to
the sauce and pour it into a 1½-quart casserole or 6 ramekins.
Sprinkle the mixture with cheese. Bake, uncovered, at 350°F for
20 minutes. Serves 6.

Do not discard crab fat as it enhances the flavor of crab
meat dishes.

Microwave Crawfish Étouffée

⅓ cup flour
⅓ cup vegetable oil
2 large onions, chopped
1 small bunch green onions, finely chopped
1 bell pepper, chopped
3 cloves garlic, crushed
1 (16 ounce) can tomatoes, whirled in blender or food processor
2-2½ pounds peeled crawfish tails (reserve fat)
½ lemon, juiced
½ teaspoon liquid crab boil
Tabasco sauce to taste
Salt and pepper to taste
2 cups water
1½ cups rice, cooked

Mix the flour and oil in a 4-cup Pyrex measure. Microwave on high
for 5 to 6 minutes, or until the roux is light brown. To the roux
add the onion, green onion, bell pepper, and garlic. Stir and
microwave on high for 2 to 3 minutes. Transfer to à 3-quart
Pyrex dish. Add the tomatoes and mix well. Add the crawfish tails,
fat, lemon juice, crab boil, Tabasco sauce, salt, pepper, and
water. Microwave on medium for 5 to 6 minutes to blend the
flavors. Serve over rice. Serves 6.

Boiled Crawfish

20 pounds crawfish
12 lemons, halved and squeezed (reserve juice)
2 bunches celery, halved
12 onions, quartered
6 (3 ounce) bags crab boil (see page 203)
2 heads garlic
3 teaspoons cayenne
4 ears corn on the cob
4 Irish potatoes

Purge the crawfish by soaking in heavily salted water for 15
to 20 minutes. Do this at least 2 times, or until the water is clear.
While purging the crawfish, have 5 gallons of water heating in a
15-gallon pot. Add the lemons, lemon juice, celery, onions,
crab boil, garlic, and cayenne. After it comes to a boil add
the crawfish, corn, and potatoes. Return to a boil and continue
boiling for 10 minutes. Turn the heat off and let them stand
for 30 minutes. This allows the crawfish to cook a little
longer and to absorb the seasonings. Drain and serve with the
corn, potatoes, crackers, and beer. Southerners love back yard
seafood boils and allow 5 pounds per person.

8 pounds of crawfish yield 1 pound of crawfish meat.

Crawfish Étouffée

2 cloves garlic, minced
2 large onions, chopped
¼ cup chopped celery leaves
2 tablespoons butter
2 pounds peeled crawfish tails (reserve fat)
1 tablespoon Worcestershire sauce
Dash of Tabasco sauce
½ lemon, juiced
Salt and pepper to taste
¼ cup chopped parsley
2 cups rice, cooked

In a Dutch oven sauté the garlic, onion, and celery
leaves in the butter. Add the fat, Worcestershire sauce, Tabasco
sauce, and lemon juice. Cover the pan and simmer the mixture
for 30 minutes over low heat. Add the crawfish tails, salt, and
pepper. Continue cooking for 20 minutes. Add the parsley and serve
over the rice. Serves 8.

Creole Crawfish Étouffée

1 cup butter
1 cup finely chopped white onion
½ cup finely chopped celery
1 cup finely chopped green onion
1 teaspoon minced garlic
2 tablespoons flour
1 cup whole tomatoes (preferably fresh)
2 cups Fish Stock (see Index)
2 teaspoons salt
1 teaspoon pepper
1 tablespoon Worcestershire sauce
1½ cups crawfish meat
Dash of cayenne
1 cup rice, cooked

In a large saucepan melt the butter. Add the onion, celery,
and green onion and sauté until tender. Add the garlic
and continue cooking 1 minute. Gradually add the flour and stir
constantly until golden brown. Add the tomatoes and blend in
the stock. Simmer the mixture for 10 minutes. Add the salt,
pepper, Worcestershire sauce, crawfish, and cayenne. Cook
slowly 15 to 20 minutes, stirring occasionally. Serve over hot
fluffy rice. Serves 4.

Crawfish dishes prepared with highly seasoned sauces
or gravies are equally good refrigerated and reheated within
the next 2 days.

Crawfish Pie

½ cup unsalted butter

¼ cup flour

3 tablespoons tomato sauce

1 medium onion, finely chopped

½ bell pepper, finely chopped

½ cup finely chopped celery

4 green onion bottoms, chopped

2 cloves garlic, minced

2 tablespoons dry vermouth

2 pounds peeled crawfish tails

4 green onion tops, chopped

2 teaspoons salt

1 teaspoon cayenne

1 (10 ounce) package frozen Pepperidge Farm patty shells, thawed

In a large saucepan melt the butter over medium heat. Whisk in the flour and cook, stirring frequently, until the roux turns dark golden brown. Stir in the tomato sauce, onion, bell pepper, celery, green onion bottoms, and garlic. Add the vermouth and reduce the heat. Cook, covered, stirring occasionally, for 1 hour. Stir in the crawfish tails, green onion tops, salt, and cayenne. Cook, covered, for 20 minutes. Remove the cover and continue cooking for 20 minutes. Transfer the mixture to a medium bowl and cool for 30 minutes. On a floured surface roll out 4 of the patty shells to form the bottom pastry crust, transfer the crust to a 9″ pie pan, and fill it with the crawfish mixture. Roll out the remaining 2 patty shells to form the top crust, place it on top of the pie, and seal the edges. Bake at 400°F for 30 to 35 minutes or until golden brown.

Fried Crawfish Tails

1 pound crawfish tails

Salt and pepper to taste

2 eggs

¼ cup milk

1 cup flour

¼ teaspoon cayenne

Cooking oil

Season the cleaned crawfish tails with salt and pepper. In a small bowl beat the eggs and add the milk, mixing well. In a medium bowl mix the flour, cayenne, salt, and pepper. Dip each crawfish tail in the egg mixture and then in the flour. Fry the crawfish in deep hot oil until they are a light golden color, being careful not to overcook them. Transfer the crawfish to paper towels to drain. Serve them on a heated platter. Serves 2-4.

Boil only live crawfish. A straight crawfish tail indicates that the crawfish was not alive when boiled.

Seafood

Fish Stock

2 pounds fish trimmings (about 2 quarts)
2 medium onions, thinly sliced
1 cup white wine
1 lemon, juiced
6-8 parsley stems (do not use leaves)
1 bay leaf
¼ teaspoon salt
⅛ teaspoon white pepper

Place all of the ingredients in a 6-8 quart enameled or stainless steel pot and cover with water. Bring to a simmer and skim carefully. Simmer, uncovered, for 30 minutes. Strain the stock into a large saucepan, let it cool, and skim it again. Refrigerate the stock until it is needed (will keep 2 to 3 days in the refrigerator).
NOTE: If fish trimmings are unavailable, bottled clam juice and white wine (6 cups clam juice to 2 cups wine) may be substituted for the fish stock.

Pompano en Papillote

4 pompano fillets
2 cups water
1 lemon, juiced
2 bay leaves
Dash of thyme
1 teaspoon salt
½ teaspoon pepper
2 tablespoons butter
2 tablespoons flour
1 (4 ounce) can mushrooms, chopped
1 dozen cooked shrimp, chopped
1 dozen oysters, chopped
4 green onions, chopped
2 cloves garlic, chopped
¼ cup dry white wine

Poach the fillets of pompano for 5 minutes in the water seasoned with the lemon juice, bay leaves, thyme, salt, and pepper. Using a slotted spatula, carefully remove the fillets and set aside. Strain and reserve the fish stock. In a saucepan melt the butter and blend in the flour. Add the reserved fish stock slowly, stirring constantly, until a medium sauce consistency is reached. Add the mushrooms, shrimp, oysters, green onion, and garlic. Bring to a rolling boil. Add the wine and reduce the heat. Cut 4 (11″ x 14″) pieces of foil into heart shapes. Place each fillet on the right half of a heart-shaped piece of buttered foil. Top each fillet with ¼ of the sauce. Fold the left side of the heart over and crimp the edges together tightly, creating a well-sealed package. Bake on a cookie sheet at 400°F for 15 minutes. Serve in the foil packages. Serves 4.

An elaborate congealed fish

Redfish Glacé

1 teaspoon Worcestershire sauce
½ teaspoon Tabasco sauce
1 tablespoon vinegar
3 tablespoons salt
1 onion
1 bay leaf
1 sprig thyme
1 rib celery, quartered
½ lemon
3 pounds red snapper or redfish
2 tablespoons unflavored gelatin
14 green olives, pitted
14 ripe olives, pitted
1 (2 ounce) can pimientos
1 (5 cup) fish-shaped mold, lightly oiled
Lettuce

In a large pot combine 1½ quarts water with the first 9 ingredients.
Bring the water to a boil and simmer it for 30 minutes. Add
the fish and poach 10 minutes per inch of thickness. Transfer the
fish to a platter and set it aside. Strain the fish stock and
reserve it. Soak the gelatin in ¼ cup cold water; then dissolve
it in 2 cups of the hot fish stock. Slice all of the olives
to fit the scale depressions in the mold. Line the mold scales
with alternate slices of green and ripe olives. Follow the
design of the fish tail and fin with thin strips of pimiento and,
in the same manner, use the pimiento to mark the gill and mouth.
Around the eye, curve a small strip of pimiento and place a small
piece of black olive inside the pimiento to form the eye. Using
a fork, flake the fish. Fill the mold with the flaked fish until
it is ¾ full. Pour the gelatin mixture over the fish. Chill
the fish, covered, until it is firm. Arrange the lettuce leaves
on a large platter and unmold the fish on it. Serve the fish
with Hollandaise Sauce (see Index).

Trout Katherine

4 white or speckled trout fillets
Salt and pepper to taste
1 tablespoon lemon juice per fillet
1 teaspoon Worcestershire sauce per fillet
1 cup butter

Season the fillets with salt, pepper, lemon juice, and Worcestershire
sauce on each side. In a large heavy skillet melt the butter. Sauté
the fillets over moderately high heat for 2 to 3 minutes on
each side or until golden brown. Serves 4.

Trout St. Charles

⅔ cup butter or margarine
2 tablespoons flour
1 teaspoon salt
Dash of cayenne
¾ cup light cream
½ cup dry white wine
20 ounces trout fillets
½ teaspoon pepper
Toasted slivered almonds
Parsley

In a saucepan melt ½ cup of the butter. Blend in flour, ½
teaspoon of the salt, and cayenne. Gradually add the cream and
wine, stirring, until thick and smooth. Keep the mixture warm.
Place the trout, skin side down, in a buttered shallow baking
pan. Melt the remaining butter. Brush the trout with the melted
butter and season with ½ teaspoon of the salt and pepper. Place
the pan on the top shelf of the broiler. Broil for 5 to 6 minutes.
Just before serving, pour the sauce over the trout
and garnish with the almonds and parsley. Serves 3-4.

Trout Marguery

2 cups medium White Sauce (see Index)
2 tablespoons butter
½ cup finely chopped onion
2 cloves garlic, minced
1 rib celery, chopped
1 bay leaf
1 slice lemon
¼ teaspoon thyme
1 sprig parsley
2 rings bell pepper
1 (4 ounce) can mushrooms, drained
1 pound cooked shrimp, peeled and deveined
4 ounces smoky cheese
6 medium fillets Broiled Trout (see Index)

In a medium saucepan make the White Sauce. In a small
skillet melt the butter over medium heat. Add the onion,
garlic, and celery and sauté until light brown and
add to the white sauce. In a small cheesecloth bag put the bay
leaf, lemon, thyme, parsley, and bell pepper. Place the
seasoning bag in the white sauce and allow it to
remain in the white sauce for 30 minutes. Remove the seasoning bag.
Add the mushrooms and shrimp. Cook over low heat for 15
to 20 minutes. Immediately before serving, add the
cheese, stirring constantly, until it is melted. Pour the sauce
over the Broiled Trout. Serves 6.

Redfish Courtbouillon

1 (6 pound) redfish
4 tablespoons butter
4 tablespoons flour
1½ cups chopped onion
2 green onions, chopped
2 tablespoons chopped bell pepper
3 cloves garlic, minced
1 (14 ounce) can tomato sauce
3 tablespoons chopped parsley
2 bay leaves
¼ teaspoon thyme
2 teaspoons salt
¼ teaspoon pepper
3-4 cups hot water
1½ cups rice, cooked

Cut the fish in 2-inch cross sections. In a large heavy pot
melt the butter over medium heat. Add the flour, stirring constantly,
until a dark brown color is reached. Add the onions, bell pepper, and
garlic. Continue cooking, stirring often, until the vegetables
are soft. Add the tomato sauce and cook for 15 minutes.
Add the parsley, bay leaves, thyme, salt, and pepper.
Gradually stir in the hot water. Cover and cook over
low heat for 30 minutes. Place the fish in a baking pan and
cover it with gravy. Bake at 350°F for 30 to 45 minutes. Serve
with rice. Serves 6.

Trout Amandine

4 (6-8 ounce) trout fillets
Salt and pepper to taste
½ cup flour
⅓ cup cooking oil
½ cup butter
½ cup sliced almonds
1 lemon, thinly sliced
1 tablespoon chopped parsley

Season the trout with salt and pepper. Dredge with flour. In
a large heavy skillet heat the oil over moderately high heat.
Add the fillets and sauté them until golden brown on
both sides. Transfer them with a slotted spatula to paper towels
to drain, then to a heated platter to keep warm. In a small
skillet melt the butter. Add the almonds and sauté until light golden
brown. Pour the almond mixture over the trout and
garnish with lemon and parsley. Serves 4.

Skinning is not desirable with delicate flavored fish because the
skin helps to retain the flavor and juices.

Baked Red Snapper

4 large onions, chopped
½ cup butter
4 cups bread cubes
¼ cup white wine
Salt and pepper to taste
1 (6-8 pound) red snapper
1 tablespoon olive oil
1 clove garlic, minced
2½ cups canned tomatoes
6 cups water
3 sprigs parsley
1 bay leaf
¼ teaspoon thyme leaves
1 whole clove
2 cups chopped celery

In a large skillet sauté half of the onions in half of the butter
until they are brown around the edges. Add the bread cubes and wine.
Fry the mixture for 10 minutes, stirring. Add the salt and
pepper. Remove the mixture from the heat and allow it to cool. Wash
the fish and dry it with paper towels. Rub the cavity
with the olive oil, salt, and pepper. Stuff the cavity
with the bread mixture and place it in a generously buttered, large
baking pan. In a large skillet sauté the remaining onion and
the garlic in the remaining butter. Add the tomatoes, water,
parsley, bay leaf, thyme, clove, and celery and mix
well. Pour the sauce over the fish and bake it at 350°F for
20 minutes. INCREASE OVEN TEMPERATURE to 450°F and
continue baking for 20 minutes or until done. Transfer the
fish to a warm serving platter. Serve the fish with the sauce
spooned over it. Serves 4-6.

Trout Meunière

2½ cups peanut oil
3 (2½ pound) trout fillets, halved
1 cup flour
1 cup butter
2 tablespoons lemon juice
2 teaspoons Worcestershire sauce
1 teaspoon salt
¼ cup chopped parsley

In a frying pan preheat the oil to 350°F. Test the temperature
by dropping a small amount of water in the oil; if it pops the oil is hot
enough. Dredge the trout evenly in the flour and fry it, 2 pieces at a
time, over medium heat, for 5 to 7 minutes on each side. Transfer the
fried fillets to a heated platter and keep them warm. In a
heavy saucepan melt the butter and brown it lightly.
Stir in the lemon juice, Worcestershire sauce, salt, and
parsley and heat thoroughly. Pour some of the sauce over the fillets
and serve the remaining portion in a sauceboat. Serves 6.

Stuffed Flounder

½ cup butter
1 onion, finely chopped
1 bell pepper, finely chopped
2 cloves garlic, pressed
1 cup diced celery
½ loaf stale French bread, cut in cubes
1 cup water
¼ cup chopped green onion
¼ cup chopped parsley
1 cup lump crab meat
½ cup chopped cooked shrimp
Salt and pepper to taste
2 tablespoons lemon juice
6 (1 pound) flounders
6 tablespoons white wine
Parsley
Lemon wedges

In a large skillet melt ¼ cup of the butter over medium heat. Add the onion, bell pepper, garlic, and celery and sauté for 10 minutes. In a bowl soak the bread in the water for a few minutes and squeeze it dry. Add the bread to the mixture in the skillet. To this combination add the green onion, parsley, crab meat, shrimp, seasonings, and 1 tablespoon of the lemon juice and cook over low heat for 15 minutes, stirring occasionally. Slit the skin of the flounders on the dark side lengthwise down the center of the fish. On both sides of the slit form the pockets by running the knife between the skin and the meat. Fill these pockets with the stuffing. Place the flounder in a buttered shallow baking pan. Melt the remaining butter, add the remaining lemon juice, and brush the fish with this mixture. Bake the fish at 350°F for 30 minutes. During the last 5 minutes of baking, pour 1 tablespoon of the wine over each of the flounders. Serve the flounders garnished with parsley and lemon wedges. Serves 6.

Broiled Trout

6 medium trout fillets
Salt and pepper to taste
½ cup butter or margarine
2 teaspoons Worcestershire sauce
2 teaspoons lemon juice
Dash of Tabasco sauce
¼ teaspoon garlic powder
Fresh parsley
Lemon slices

Place the fillets on aluminum foil in a shallow pan. Season the fillets with salt and pepper. In a small saucepan melt the butter. Add the Worcestershire sauce, lemon Juice, Tabasco sauce, and garlic powder. Pour the sauce over the fillets and place the pan under a preheated broiler for 10 to 12 minutes, or until brown, without turning. Garnish the fillets with fresh parsley and lemon slices. Serves 6.

Named for the founder of New Orleans, Jean Batiste le Moyne,
Sieur de Bienville

Oysters Bienville

½ cup butter
1 cup finely chopped green onion or yellow onion
½ cup flour
2 cups chicken broth or fish stock, warmed
1½ pounds Boiled Shrimp (see Index), peeled and finely chopped
½ pound fresh mushrooms, finely chopped
3 egg yolks
½ cup half-and-half cream
½ cup white wine
1 teaspoon salt
1 teaspoon white pepper
½ teaspoon cayenne
6 pie pans filled with rock salt
3 dozen oysters on the half shell
¼ cup bread crumbs
½ cup grated Parmesan cheese
⅛ teaspoon paprika

In a heavy 3-quart saucepan melt the butter. Add the onion and
sauté until tender. Slowly blend in the flour over low heat, stirring
constantly, until lightly browned. Gradually add the warm
broth, stirring constantly. Simmer over medium heat for 10
minutes, or until the sauce is very thick. Stir in the shrimp and
mushrooms. Continue cooking for 5 minutes and remove from
heat. Whisk together the egg yolks, cream, and wine. Very slowly
pour a little of the warm sauce into the egg mixture, stirring
constantly, to avoid curdling. Stir the egg mixture into the sauce
and add the salt, pepper, and cayenne. Return to low heat,
stirring constantly, until thickened. (Sauce must be very thick so
that it will sit on top of the oysters.) Arrange a layer of rock salt in
the bottom of each of 6 pie pans. Pour the excess liquid from
each oyster and place 6 oysters in their shells in each pan. Bake at
375°F for 7 minutes. Remove pans from the oven. INCREASE
OVEN TEMPERATURE to 400°F. Oysters will have produced
more liquid and it must be poured off. Spoon the sauce over each
oyster. Combine the bread crumbs, cheese, and paprika and
top each oyster with this mixture. Return to the oven and bake
at 400°F for 10 minutes, or until the tops are lightly browned.
Serve immediately. Serves 6.

Louisiana oysters are salty and moderation should be used when
adding salt to oyster dishes.

Artichoke Oysters Harrison

3 artichokes, boiled
½ cup butter
½ cup flour
2 cloves garlic, chopped
1 onion, chopped
3 dozen oysters (reserve liquor)
1 (4½ ounce) can mushrooms (reserve liquid)
Salt and pepper to taste
½ teaspoon thyme
¼ teaspoon Tabasco sauce
¼ teaspoon rosemary
Worcestershire sauce to taste
¼ teaspoon marjoram
1 lemon, thinly sliced
2 ounces dry sherry
½ cup chopped parsley
Bread crumbs

Remove the leaves from the artichokes. Scrape the leaves and
reserve the scrapings. Chop the bottoms. In a skillet
make a dark brown roux with the butter and flour. Add the garlic and
onion and sauté until tender. Add the oyster liquor
and liquid from the mushrooms. Simmer the mixture for 30
minutes. Add water if more liquid is needed. Add the mushrooms,
artichoke bottoms, scrapings, seasonings, oysters, and
lemon slices and continue cooking for 10 minutes. Remove from heat
and add the sherry. Transfer the mixture to a buttered
baking dish. Top with the parsley and bread crumbs. Bake
at 400°F for 10 minutes. Serves 4-6.

Oyster Mélange

¼ pound ground pork
3 pounds ground beef
3 onions, finely chopped
3 green onions, finely chopped
3 ribs celery, finely chopped
½ bell pepper, finely chopped
½ bunch parsley, finely chopped
¼ cup flour
6 dozen oysters (reserve ½ cup liquor), chopped
Red pepper to taste
Salt and pepper to taste
8 large patty shells

In a heavy skillet brown the pork and beef. Add the onion,
green onion, celery, bell pepper, and parsley and mix well. Add
the flour and cook until the vegetables are well done.
Add the oysters and ½ cup of the oyster liquor or enough to make a
thick gravy. Add the red pepper, salt, and pepper. Continue cooking
for 5 minutes. Spoon the mixture into the patty shells.
Bake at 350°F for 10 minutes or until hot. Serves 8.

Oysters Italiano

½ cup olive oil
¼ cup flour
2 bunches green onions, finely chopped
4 cloves garlic, finely chopped
1 small bell pepper, finely chopped
3 tablespoons finely chopped parsley
1 cup Italian seasoned bread crumbs
1 (10½ ounce) can cream of mushroom soup
½ (10½ ounce) can cheese soup
2 tablespoons Worcestershire sauce
1 teaspoon oregano
¼ cup dry vermouth
½ teaspoon Angostura bitters
1 teaspoon Tabasco sauce
1 (4 ounce) can mushroom stems and pieces, drained
2 (1 pint) jars oysters, well drained

In a large heavy skillet heat ¼ cup of the olive oil. Blend in the flour and stir over medium heat until the flour is browned. Add the remaining olive oil, green onion, garlic, bell pepper, and parsley. Cook over low heat until the onion is tender, stirring constantly. Add the bread crumbs and blend. Add the undiluted soups and stir until blended. Add the Worcestershire sauce, oregano, vermouth, and bitters and blend well. Add the Tabasco sauce, a few drops at a time, and mix well. Add the mushrooms and oysters and cook over low heat, stirring constantly, for 20 minutes. Fill 8 ramekins with the mixture and garnish with parsley. Serve with French bread and salad. If prepared in advance, bake at 350°F for 15 minutes before serving. Serves 8.

Fried Oysters

1½ pints or 2 dozen freshly shucked oysters
Vegetable oil
1 cup very finely ground yellow corn flour or ¾ cup corn meal and ¼ cup flour
2 teaspoons salt
¾ teaspoon pepper
⅛ teaspoon cayenne

Drain the oysters in a colander. In a deep fryer heat the oil to 375°F. In a bowl combine the corn flour, salt, pepper, and cayenne and mix thoroughly. Roll the oysters, a few at a time, in the flour mixture until they are evenly coated. Fry the oysters, a few at a time, maintaining the temperature of the oil near 375°F at all times, for 2 minutes, or until they are golden brown. Remove the oysters with a slotted spoon, drain them on paper towels, and serve them hot. Serves 2.

Oysters Oregano

¼ cup butter
1 large onion, chopped
½ teaspoon thyme
¾ teaspoon oregano
3 cloves garlic, finely chopped
2 tablespoons chopped parsley
¼ teaspoon red pepper
Salt and pepper to taste
4 dozen oysters with liquor
1 cup Italian-style bread crumbs
½-¾ cup Parmesan cheese

In a skillet melt the butter. Add the onion and sauté until limp. Add all of the seasonings and mix well. Add the oysters and when the edges curl, add the oyster liquor. Fold in the bread crumbs. Transfer the mixture to a buttered casserole. Sprinkle the dish heavily with Parmesan cheese. Bake at 350°F for 15 to 20 minutes. Serves 4.

Creole Jambalaya

1 recipe Basic Creole Stock (see Index), omit bell pepper
½ (8 ounce) can tomato sauce
1½ quarts water
3 cups uncooked rice
¼ cup chopped green onion tops
¼ cup chopped parsley
4 dozen raw oysters, drained
Salt and pepper to taste

In a large saucepan combine the stock, tomato sauce, and water and blend well. Bring the mixture to a boil. Stir in the rice, onion tops, and parsley and cook, covered, over low heat for 20 minutes, or until the rice is almost tender. Stir in the oysters. Continue cooking, covered, over low heat for 5 minutes, or until the rice is tender and the oyster edges begin to curl. If necessary, add more water during cooking. Season the jambalaya with salt and pepper. Serves 8-10.

Allow 6 to 8 large fried oysters per serving.

Oysters Poulette

3 tablespoons cooking oil
4 tablespoons butter
5 tablespoons flour
3 dozen oysters (reserve 1 cup liquor)
1 cup cooked peeled shrimp
1 cup milk
2 tablespoons chopped onion
¼ teaspoon finely chopped parsley
1 tablespoon chopped bell pepper
3 tablespoons lemon juice
1 teaspoon Worcestershire sauce
1 teaspoon paprika
Salt and pepper to taste
3 egg yolks, beaten
8 patty shells

In a heavy saucepan combine the oil and butter over medium heat until the butter melts. Blend in the flour for 1 minute. Add the oysters, oyster liquor, and all other ingredients except the eggs and patty shells. Cook over low heat, stirring constantly, for 15 minutes, or until the sauce is thick. Stir the egg yolks into the mixture and continue cooking for 3 minutes. Serve the poulette sauce immediately in patty shells. Serves 4.

Shrimp Vermouth

4 tablespoons butter
½ cup sliced green onion
½ pound fresh mushrooms, sliced
3 pounds Boiled Shrimp (see Index), peeled and deveined
2 teaspoons rosemary, crushed
2 teaspoons lime juice
1 tablespoon lemon juice
½ cup dry vermouth
Salt and pepper to taste
1½ cups sour cream
Vermouth Rice (see Index)

In a large heavy skillet melt the butter. Add the green onion and mushrooms and sauté until the green onion is soft. Add the shrimp and rosemary and continue cooking for 5 minutes. Add the lime juice, lemon juice, and vermouth and cook an additional 3 minutes. Season with salt and pepper. Just before serving, add the sour cream and cook slowly, over low heat, until the mixture is thoroughly heated. High temperature will curdle the cream. Serve with the Vermouth Rice. Serves 6.

Shrimp Newburg

3-5 tablespoons butter or margarine
2 medium onions, chopped
3 ribs celery, chopped
6 tablespoons flour
2 cups milk
¼ teaspoon salt
¼ teaspoon pepper
Dash of cayenne
1 teaspoon Worcestershire sauce
¼ cup cream sherry
2 egg yolks, slightly beaten
1 cup half-and-half cream
2 pounds Boiled Shrimp (see Index), peeled and deveined
Toast points or patty shells

In a heavy 5-quart pot melt the butter. Add the onion and celery and sauté until limp. Gradually stir in the flour, adding more butter if necessary. Blend well but do not brown. Gradually stir in the milk, stirring constantly, until the sauce has thickened. Add the salt, pepper, cayenne, Worcestershire sauce, and sherry. Whisk together the egg yolks and half-and-half cream and gradually add it to the sherry sauce. Fold in the shrimp. Transfer the mixture to the top of a double boiler and cook for 15 minutes. Serve over toast points or in patty shells. Serves 6.

Simple Shrimp Creole

2 tablespoons butter or margarine
½ cup minced onion
2 tablespoons flour
1 bay leaf, crushed
¼ cup diced celery
1 teaspoon minced parsley
½ cup minced bell pepper
Dash of cayenne
¼ teaspoon Tabasco sauce
½ teaspoon salt
1 (6¼ ounce) can tomato paste
3 cups water
2 cups cooked shrimp
1 cup rice, cooked

In a large heavy skillet melt the butter. Add the onion and sauté until limp, but not brown. Blend in the flour. Add the bay leaf, celery, parsley, bell pepper, cayenne, Tabasco sauce, salt, tomato paste, and water. Cook for 30 minutes over low heat, stirring occasionally, until thickened. Stir in the shrimp and simmer for 20 minutes. Serve over rice. Serves 4.

Boiled Shrimp

---

1 gallon water

1½ tablespoons liquid crab boil or 1 bag crab boil

1 cup salt

2 lemons, halved

1 teaspoon cayenne

1 tablespoon salad oil

2 ribs celery with leaves, quartered

1 onion, quartered

6 cloves garlic, halved

3-5 pounds raw shrimp

In a large pot bring the water to a boil. Add the crab boil and other seasonings and continue boiling for 30 minutes. Add the shrimp. When the water returns to a boil, cook for 10 to 15 minutes depending on the size of the shrimp. In a colander drain the shrimp and rinse them under cool water to stop the cooking process. If prepared crab boil is not available, the following ingredients may be substituted.

1½ teaspoons Tabasco sauce or cayenne

1 teaspoon allspice

10 whole cloves

5 bay leaves, crushed

1 teaspoon celery seed

1 tablespoon dill seed

¼ cup coriander seed

¼ cup mustard seed

Shrimp Paella

---

3 tablespoons butter

¾ cup chopped onion

1 clove garlic, finely chopped

1 pound raw shrimp, peeled and deveined

13 ounces chicken broth

½ teaspoon salt

⅛ teaspoon cayenne

5 ounces uncooked saffron or curried rice

¼ cup raisins

1 avocado, peeled and cut in ½-inch cubes

1 tomato, peeled and cut in ½-inch cubes

In a large skillet melt the butter. Add the onion and garlic and sauté until tender. Add the shrimp, chicken broth, salt, and cayenne. Stir in the rice. Bring the mixture to a boil, stirring occasionally. Reduce the heat, cover, and simmer for 20 minutes. Uncover and continue cooking until all the liquid is absorbed. Fold in the raisins, avocado, and tomato. Serves 4.

Barbecued Shrimp Napoleon

6 pounds large raw shrimp, heads and shells on
3 cups butter
6 tablespoons pepper
3 lemons, sliced
3 oranges, sliced

Wash the shrimp in cold water. Drain for 1 hour. Place the
shrimp in a large baking pan. Place the sticks of
butter on top of the shrimp. Sprinkle with pepper, covering
the entire top surface. Arrange the lemon and orange slices on top of
the shrimp. Bake at 350°F for approximately 45 minutes, stirring
gently, and turning the shrimp over every 15 minutes. (If shells begin
to crinkle, the shrimp is being overcooked and will be
difficult to peel.) Serve the shrimp, unpeeled, in the
sauce with hot French bread for dunking. Serves 6.

Shrimp Sauterne

(New Orleans Style)

1/3 cup olive oil
6 tablespoons butter
6 cloves garlic, minced
2 bay leaves
1 teaspoon rosemary
1 teaspoon oregano
1 teaspoon crushed whole peppercorns
1 teaspoon salt
2 pounds raw shrimp, peeled and deveined
1/4 cup sauterne wine
1 lemon, juiced
1 (8 ounce) loaf French bread

In a large skillet heat the oil and butter. Add the seasonings and
shrimp. Sauté for 10 to 15 minutes. Add the wine and lemon juice.
Simmer for 5 to 10 minutes. Serve with hot French bread
for dipping in the sauce. Serves 4-6.

1½ to 2 pounds of heads-on shrimp in the shell yield 1 pound
peeled shrimp.

Shrimp Patties

½ pound raw shrimp, peeled and deveined
½ pound fresh pork shoulder, chopped
1 teaspoon grated lemon peel
½ cup chopped green onion
1 teaspoon salt
½ teaspoon pepper
2 tablespoons peanut oil
Soy sauce to taste

In a food processor combine the shrimp, pork, lemon peel,
green onion, salt, and pepper. Process until the mixture
is smooth and pasty. Shape the mixture into round cakes ⅓-inch
thick. Chill for 1 hour. In a heavy skillet heat the oil
over medium heat. Add the cakes. During the frying process,
press the cakes with a spatula and cook until browned. Turn
and brown the other side. Serve hot with a dash of soy sauce.
Serves 6.

Shrimp Étouffée

½ cup butter
2 cloves garlic, minced
4 green onions, chopped
1 bay leaf
½ lemon, juiced
Salt and pepper to taste
1 teaspoon rosemary
¼ cup white wine
2 pounds raw shrimp, peeled and deveined
¼ cup chopped parsley
1 cup rice, cooked

In a medium skillet melt the butter. Add the garlic and green
onion and sauté until soft. Add the bay leaf, lemon
juice, salt, pepper, rosemary, and ½ of the wine. Simmer for 10
minutes. Remove the bay leaf, add the shrimp, and continue cooking
for 20 minutes. Add the remaining wine and parsley. Serve
over the rice. Serves 4-6.

Drain oysters in a colander and dry them between sheets of paper
towels before frying.

Curried Shrimp

6 tablespoons butter
½ cup chopped onion
½ cup chopped bell pepper
2 cloves garlic, minced
2-3 teaspoons curry powder
2 tablespoons lemon juice
¾ teaspoon salt
½ teaspoon ground ginger
Cayenne to taste
Dash of nutmeg
Dash of paprika
Dash of chili powder
3 cups cooked shrimp
Saffron rice, cooked

In a medium skillet melt the butter. Add the onion, bell
pepper, and garlic and sauté until soft. Add the
remaining seasonings and simmer for 1 minute. Add the
cooked shrimp and continue cooking until it is thoroughly heated.
Serve the shrimp over the cooked saffron rice. Serves 4-6.

Shrimp Curry

½ cup butter
½ cup flour
¼ cup chopped onion
¼ cup chopped celery
2 teaspoons mild curry powder
1 teaspoon hot curry powder
Pinch each of nutmeg, ginger, ground cloves
Salt to taste
3½ cups milk
¼ cup sherry
2 pounds raw shrimp, peeled and deveined
1-1½ cups rice, cooked
Assorted condiments: peanuts, chutney, sliced bananas, sliced egg, bacon, pineapple chunks, raisins, minced green onion

In a large saucepan melt the butter over medium heat. Add the flour,
stirring constantly, until frothy but not brown. Add the
onion and celery and sauté until tender. Stir in the
spices and salt. Gradually add the milk and sherry, stirring constantly.
Simmer the mixture for 10 minutes, stirring frequently.
Add the shrimp and continue cooking for 20 minutes. Serve with
fluffy rice and assorted condiments. Serves 4-6.

Shrimp are graded by count per pound: jumbo (15-20), large
(20-25), medium (25-35), and small (35-45).

Shrimp Supreme

½ cup butter
1¼ teaspoons garlic salt
¼ cup chopped onion
1 bunch fresh parsley, finely chopped
½ teaspoon pepper
3 dashes Tabasco sauce
2 pounds raw shrimp, peeled and deveined
2 tablespoons cornstarch, softened in 2 tablespoons water
1 pint half-and-half cream
10 ounces Monterey Jack cheese, cubed
2 egg yolks, well beaten
Seasoned French bread crumbs

In a skillet melt the butter. Add the garlic salt, onion, parsley,
pepper, and Tabasco sauce. Sauté until the onion and parsley are
soft. Add the shrimp and cook until the shrimp are pink and tender.
Remove the shrimp, using a slotted spoon, and set aside. Lower
the heat and slowly add the cornstarch and half-and-half
cream, stirring, until slightly thickened. Add the
cheese and stir until melted. Stir in the egg yolks and continue cooking
until thick. Remove from heat. Place the shrimp in a buttered Pyrex
dish, pour the sauce over the shrimp, and sprinkle with
seasoned bread crumbs. Bake the dish at 350°F until
it is hot and bubbly. Serves 8.

Shrimp Remoulade

½ cup tarragon vinegar
2 tablespoons ketchup
1 tablespoon paprika
½ teaspoon cayenne
1 teaspoon salt
1 clove garlic, minced
4 tablespoons horseradish
2 tablespoons Creole mustard
1 tablespoon Dijon-style mustard
1 cup vegetable oil
¾ cup minced green onion
¾ cup minced celery
3 pounds Boiled Shrimp (see Index), peeled and deveined
Lettuce, shredded

Blend the vinegar, ketchup, paprika, cayenne, salt, garlic, horseradish,
and mustards in a blender. Continue to blend, adding the
oil slowly. Add and mix in the onion and celery. Chill the sauce
overnight. Arrange beds of lettuce on salad plates, top with
the shrimp, and cover with the chilled sauce. Serves 8.

Greek Shrimp

1⅓ cups chopped celery
1 ⅓ cups chopped onion
⅓ cup margarine
2 pounds raw shrimp, peeled
4 cups cooked rice
1½ teaspoons Cavender's Greek seasoning
½ pound Feta cheese, crumbled
¾ cup Greek olives
2 (16 ounce) cans tomato wedges

In a skillet sauté the celery and onion in the margarine until it
is limp. Add the shrimp, rice, seasoning, cheese, olives, and
tomatoes. Transfer the mixture to a 2-quart casserole dish and bake
at 350°F for 25 minutes or until it is bubbly and the shrimp
are cooked. Serves 6-8.

Shrimp and Spaghetti Gratin

3 pounds raw shrimp, heads removed
2 teaspoons salt
3 tablespoons pepper
½ teaspoon basil
½ teaspoon thyme
¼ teaspoon garlic powder
1 teaspoon prepared barbecue sauce
1 tablespoon parsley flakes
1 tablespoon lemon juice
1 tablespoon Worcestershire sauce
1½ cups butter, cut in 1-inch slices
8 ounces spaghetti, cooked and drained
8 ounces Velveeta cheese, grated

Wash the shrimp in cold water and drain them for 1 hour. In a large
shallow baking pan arrange the shrimp evenly. Combine the herbs,
spices, and seasonings and sprinkle the mixture over the shrimp. Add the
lemon juice, Worcestershire sauce, and butter. Bake the shrimp mixture,
uncovered, at 350°F for 25 minutes, stirring occasionally. When the
shrimp are cool enough to handle, peel and discard the shells. Much of
the spicey seasoning will be lost with the shells, but don't worry — there
will be plenty left for this spicey dish so typical of New Orleans cooking.
Transfer the sauce in the bottom of the baking pan to a container with a
pouring lip. Divide the spaghetti into 4 or 6 individual casseroles.
Arrange the shrimp on the spaghetti and pour ¼ cup of the sauce over
each serving. Top each casserole with cheese and bake at 350°F until the
cheese is melted and bubbly. Serves 4-6.

Frozen shrimp should be defrosted and dried thoroughly
before cooking.

Seafood Casserole

½ cup butter
¾ teaspoon onion salt
¾ teaspoon garlic salt
¼ cup chopped onion
1 bunch parsley, finely chopped
½ teaspoon pepper
¼ teaspoon Tabasco sauce
2 pounds raw shrimp, peeled and deveined, or 1 pound crab meat
2 tablespoons cornstarch, softened in 1 tablespoon water
1 pint half-and-half cream
10 ounces Monterey Jack cheese, grated
3 egg yolks, well beaten
Seasoned French bread crumbs

In a large skillet melt the butter over medium heat. Add the
onion salt, garlic salt, onion, parsley, pepper, and Tabasco sauce and
sauté until the onion is tender. Add the shrimp and
continue cooking until the shrimp are pink. Remove the shrimp and
reserve them. Combine the cornstarch and cream. Gradually
add the cream mixture to the skillet and cook over
low heat, stirring constantly, until the sauce is slightly thickened. Add
the cheese, stirring constantly, until the cheese is melted. Stir
in the egg yolks and continue cooking until the sauce
is thick. Remove from heat. Arrange the shrimp in a buttered
casserole. Pour the sauce over the shrimp. Cover
the top with bread crumbs. Bake at 350°F until golden
brown and bubbly. When substituting crab meat for shrimp,
add the crab meat to the sauce immediately before
transferring the sauce to the casserole. Serves 8-10.

Shrimp Creole

2 cups Basic Creole Stock (see Index)
2 (6 ounce) cans tomato paste
1 (8 ounce) can tomato sauce
½ cup water
4 pounds raw shrimp, peeled and deveined
Salt and pepper to taste
2-2½ cups rice, cooked

In a large heavy saucepan combine the stock, tomato paste,
and tomato sauce and blend. Add enough of the water
to create the consistency of a thick sauce. Bring the mixture to a boil.
Add the shrimp, cover, and simmer for 10 to 15 minutes,
or until the shrimp are tender. Season the dish with salt and
pepper. Serve the Shrimp Creole over fluffy rice. Serves 8-10.

To thaw frozen shrimp quickly, place them in cold tap water.

Batter-Fried Butterfly Shrimp

2 pounds raw large shrimp
Cooking oil
1 cup flour
1 teaspoon salt
1 teaspoon baking powder
1 tablespoon salad oil
1 cup stale beer
¼ teaspoon Tabasco sauce

Peel and devein the shrimp, leaving the tail on. With a
sharp knife cut each shrimp almost in half, lengthwise down the
back. Spread the shrimp out in the butterfly shape and pat
them dry with paper towels. Heat the oil for deep frying
to 375°F. Holding each shrimp by the tail, dip it in the Beer Batter.
Fry the shrimp until golden. Transfer the shrimp to
paper towels to drain. Serve the shrimp with Tartar Sauce
(see Index).

BEER BATTER:
In a medium bowl sift together the flour, salt, and baking
powder. Make a well in the center of the dry mixture and
pour in the oil, beer, and Tabasco sauce in a stream,
stirring constantly, until the batter is smooth. Allow the batter
to stand, covered, for 3 hours at room temperature. Stir the batter
before using it. Serves 4.

Easy Shrimp Newburg

4 quarts water
¼ cup salt
5 pounds raw shrimp
½ cup margarine
2 bell peppers, chopped
1 heaping tablespoon flour
3 (10½ ounce) cans cream of mushroom soup
½ pound extra sharp Cheddar cheese, grated
Dash of Tabasco sauce
2 jiggers sherry
1 bottle stuffed olives, drained and chopped

In a large stock pot bring the water to a boil and add the salt
and shrimp. Allow the water to return to a boil and cook the
shrimp for 10 minutes. Drain the shrimp, rinse with cold
water, and peel. In a Dutch oven melt the margarine. Add the bell
pepper and sauté. Add the flour and cook for 2 minutes.
Add the mushroom soup and cheese and cook until the cheese is
melted. Add the remaining ingredients and stir. Serve hot.
The Shrimp Newburg may be frozen. Serves 8-10.

Shrimp are best frozen headless, in their shells, and completely
submerged in water.

Shrimp Cotillion

¾ cup dry vermouth
¾ cup water
1 small onion, halved
1 rib celery with leaves, quartered
1 pound fresh or frozen scallops
½ cup butter
6 tablespoons flour
1 teaspoon paprika
1 cup half-and-half cream
1¾ teaspoons salt
¼ teaspoon white pepper
2 dashes Tabasco sauce
1 tablespoon lemon juice
2 tablespoons butter
1 cup sliced fresh mushrooms
1 pound Boiled Shrimp (see Index), peeled and deveined
Rice Pilaf (see Index)

In a saucepan boil the vermouth, water, onion, and celery for
4 minutes. Add the scallops and simmer for 8 minutes. With a slotted
spoon remove the scallops. Strain the liquid and reserve. In
a large heavy skillet melt ½ cup butter over medium heat.
Blend in the flour, stirring constantly. Add the paprika,
reserved liquid, half-and-half cream, salt, pepper, Tabasco sauce,
and lemon juice. Simmer the mixture, stirring constantly, until
slightly thickened. In a small skillet melt 2 tablespoons butter. Add
the mushrooms, sauté, and transfer to the cream sauce. Stir
in the scallops and shrimp and simmer over low heat until
thoroughly heated. Serve over the Rice Pilaf. Serves 6.

Baked Stuffed Shrimp

2 pounds raw jumbo shrimp
1 tablespoon margarine
1 tablespoon lemon juice
⅛ teaspoon salt
⅛ teaspoon pepper

Peel the shrimp leaving the tails on and split them halfway
through, lengthwise down the back, and spread them into
a butterfly shape. In a heavy saucepan melt the margarine. Add the
lemon juice, salt, and pepper. Add the shrimp and sauté over low heat
until pink. Transfer the shrimp to a plate to cool
and reserve the drippings in the saucepan.

STUFFING:

3 tablespoons margarine
1 large onion, finely chopped
½ medium bell pepper, finely chopped
2 green onions, finely chopped
2 sprigs parsley, finely chopped
1 rib celery, finely chopped
1¾ cups stale bread pieces
2 eggs, beaten
1 pound crab meat
1 pound raw shrimp, peeled, deveined, and chopped
Salt and pepper to taste
1½ cups fine bread crumbs
½ lemon, juiced

In a skillet melt 2 tablespoons of the margarine. Add the onion, bell pepper, green onion, parsley, and celery and simmer until the vegetables are limp. Add the stale bread alternately with the beaten egg. Add the crab meat and shrimp and season to taste with the salt and pepper. Remove the mixture from the heat and allow it to cool. After the stuffing has cooled, stir in the reserved drippings from the sautéed shrimp. Mound some of this mixture on the sliced side of each shrimp. Dip the entire shrimp in the bread crumbs. Place the shrimp in a well-greased baking pan, dot them with the remaining margarine, and bake the dish at 325°F for 15 minutes. Turn each shrimp over and bake for another 15 minutes, or until the shrimp are golden brown. Serve the shrimp sprinkled with the lemon juice. Serves 4-6.

Soft-Shell Crab

"The ultimate delight in seafood" is the well-deserved reputation of the soft-shell crab in New Orleans and other gourmet cities of the United States. Contrary to some beliefs, they are not a separate breed, but the same familiar blue crab at the molting stage. Crabs outgrow their shells, burst out of the old ones, and grow new ones. For the few hours after the "buster" crab has shed its old shell, the crab's shell is soft. This is the "magic stage" prized by crabbers and gourmets alike.

TO CLEAN THE SOFT-SHELL CRAB

To clean the soft-shell crab, place it on a cutting surface. Lift the shell at the points on either side of the back and remove the feathery gills. Cut off the eyes and mouth. Lift the shell gently and remove the sandbag from under the mouth. Discard all the removed parts, wash the crab in cold running water, and pat it dry with paper towels.

If you are lucky enough to acquire a big batch of soft-shell crabs at one time, they may be frozen, but do not clean them before freezing. This speeds up deterioration. The crabs should be cleaned just before cooking. For freezing, simply rinse them with cold water, pat them dry, wrap them in freezer paper, and freeze quickly.

Soft-Shell Crabs Meunière or Amandine

4 large soft-shell crabs
¾ cup butter
1 tablespoon lemon juice
¼ teaspoon white pepper

Clean the crabs and fry them according to instructions for
Fried Soft-Shell Crabs (see Index). Keep the crabs warm in
the oven at 200°F. In a heavy saucepan melt the butter over low
heat until the butter begins to turn brown. Remove from the
heat and add the lemon juice and white pepper and mix well.
Return the pan to low heat and brown for 1 minute, or
until the sauce is nut brown. Serve the crabs with
a generous portion of the meunière sauce poured over each
serving. Serves 2-4.

AMANDINE:

Prepare Soft-Shell Crabs Meunière, but just before the
butter is brown, add 1 cup blanched sliced almonds. Remove
the almonds as they brown and reserve them in a small bowl until
sauce is complete. To serve, spread the almonds over the crabs
and top them with the sauce. Serves 2-4.

A treat that will be long remembered

Fried Soft-Shell Crabs

6 Soft-Shell Crabs, To Clean (see Index)
1 cup milk
1 egg
Salt and freshly ground pepper to taste
1½ cups flour
Cooking oil
Lemon wedges
Tartar Sauce (see Index)

In a large bowl beat together the milk and egg until well
blended. Season the crabs with the salt and pepper. Soak the crabs
in the milk mixture for 15 minutes, turning frequently. Dredge
the crabs in the flour and shake off the excess flour. In a deep fryer or
large pot heat the oil to 365°F or very hot, but not boiling.
Lower the crabs into the oil, being careful not to overcrowd
the pot. The crabs should have room to float on the surface
of the oil. Fry the crabs for 5 to 6 minutes, or until they are
golden brown. Transfer the crabs to paper towels to drain.
Serve the crabs piping hot, accompanied by lemon wedges and
tartar sauce.

When frying seafood, the seafood and the batter must both be cold
and the oil extremely hot. This prevents the batter from
becoming saturated with grease. Cook only a few pieces at a time.

Stuffed Soft-Shell Crabs

SAUCE:
1½ cups dry vermouth
1½ teaspoons salt
½ teaspoon pepper
¼ teaspoon cayenne
2 pounds raw shrimp, peeled and deveined
¾ cup butter
1 cup finely chopped onion
½ cup finely chopped green onion
2 cloves garlic, pressed
4 tablespoons flour
6 Soft-Shell Crabs, To Clean (see Index)
2 eggs
⅓ cup milk
Salt and pepper to taste
Cayenne to taste
1 cup flour
Cooking oil
1 cup sour cream
Lemon wedges

In a Dutch oven combine the vermouth, salt, pepper, and cayenne. Add the shrimp and boil them for 8 minutes. Drain the shrimp and reserve the liquid. Allow the shrimp to cool. In a large skillet melt the butter over low heat. Add the onion, green onion, and garlic and sauté for 20 minutes, or until the onion is translucent. Add the flour, stirring constantly, for 2 minutes. Gradually add the heated shrimp stock to make a medium-thick white sauce. Slice the shrimp lengthwise. Insert the slices of shrimp in the slit in the center of the crab and in each point from which the feathery gills were removed. Use as many shrimp as possible. Add any remaining shrimp to the white sauce. Combine the eggs, milk, salt, pepper, and cayenne. Dip the crabs in this mixture until they are well coated. Dredge the crabs in the flour and fry them in hot oil until they are golden brown. Transfer the fried crabs to paper towels to drain. Reheat the white sauce and add the sour cream at the last moment. Do not boil the sauce. Serve the crabs hot, covered with the sauce, and garnished with lemon wedges. Serves 6.

Seafood

Especially good with shrimp, crab claws, or crab bodies, cleaned and halved

Seafood Marinade

½ cup vegetable oil
¼ cup white vinegar
¼ cup water
1 (0.9 ounce) envelope Good Seasons mild Italian dressing
4 cloves garlic, minced
6 ribs celery, chopped
2 white onions, chopped
Salt and pepper to taste

In a bowl mix together all of the ingredients well. Pour the marinade over boiled seafood. Marinate the seafood overnight.

Herb Sauce for Poached Fish

¼ cup butter
2 teaspoons Dijon-style mustard
1 lemon, juiced
Salt and pepper to taste
½ teaspoon ground nutmeg
2 teaspoons chopped parsley
1 teaspoon chopped chive
3 egg yolks

In the top of a double boiler combine the butter, mustard, lemon juice, salt, pepper, nutmeg, parsley, and chive. Place over simmering water and whisk together until the butter melts. Beat the egg yolks until thick and lemon colored and stir them into the butter-mustard mixture. Continue beating vigorously over simmering water until the sauce thickens. Serve immediately over poached fish. Makes ¾ cup.

Tartar Sauce

2 egg yolks
1½ teaspoons Dijon-style mustard
1 teaspoon lemon juice
1¼ cups vegetable oil
1 teaspoon chopped pickle
1 teaspoon finely chopped onion
1 teaspoon parsley

In a food processor combine the eggs, mustard, lemon juice, and 1 tablespoon of the oil. Process for 30 seconds. To this mixture slowly add the remainder of the oil. Add the pickles, onion, and parsley and process for 5 seconds.

Seafood Cocktail Sauce

¾ cup chili sauce or ketchup
2-4 tablespoons lemon juice
2-3 tablespoons horseradish
2 teaspoons Lea and Perrins Worcestershire sauce
3 drops Tabasco sauce
Salt to taste

In a bowl combine all of the ingredients and mix thoroughly.
Chill. Serve the sauce with seafood cocktails such as shrimp, crab,
or oysters. Makes 1 cup.

Sauce Pecandine

½ cup butter
⅔ cup chopped pecans
3 drops Tabasco sauce
1 tablespoon chopped parsley

In a heavy saucepan over low heat melt the butter. Add the
remaining ingredients and simmer for 2 to 3 minutes. Pour the sauce
over broiled fish fillets and serve immediately. Makes
sauce for 1½ pounds fish.

Crab Boil

1½ teaspoons Tabasco sauce or cayenne pepper
1 teaspoon allspice
10 whole cloves
5 bay leaves, crushed
1 teaspoon celery seed
1 tablespoon dill weed
¼ cup coriander seed
¼ cup mustard seed

This recipe is equivalent to 1 (3 ounce) bag of crab boil
OR 1½ tablespoons liquid crab boil.

Mayonnaise seasoned with lemon juice, dill, oregano, and Dijon
mustard is a good accompaniment to fried soft-shell crabs, shrimp, or
oysters.

VEGETABLES
Vegetables are a much-neglected part of cooking. Boiled briefly, with only a little water, or steamed, or stir-fried, they are firm, tender, and delicious. Overcooked, they lose most of their vitamins and flavor, and emerge as a limp mass only the very hungry will enjoy. As the central ingredient of a well-seasoned dish, the vegetable can be the highlight of the meal.

VEGETABLES

Reflections in the water from the typical summer afternoon rain (a way of life in semi-tropical New Orleans) in famed Pirates Alley simply multiply the already present beauty of buildings from another age. These buildings still serve New Orleanians and tourists alike in this vibrant, romantic community called the Vieux Carré (better known as the French Quarter).

Stuffed Artichokes

2 artichokes
4 quarts water, salted
2 lemons, juiced
1 tablespoon olive oil
½ cup Italian bread crumbs
½ cup grated Parmesan cheese
1 teaspoon salt
¼ cup olive oil
1 teaspoon garlic powder

With a sharp knife remove the top ⅓ from the artichokes.
With scissors snip the thorns from the tips of the remaining
leaves. Soak the artichokes in lightly salted water to clean and rinse.
In a Dutch oven combine the salted water, ½ of the lemon juice, and
olive oil. Over high heat bring the mixture to a rolling boil.
Lower the artichokes into the boiling water and boil for 15 minutes.
Remove the artichokes from the water and allow to cool. Using
a large sturdy spoon open the artichokes and remove the chokes
(fuzzy matter on the rim of the interior of the heart) and the
lighter tender leaves on the inside that are undeveloped. Return
the artichokes to the water in the Dutch oven and continue cooking
over medium heat for 30 minutes, or until the hearts are fork
tender. Remove the artichokes from the water and drain. Prepare
the stuffing by combining the bread crumbs, cheese, and salt.
When the artichokes have cooled, place about 2 tablespoons of the
stuffing over each heart and then place the balance by tablespoonfuls
at the base of each leaf. In a measuring cup with a pouring lip
combine the olive oil, remaining lemon juice, and garlic powder. Place
the stuffed artichokes, stem down, in a colander and drizzle the oil
mixture slowly over them. Place the colander over a pot of boiling
water, being certain that the water does not touch the colander.
Steam the artichokes, covered, for 20 minutes, or until the
cheese has melted and the stuffing is moist. Serve the artichokes
immediately. Serves 2.
NOTE: Artichokes may be prepared and stuffed in advance and
steamed 20 minutes before serving.

Artichokes with Lemon Butter

2 artichokes
½ cup butter
1 lemon, juiced
Salt to taste

Prepare and boil the artichokes according to the directions in
Stuffed Artichokes. In a small saucepan melt the butter.
Stir in the lemon juice and salt. Serve the artichokes whole
with the lemon-butter mixture as a dipping sauce for the
artichoke leaves.

Artichoke Casserole

1 (6 ounce) jar marinated artichokes
1 (14 ounce) can artichoke hearts, drained and quartered
1½ cups Italian bread crumbs
¼ pound Romano cheese, grated
6 cloves garlic, chopped
1 (4 ounce) can mushrooms, drained
½ cup olive oil
Salt and pepper to taste
Asparagus spears
4-5 hard-boiled eggs, sliced

In a medium bowl combine the artichokes, artichoke hearts, bread crumbs, cheese, garlic, mushrooms, olive oil, salt, and pepper and mix thoroughly. Transfer the mixture to a buttered 9″ x 9″ casserole and garnish with the asparagus spears and egg slices. Bake the casserole, covered, at 350°F for 45 minutes. Remove the cover and continue baking for 15 minutes. Serves 4.

Tips for Cooking Dried Beans

Wash and sort the beans. Cover the beans with water and boil for 2 minutes. Remove from the heat and let the beans soak for at least 1 hour. Even if you plan to soak the beans overnight, this method keeps the beans from souring. This short-soak method helps retain the vitamins, cuts cooking time considerably, and produces beans with fewer hard skins than those soaked overnight. Add the salt and flavorings only after soaking. Salt has a tendency to toughen the beans which causes them to take longer to cook. In order to prevent the beans from boiling over, add 1 tablespoon bacon grease or butter, a piece of slab bacon, or seasoning ham with some fat on it. One cup of dried beans yields, depending on the variety and size of the beans, 2-2¾ cups cooked beans. Nutritionally, beans are high in protein, but they require the addition of rice to be a complete protein.

Creole Cooked Red Beans

1 pound dried red beans
1 ham bone
8-10 cups water
1 (8 ounce) can tomato sauce
2 teaspoons garlic salt
¼ teaspoon Tabasco sauce
1 teaspoon Lea and Perrins Worcestershire sauce
½ pound ham, diced
½ pound hot sausage, sliced
½ pound smoked sausage, sliced
½ cup chopped celery
1 cup chopped onion
3 cloves garlic, pressed
2 bay leaves
Salt and pepper to taste
¼ cup chopped parsley
2 cups rice, cooked

Prepare the beans according to the instructions in Dried Beans, Tips for Cooking (see Index). In a large pot place the ham bone, water, tomato sauce, garlic salt, Tabasco sauce, Worcestershire sauce, and beans. Cook, uncovered, over low heat. In a skillet sauté the ham and sausage until the grease is rendered. Transfer the ham and sausage to the bean pot. To the grease in the skillet add the celery, onion, and garlic and sauté until soft. Pour this mixture into the bean pot. Add the bay leaves, salt, and pepper and continue cooking for 2 to 2½ hours, or until the beans are soft and creamy. Add water while cooking if necessary. Remove the bay leaves and add the parsley. Serve the beans over rice. Serves 6-8.

Black-Eyed Peas

6 slices bacon
½ medium white onion, chopped
4 dashes Tabasco sauce
1 teaspoon sugar
Dash of garlic powder
Salt and pepper to taste
½ pound dried black-eyed peas

In a large saucepan fry the bacon until crisp. Remove the bacon, drain, and sauté the onion in the bacon grease. Add the remaining seasonings and peas and fill the pot with water. Bring the water to a rolling boil, reduce the heat, and cook, covered, for 2 hours, or until the water is reduced to the level of the peas. Add ½ cup more water and simmer until the peas are soft and the liquid is thickened. Serves 4.

Angelic White Beans

1 cup dried large lima beans
6 slices bacon, cut in ½-inch pieces
½ medium white onion, diced
1¼ teaspoons garlic salt
5 drops Tabasco sauce
Salt and pepper to taste
4 bay leaves

Prepare the beans according to Dried Beans, Tips for
Cooking (see Index). In a 6-quart pot fry the bacon
over moderately high heat until crisp. Remove the bacon and
reserve it. To the bacon grease add the onion, garlic salt, Tabasco
sauce, salt, and pepper and sauté until the onion is limp. Add a small
amount of water to the mixture and stir, scraping the
bottom of the pot. To this mixture add the reserved bacon,
beans, and the water in which they have been soaked. Fill the
pot with water to within 1 inch of the top and bring the
mixture to a slow boil. Add the bay leaves and cook, stirring
occasionally, until the water is reduced to the level of the
beans. Cook the beans a total of 3 to 4 hours, or until the
beans are tender, adding water as needed. Serves 4-6.

Old-Fashioned Green Beans

4-6 slices bacon
1 large onion, chopped
1½-2 pounds green beans, snapped
½ cup water
Salt and pepper to taste
6-8 new potatoes (optional)
1 cube chicken bouillon (optional)
¼ teaspoon sugar (optional)

In a heavy pot fry the bacon until crisp over medium heat,
remove the bacon, and drain. Add the onion to the bacon grease
and sauté until limp. Add the green beans, water, salt, pepper,
and any of the optional ingredients. Simmer the mixture, covered,
for 45 minutes or until tender. Transfer the green bean mixture to
a serving dish and crumble the bacon over the top of the
beans. Serves 6-8.

Vegetable Topping: Beat together 1 (8 ounce) package cream
cheese, ⅓ cup milk. Stir in ¼ cup chopped nuts.

Broccoli Pie

4 frozen Pepperidge Farm patty shells
1 (10 ounce) package chopped broccoli
6 eggs
1 (3 ounce) package cream cheese (at room temperature)
¼ cup grated sharp cheese
2 tablespoons finely chopped green onion
2 tablespoons finely chopped parsley
½ teaspoon salt
½ teaspoon pepper
2 tablespoons Parmesan cheese

Thaw the patty shells in the refrigerator for 2 hours. Roll the
patty shells out on a lightly floured surface for a 10″ pie plate.
In a medium saucepan cook the broccoli according to package
directions and drain. In a medium bowl combine the eggs, cream
cheese, and sharp cheese and beat well. Stir in the broccoli, green
onion, parsley, salt, and pepper. Turn the mixture into the
pie shell and top with the Parmesan cheese. Bake the pie at
425°F for 20 minutes, or until there is a crown. Serves 4-6.

Broccoli Casserole

¼ cup butter
½ large onion, chopped
2 packages fresh broccoli, chopped
1 (8 ounce) can large mushroom buttons (reserve liquid)
1 (10¾ ounce) can mushroom soup
1 (8 ounce) roll garlic cheese
¼ cup chopped almonds
¼ cup butter
1 teaspoon garlic powder
½ cup bread crumbs
Paprika

In a deep heavy skillet melt ¼ cup butter over medium heat. Add
the onion and sauté until soft. Add the broccoli and mushrooms and
sauté until the broccoli is limp. Stir in the soup, mushroom
liquid, and cheese, stirring, until the cheese is melted. Pour the
mixture into a large buttered casserole and scatter the almonds
on top. In a small saucepan melt ¼ cup butter over low heat. Add
the garlic powder and bread crumbs and blend until the crumbs
are moist. Top the casserole with the bread crumb mixture,
sprinkle with paprika, and bake at 300°F for 1 hour. Serves 8.

Dried herbs are more concentrated than fresh herbs.
If a recipe calls for dried herbs and you prefer fresh
ones, double the amount indicated.

Great for leftover rice
Broccoli Rice Casserole

¼ cup margarine
1 onion, chopped
1 (10 ounce) package chopped broccoli
1 (10 ¾ ounce) can mushroom soup
1 (8 ounce) jar Jalapeño Cheez Whiz
2 cups cooked rice
2 (4 ounce) cans sliced mushrooms, drained
1 (8 ounce) can water chestnuts, drained and chopped

In a large skillet melt the margarine over medium heat. Add the onion and sauté until translucent. Add the broccoli and continue cooking for 5 minutes or until tender. Add the soup and Cheez Whiz, stirring, until the cheese melts. Stir the broccoli mixture into the rice. Fold in the mushrooms and water chestnuts. Transfer the mixture to a buttered 2-quart casserole. Bake the casserole at 350°F for 25 to 30 minutes. Serves 6-8.

Fancy Cabbage Casserole

2 medium cabbages, cored and quartered
½ cup butter
2 onions, chopped
1 bell pepper, chopped
3 cloves garlic, chopped
½ pound Velveeta cheese
Salt and pepper to taste
1 cup bread crumbs
½ pint half-and-half cream
2 tablespoons grated Cheddar cheese

Boil the cabbage in a small amount of water until tender. Drain, cool, and chop finely. In a large pot melt the butter over medium heat. Add the onion and sauté until wilted. Add the bell pepper, garlic, and cabbage and continue cooking the mixture until the bell pepper is tender. Stir in the Velveeta cheese, salt, pepper, and ½ cup of the bread crumbs and continue stirring until the cheese melts. Transfer the mixture to a buttered 2-quart casserole. Add the cream. Combine the remaining bread crumbs with the Cheddar cheese and cover the top of the casserole with this mixture. Bake the casserole at 350°F for 15 minutes or until bubbly. Serves 8-10.

Spicy Cabbage Casserole

1 pound ground beef
1 large onion, chopped
2 cloves garlic, minced
½ bell pepper, chopped
½ teaspoon oregano
1 teaspoon salt
½ teaspoon pepper
1 (10 ounce) can Ro-tel tomatoes, chopped
1 (8 ounce) can tomato sauce
½ cup uncooked rice
1 cabbage, shredded
½ cup grated American cheese

In a deep heavy skillet over moderately high heat combine the beef, onion, garlic, bell pepper, oregano, salt, and pepper, stirring constantly, until brown. Add the tomatoes, tomato sauce, and rice and mix thoroughly. In a buttered 9"x13" casserole arrange layers of the meat mixture, the cabbage, and the cheese. Bake the casserole, covered, at 350°F for 1½ to 2 hours. Serves 4-6.

Cabbage Mélange

2 tablespoons cooking oil
2 cups shredded cabbage
1 large onion, sliced
1 cup diced celery
½ medium bell pepper, chopped
1 tomato, chopped
Salt and pepper to taste
1 teaspoon sugar
Soy sauce to taste

In a large heavy skillet heat the oil over medium heat. Add the remaining ingredients except the soy sauce. Stir the mixture until the vegetables are lightly coated with the oil. Cook, covered, for 5 minutes. Sprinkle the mixture with soy sauce. Serve hot. Serves 6.

Vegetables that grow underground, i.e. beets, potatoes, carrots should start cooking in cold water; conversely, those that grow above ground, i.e. corn, peas, beans should start cooking in boiling water.

Vegetables

Sweet and Sour Cabbage

4 tablespoons bacon grease
1 small onion, finely chopped
1 red cabbage, shredded
⅛ cup vinegar
¾ cup water
2 tablespoons sugar
Salt and pepper to taste
1 large apple, pared and sliced

In a heavy pot heat the bacon grease over medium heat. Add the onion and sauté until golden brown. Add the cabbage, vinegar, water, sugar, salt, and pepper and stir gently. Arrange the apple slices on top of the mixture. Cook the mixture, covered, over low heat for 20 minutes. Serves 6.

Tangy Mustard Cauliflower

1 medium head cauliflower
1 teaspoon salt
½ cup mayonnaise
½ tablespoon minced onion
1 teaspoon prepared mustard
½ cup grated Cheddar cheese

In a medium saucepan cover the cauliflower with water and add the salt. Simmer the cauliflower until it is tender. With a slotted spoon transfer it to an 8″ x 8″ baking dish. In a bowl combine the mayonnaise, onion, and mustard, mixing well. Spread the mixture over the top and around the sides of the cauliflower. Sprinkle with the cheese. Bake the cauliflower at 350°F for 10 minutes, or until the cheese melts. Serves 4-6.

Sweet and Sour Carrots

1 pound carrots, diagonally sliced
1 bell pepper, cut in 1-inch pieces
⅓ cup sugar
1 tablespoon cornstarch
½ teaspoon salt
1 (16 ounce) can unsweetened pineapple chunks (reserve ½ cup juice)
2 tablespoons vinegar
2 teaspoons soy sauce

In a large saucepan over medium heat cook the carrots in water to cover for 15 minutes. Add the bell pepper and cook, covered, for 3 minutes. In another saucepan combine the sugar, cornstarch, and salt. Stir in the pineapple juice, vinegar, and soy sauce and cook until bubbly. Stir in the carrots and pineapple. Heat the mixture thoroughly and serve. Serves 4-6.

Company Carrots

2 pounds carrots, cut in strips
½ cup mayonnaise
1 tablespoon minced onion
1 tablespoon horseradish
Salt and pepper to taste
6 saltine crackers, crumbled
1 tablespoon parsley flakes
Paprika
Butter

In a saucepan cook the carrots in boiling salted water until tender. Drain the carrots and reserve ¼ cup of the liquid. Arrange the carrots in a shallow 1½-quart baking dish. In a bowl combine the mayonnaise, carrot liquid, onion, horseradish, salt, and pepper. Pour the mixture over the carrots. Sprinkle the casserole with the cracker crumbs, parsley flakes, and paprika and dot with butter. Bake the dish, uncovered, at 375°F for 20 to 25 minutes. Serves 6-8.

Carrots Thetis

2 pounds carrots
½ onion
½ bunch celery
½ bell pepper
½ cup butter
½ teaspoon MSG
¼ teaspoon rosemary
¼ teaspoon garlic salt
¼ teaspoon seasoned salt
¼ teaspoon lemon pepper
1 pint fresh mushrooms, sliced
¼ cup liquid brown sugar
3 tablespoons Worcestershire sauce
½ cup cooking sherry

Put the carrots, onion, celery, and bell pepper through a food processor fitted with the thin slicing disk or slice them thinly by hand. In a large skillet or pot with a lid melt the butter. Add the vegetables and seasonings and sauté gently for 15 minutes. Add the mushrooms, sugar, Worcestershire sauce, and sherry. Stir the mixture until it is thoroughly heated and the vegetables are limp but not soggy. Serves 12.

Scalloped Corn

2 cups cooked whole kernel corn
2 eggs, beaten
½ teaspoon salt
¼ cup chopped olives
½ cup corn flake crumbs
¾ cup milk
2 tablespoons butter or margarine

In a bowl combine the corn, eggs, salt, and olives. Transfer
½ of the mixture to a greased 1-quart baking dish. Cover with
½ of the crumbs. Add the remaining corn mixture and crumbs.
Pour the milk over the casserole and dot the top with
butter. Bake the casserole at 350°F for 30 minutes. Serves 4.

Old-Fashioned Corn

3 slices bacon
1 medium onion, chopped
1 (10 ounce) can whole tomatoes
1 (16 ounce) can whole kernel corn, drained
Freshly ground pepper to taste
Salt to taste
Pinch of sugar

In a skillet fry the bacon until it is crisp. Add the onion and
sauté until it is translucent. Add the tomatoes, corn, pepper, salt,
and sugar. Simmer the mixture until thoroughly heated. Serves 4.

Corn Soufflé

¼ cup butter
¼ cup flour
⅔ cup milk
1 cup cream-style corn
3 eggs, separated
½ teaspoon salt
¼ cup grated American cheese
1 tablespoon chopped bell pepper

In a saucepan melt the butter. Add the flour and blend. Stir
in the milk and corn and cook until it is thick. Remove from heat.
Beat the egg yolks. Add the egg yolks, salt, cheese, and bell
pepper. In a large bowl beat the egg whites until stiff peaks form
and fold them into the corn and cheese mixture. Spoon the
mixture into a buttered 2-quart casserole and bake at 350°F for
45 minutes or until set. Serve immediately. Serves 6.

Seafood-Stuffed Eggplant

2 small eggplants, halved
1 tablespoon lemon juice
4 tablespoons olive oil
1 large onion, finely chopped
1 tablespoon finely chopped parsley
½ cup finely chopped bell pepper
3 cloves garlic, minced
1 pound raw shrimp, peeled and deveined
2-3 slices stale bread, crumbled
1 tablespoon Worcestershire sauce
Salt and pepper to taste
⅓ cup grated Romano cheese
½ pound crab meat
2 eggs, slightly beaten
Italian-style bread crumbs
Butter

In a Dutch oven parboil the eggplants in water to cover with the lemon juice. Drain and cool. Scoop the pulp of the eggplant from the shell, being careful not to break the shell, and chop the pulp. In a Dutch oven heat the olive oil and sauté the onion, parsley, bell pepper, and garlic until tender. Add the shrimp and continue cooking for 5 minutes, stirring constantly. Add the pulp and cook for 5 minutes. Remove from heat. Stir in the bread, Worcestershire sauce, salt, pepper, cheese, and crab meat and mix well. Gradually add the eggs, stirring constantly.
Fill the eggplant shells with this mixture. Sprinkle with the bread crumbs and dot each with butter. Arrange the eggplant in a shallow baking pan with ¼ inch of water added. Bake at 350°F for 45 minutes. Serves 4.

Eggplant Soufflé

1 large or 2 small eggplants, peeled and chopped
1 onion, chopped
1 bell pepper, chopped
2 eggs, well beaten
1 teaspoon salt
½ teaspoon pepper
½ teaspoon baking powder
2 tablespoons flour
1 cup milk
1 cup grated Cheddar cheese
½ cup seasoned bread crumbs

In a large pot parboil the eggplant, onion, and bell pepper in salted water until soft. Remove from heat and drain. Add the remaining ingredients except the bread crumbs and stir until well blended. Pour into a buttered 1½-quart casserole. Sprinkle the seasoned bread crumbs on the top. Bake the casserole at 375°F for 25 minutes or until firm. Serves 4-6.

Lamb-Stuffed Eggplant

2 eggplants
1 tablespoon olive oil
½ cup minced onion
3 cloves garlic, minced
1 (8 ounce) can tomato sauce
¼ cup water
½ cup uncooked quick cooking rice
2 tablespoons finely chopped parsley
½ teaspoon salt
¼ teaspoon pepper
2 cups diced cooked lamb

Slice the eggplants in half lengthwise. Remove the pulp from the eggplants, leaving a 1-inch thick shell. In a large heavy skillet heat the oil over medium heat. Add the onion and garlic and sauté until soft. Add the eggplant pulp. Stir in the tomato sauce and water and continue cooking for 10 minutes. Remove the mixture from the heat, stir in the remaining ingredients, and mix well. Stuff the eggplant shells with the mixture. Arrange the stuffed eggplants in a buttered 9"x13" baking dish. Add ¼ inch boiling water to the bottom of the baking dish. Bake the dish, covered, at 350°F for 1 hour, or until the eggplant is tender. Serves 4.

Stuffed Mirlitons

4 large mirlitons
3 tablespoons shortening
1 large onion, chopped
1 clove garlic, crushed
½ cup chopped celery
¾ pound cooked shrimp
Salt and pepper to taste
½ cup grated sharp Cheddar cheese
½ cup buttered bread crumbs

In a saucepan boil the mirlitons until fork tender. Cut the mirlitons in half, remove seeds, and scoop out inside leaving the shells intact. In a large heavy skillet melt the shortening. Add the onion and garlic and sauté until translucent. Add the celery and cook until tender. Remove the excess water from the mirliton meat and mash. Combine the mashed mirliton with the shrimp, salt, pepper, cheese, ¼ cup of the bread crumbs, and the vegetable mixture. Fill the mirliton shells with this mixture and cover the tops with the remaining bread crumbs. Bake at 350°F for 20 minutes, or until the tops are browned. Serves 4.

Mushrooms Florentine

¼ cup butter
¼ cup chopped onion
1 pound fresh mushrooms
2 (10 ounce) packages frozen chopped spinach, cooked and drained
1 cup grated mozzarella, Monterey Jack, or Romano cheese
1 teaspoon salt
¼ teaspoon garlic salt

In a medium skillet melt the butter. Add the onion and mushrooms and sauté for 5 minutes. Stir in the remaining ingredients and transfer the mixture to a 9″ x 9″ baking dish. Bake the casserole at 350°F for 20 minutes. Serves 6-8.

Mushrooms and Artichokes

½ cup butter
½ pound fresh mushrooms, washed and thinly sliced
1 (14 ounce) can artichoke hearts, drained and mashed
Salt and pepper to taste
Garlic powder to taste

In a heavy saucepan melt the butter. Add the mushrooms and sauté until they are golden brown. Add the artichoke hearts, salt, pepper, and garlic powder. Simmer the mixture for 30 minutes or until almost dry. Serves 4-6.

French Fried Mushrooms

½ cup flour
1 teaspoon baking powder
Milk
1 pound fresh mushrooms, washed
Salt to taste

In a bowl combine the flour, baking powder, and enough milk to make a batter the consistency of a thick cream. Dip the mushrooms in the batter. Deep fry at a high temperature for 2 to 3 minutes. Drain on absorbent paper towels. Sprinkle with salt. Serve hot. Serves 6-8.

Potatoes Orleans

1½ pounds red potatoes, peeled
1 medium onion, grated
3 tablespoons peanut oil
6 tablespoons butter
Salt and pepper to taste
1 teaspoon chopped parsley

Using a food processor grate the potatoes. Soak and drain the grated potatoes several times in cold water to remove the starch. Drain the potatoes and squeeze them dry in a cloth kitchen towel. Combine the potatoes and onion. In a large non-stick skillet heat the oil and 3 tablespoons of the butter over medium heat. Add the potato-onion mixture. Using a spatula press the potatoes into the bottom of the skillet, spreading them evenly to the edges. Cook for 15 to 20 minutes or until crisp. Season with salt and pepper. Invert the skillet on a large plate or cookie sheet. Melt the remaining butter in the skillet and return the potato round to the skillet. Fry the remaining side for 15 minutes or until crisp. Season again with salt and pepper. Transfer the potato round to a warm serving platter, cut in wedges, and garnish with parsley. Serve immediately. Serves 6.

Buffet Potatoes

4 medium baking potatoes, peeled
3 tablespoons butter or margarine
Salt and pepper to taste
¼ cup chopped parsley
½ cup grated sharp Cheddar cheese
½ cup light cream or milk

Cut the potatoes into French fry strips. Place the strips in the center of a large piece of heavy aluminum foil shaped like a baking dish. Dot the potatoes with the butter and sprinkle them with salt, pepper, parsley, and cheese. Pour the cream over the mixture. Bring the foil edges up to cover the potatoes. Seal all edges, but do not press tightly. Place the foil with the potatoes on a cookie sheet and bake at 425°F for 40 to 50 minutes. To serve, place the foil-wrapped potatoes in a basket or on a platter and fold back the edges of the foil. Serves 4.

The secret to good fries is a heavy skillet, steady heat, and not turning the potatoes until they are browned.

Spinach with Artichoke Hearts

3 slices pimiento cheese
1 (10¾ ounce) can cream of mushroom soup
2 (10 ounce) packages frozen chopped spinach
1 (9 ounce) package frozen artichoke hearts
½ cup seasoned bread crumbs

In a saucepan combine the cheese and soup over low heat.
Cook the mixture, stirring constantly, until the cheese melts. In
another saucepan cook the spinach according to package
directions without salt and drain well. Add the soup mixture to
the spinach. Cook the artichokes, separately, according to
package directions and drain. Place ½ of the spinach-soup mixture
in a buttered 2-quart casserole. Top it with the artichoke
hearts and cover with the remainder of the spinach-soup mixture.
Top the dish with the seasoned bread crumbs. Bake the dish
at 350°F for 30 minutes. Serves 6-8.

Spinach Elegante

1 pound fresh spinach
¼ cup sour cream
2 tablespoons butter
2 tablespoons horseradish
½ teaspoon salt
¼ teaspoon dried tarragon leaves, crushed
Pepper to taste

Wash the spinach and tear it into pieces. In a saucepan cook the
spinach for 5 minutes in the water which clings to leaves from
washing. Drain the spinach, squeezing out all the moisture. In a
saucepan combine the spinach with the sour cream, butter,
horseradish, salt, tarragon, and pepper and heat
thoroughly. Serves 4.

Spinach Cheese Pie

1 (10 ounce) package frozen spinach
3 tablespoons margarine
1 tablespoon flour
½ cup heavy cream
1 cup grated Monterey Jack or mozzarella cheese
Salt and pepper to taste
1 (9 inch) pie shell, baked

Cook the spinach according to package directions and drain.
In a saucepan melt the margarine over medium heat and gradually
stir in the flour. When the mixture thickens, stir in the
cream. Add ½ cup of the cheese and stir until it is melted.
Fold in the spinach, salt, and pepper. Pour the mixture into
the baked pie shell. Sprinkle the top of the pie with the
remaining cheese. Bake the pie at 350°F for 10 to 15
minutes. Serves 8.

Stuffed Zucchini Italiano

6 medium zucchini
1 pound ground round
1 cup Italian-seasoned bread crumbs
2 tablespoons grated Parmesan cheese
1 tablespoon dried onion flakes
1 egg, slightly beaten
Garlic salt to taste
Pepper to taste
Italiano Sauce
Mozzarella cheese, grated
ITALIANO SAUCE:
1 (8 ounce) can tomato sauce
1 (6 ounce) can tomato paste
2 cloves garlic, crushed
2 teaspoons sugar
1 teaspoon oregano
¾ teaspoon basil
¼ teaspoon red pepper

Scrub the zucchini with a vegetable brush under cold water.
Remove both ends from each zucchini. Drop the zucchini
into rapidly boiling water and boil, uncovered, for 10
minutes. Drain and cool. Cut the zucchini in halves
lengthwise, scoop out the pulp, and chop finely. In
a large bowl combine the zucchini pulp, meat, bread crumbs,
cheese, onion flakes, egg, garlic salt, and pepper. Fill
the shells with the meat mixture. Place the stuffed zucchini
in a lightly greased 9"x13" baking dish. Prepare the sauce
by combining all ingredients. Pour the sauce over the zucchini and
cover with mozzarella cheese. Bake the dish at 350°F for 45 minutes.
Serves 4-6.

Stuffed Acorn Squash

1 pound bulk pork sausage
1 cup pared, chopped apple
½ cup chopped onion
½ cup bread crumbs
½ teaspoon sage, crushed
¼ cup chopped pecans
¼ teaspoon freshly ground pepper
¼ teaspoon Tabasco sauce
2 medium acorn squash

In a bowl mix together the sausage, apple, onion, bread crumbs,
sage, pecans, pepper, and Tabasco sauce. Cut the squash
in halves lengthwise and scoop out the seeds and stringy portion.
Fill each half with the sausage mixture. Bake the stuffed squash,
covered, in a 9" x 13" baking dish at 375°F for 50 to 60 minutes.
Serves 4.

Squash Rockefeller

25-30 small yellow crookneck squash
2 (10 ounce) packages frozen chopped spinach
1 cup butter
1 bunch green onions, finely chopped
4 ribs celery, finely chopped
1 clove garlic, pressed
1 bunch parsley, finely chopped
½ cup boiling water
¼ teaspoon anise flavoring
1½ cups Italian bread crumbs
Salt to taste
Tabasco sauce to taste
½ cup grated Romano or Parmesan cheese

In a Dutch oven in batches parboil the squash for 10 minutes, or until it is fork tender. Drain and set aside to cool. Cook the spinach according to the package directions and drain well. In a large heavy skillet melt the butter. Add the onion, celery, and garlic, and sauté until tender. Add the spinach and parsley to the sautéed vegetables. In another bowl add the anise to the boiling water. Blend in the bread crumbs thoroughly. Add the salt, Tabasco sauce, and cheese. Add this mixture to the spinach mixture. Split the squash lengthwise and remove the seeds only. Stuff the squash with the spinach mixture. Bake, uncovered, on greased cookie sheets at 350°F for 10 to 15 minutes or until thoroughly heated. Serves 25.

Squash Cheese Bake

1 pound yellow squash, sliced
2 eggs, beaten
¼ cup finely chopped onion
½ teaspoon sage
1 cup grated Cheddar cheese
½ teaspoon salt
Paprika

Steam the squash until tender and drain it. In a large bowl blend together thoroughly the squash, eggs, onion, sage, ½ cup of the cheese, and salt. Pour the mixture into a greased casserole. Sprinkle the mixture with the paprika and the remaining cheese. Bake the casserole at 350°F for 20 to 25 minutes or until brown. Serves 4.

Squash Parmesan

5 strips bacon
¾ cup chopped onion
4 cups cooked yellow squash
1 (16 ounce) can cut green beans, drained
Salt and pepper to taste
¼ cup Italian bread crumbs
1 cup grated Parmesan cheese

In a large heavy skillet fry the bacon until crisp. In 3 tablespoons of the bacon grease sauté the onion until tender. Add the squash, green beans, and bacon. Season the mixture with the salt and pepper. Simmer the mixture for 10 minutes. Divide the squash mixture, bread crumbs, and cheese in halves and in a buttered shallow baking dish layer them alternately. Bake the dish at 350°F for 30 minutes. Serves 4-6.

Aunt Ruth's Squash Casserole

2 pounds yellow squash, sliced
1 (10¾ ounce) can cream of chicken soup
1 (8 ounce) carton sour cream
1 carrot, grated
1 onion, finely chopped
1 (2 ounce) jar pimiento, chopped
½ cup margarine, melted
1 (8 ounce) package Pepperidge Farm herb seasoned stuffing mix
Salt and pepper to taste

In a saucepan boil the squash in lightly salted water for 7 to 10 minutes and drain it. Add the remaining ingredients, reserving ½ of the stuffing mix, and mix well. Pour the mixture into a large buttered casserole and top with the remaining stuffing mix. Bake the casserole at 350°F for 45 minutes. Serves 6-8.

Springfield Sweet Potato Pie

4 medium sweet potatoes, peeled and boiled
1 cup sugar
2 eggs
¼ cup butter
½ cup milk
1 tablespoon flour
½ teaspoon baking powder
1 teaspoon vanilla
½ teaspoon cinnamon
1 (9 inch) pie shell, unbaked

In a large bowl combine all the ingredients except the pie shell and mix thoroughly. Transfer the mixture to the pie shell. Bake the pie at 350°F for 45 minutes or until light brown. Serves 4-6.

Sweet Potato Casserole

1 (2 pound 14 ounce) can sweet potatoes
2 eggs
¼ cup margarine
½ cup sugar
⅓ cup evaporated milk
1 teaspoon vanilla
TOPPING:
⅓ cup margarine
¼ cup light brown sugar
½ cup flour
1 cup chopped nuts (optional)

In a saucepan over low heat stir the sweet potatoes until thoroughly heated. Remove from heat and cream well. In a bowl mix together the remaining ingredients and add the mixture to the potatoes. Pour the mixture into a pie pan. In a small saucepan melt the margarine and add the remaining topping ingredients. Pour the topping over the potatoes. Bake the casserole, uncovered, at 350°F for 35 minutes. Serves 4-6.

Carrie's Turnips

¼ pound bacon, cut in pieces
4 medium turnips, cubed
1 small onion, finely chopped
¼ teaspoon sugar
Salt and pepper to taste
½ cup water
1 Irish potato, finely chopped

In a medium saucepan over medium heat fry the bacon for 2 minutes. Stir in the turnips, onion, sugar, salt, pepper, and water. Reduce the heat to low and simmer, covered, for 45 minutes. Add the potato and continue cooking for 20 minutes. Serves 4.

Fresh Vegetable Casserole

2 tablespoons margarine
2 large onions, sliced in rings
3 carrots, sliced
½ medium bell pepper, sliced in rings
½ pound fresh green beans, cut in 1-inch pieces
2 large tomatoes, peeled and sliced
¼ cup chopped parsley
1¾ teaspoons salt
¼ teaspoon seasoned salt
1½ teaspoons freshly ground pepper

In a skillet melt the margarine. Add the onion and sauté until
light brown. Place the onion, carrots, bell pepper, green beans,
tomatoes, and parsley in a greased 2-quart shallow casserole.
Mix lightly and add the seasonings. Bake the casserole, covered, at
350°F for 1 hour, or until the vegetables are tender, stirring
once. Serves 8.

Curried Okra and Tomatoes

2 tablespoons bacon grease
1 pound okra, sliced
1 medium onion, chopped
1 (16 ounce) can tomatoes (reserve liquid)
2 cloves garlic, minced
1 bay leaf
¼ teaspoon curry powder
½ teaspoon thyme, crushed
Salt and pepper to taste

In a large heavy skillet heat the bacon grease over medium heat. Add
the okra and onion and sauté, stirring constantly, for 20
minutes, or until the okra ceases to rope. Add the tomatoes and
reserved liquid. Stir in the garlic, bay leaf, curry powder, thyme,
salt, and pepper. Simmer the mixture, covered, for 30
minutes. Serves 4-5.

White Sauce

Thin:
1 tablespoon butter
1 tablespoon flour
1 cup milk
Salt and pepper to taste

Medium:

2 tablespoons butter

2 tablespoons flour

1 cup milk

Salt and pepper to taste

Thick:

3 tablespoons butter

3 tablespoons flour

1 cup milk

Salt and pepper to taste

In a saucepan melt the butter over low heat. Add the flour, stirring constantly, until the mixture becomes frothy. Gradually stir in the milk and continue stirring until the mixture thickens. Season with salt and pepper. Simmer the mixture for a few minutes, stirring occasionally.

CHEESE SAUCE:

1 cup medium White Sauce

½ cup grated Cheddar cheese

Stir the cheese into the White Sauce and stir constantly until the cheese is melted.

Hollandaise Sauce

3 egg yolks

1½ tablespoons lemon juice

¼ teaspoon salt

Dash of paprika

Dash of cayenne

½ cup butter, melted

Place all of the ingredients in a blender and process on low speed until thick. Transfer to a heat-proof jar, cover the jar, and refrigerate. Before serving, place the jar in a small saucepan with ½ cup water and heat over low heat until desired consistency is obtained. Makes ¾ cup.

Chantilly Sauce (Savory)

¾ cup Hollandaise Sauce

¼ cup whipping cream, whipped

Gently fold the whipped cream into the Hollandaise Sauce.

DESSERTS

Desserts are practical and ornamental at the same time. They round out a festive dinner nicely, and add flourish to a simple one. They add proteins and sugar and help people rise from the table feeling neither hungry or surfeited. Since they come as a separate course, they prolong pleasantly too-hasty family meals, and encourage conversation and sharing—and that's as much a part of good eating as the cooking is.

DESSERTS

All cities and countries have traditions. New Orleans has more than most, and one of the most popular is the annual singing of Christmas Carols in Jackson Square, highlighted by the beauty of a candle glowing in the hand of each participant. Residents come from all areas of the city and suburbs to join with the Christmas-Season tourists in this beautiful evening.

Bourbon Balls

1 cup crumbled vanilla wafers
1 cup chopped pecans
1 cup confectioners' sugar
2 tablespoons cocoa
1½ tablespoons light Karo syrup
¼ cup bourbon
Confectioners' sugar, sifted

In a large bowl combine the vanilla wafer crumbs, pecans, 1 cup confectioners' sugar, and cocoa. In another bowl combine the Karo with the bourbon and add the dry mixture. Be sure the mixture is just moist enough to form a ball. If it is not, add a small amount of bourbon. Shape into walnut-size balls and roll in the sifted confectioner's sugar. Makes 42 balls.

Butterscotch Squares

½ cup butter or margarine
2 cups brown sugar
2 eggs
1½ cups sifted flour
2 teaspoons baking powder
2 teaspoons vanilla
1 cup chopped pecans
Confectioners' sugar

In a medium saucepan melt the butter. Add the brown sugar, blend over medium heat, and set aside to cool. Add the eggs, 1 at a time, beating after each addition. Mix in flour, baking powder, vanilla, and pecans, stirring, until well blended. Spread the batter into a greased and floured 9″ x 13″ baking pan and bake at 350°F for 30 minutes. Cut the cake into squares while it is warm and dust the squares with confectioners' sugar. Makes 30 squares.

Coconut Macaroons

3 egg whites
½ cup sugar
1 tablespoon lemon juice
1 cup shredded coconut
2 tablespoons condensed milk

In a large bowl beat the egg whites until they are stiff. Add the sugar and lemon juice and beat until blended. Stir in the coconut and condensed milk. Spoon the dough by teaspoonfuls onto buttered cookie sheets. Let the dough stand several hours to dry out. Bake the macaroons at 350°F for 15 to 20 minutes. Makes 48 cookies.

Cookies

Date Bars

3 eggs
1 scant cup sugar
1 teaspoon vanilla
¼ teaspoon salt
1 cup sifted flour
1 teaspoon baking powder
1 cup chopped walnuts
1 pound chopped dates
Confectioners' sugar, sifted

In a bowl with an electric mixer cream together the eggs, sugar, and vanilla. Into another bowl sift together the salt, flour, and baking powder. Add the flour mixture to the creamed mixture and beat until smooth. Fold in the walnuts and dates. Pour the mixture into a 8″ x 8″ baking pan and bake at 350°F for 1 hour or until golden brown. With a serrated knife cut the dessert into squares while hot. When the bars are cool, sprinkle them with confectioners' sugar. Makes 32 bars.

Chocolate Drops

1 (12 ounce) package chocolate chips
3 tablespoons margarine
1 cup flour
1 (14 ounce) can condensed milk
1 teaspoon vanilla
1 ½ cups chopped nuts
Confectioner's sugar, sifted

In the top of a double boiler, over high heat, combine chocolate chips and margarine. Stir the mixture until the chocolate melts. Remove the pan from the heat. Stir in the flour, condensed milk and vanilla until thoroughly blended. Add the nuts and blend. Place cookie mixture by heaping teaspoonfuls on an ungreased cookie sheet, about 2 inches apart. Slightly depress the center of each cookie with your thumb or with a spoon. Bake at 350°F for 7 to 10 minutes. Do not brown. Transfer the cookies immediately to wire racks to cool. Dust the drops with confectioners' sugar. Makes 72-84 cookies.

Cheesecake Cookie Bars

1 cup butter (at room temperature)
1 cup sugar
1 teaspoon vanilla
2 cups self-rising flour
2 (8 ounce) packages cream cheese (at room temperature)
2 eggs
½ cup confectioners' sugar
1 cup sour cream

In a bowl with an electric mixer cream together the butter and sugar until the mixture is light and fluffy. Add ½ teaspoon of the vanilla. Gradually add the flour and mix well. Spread the mixture evenly over the bottom of an ungreased 15½" x 10½" jelly-roll pan and bake it at 350°F for 20 minutes or until lightly browned. Cool the crust. In another bowl with an electric mixer beat the cream cheese until it is smooth. Add the eggs and the remaining vanilla, continue beating until smooth. By hand stir in the sugar and fold in the sour cream. Spread the crust with the cream cheese topping and bake at 350°F for 30 to 35 minutes. Let the dessert cool and with a serrated knife cut into bars. Makes 48 bars.

French Lace Cookies

1 cup flour
1 cup finely chopped pecans
½ cup light Karo syrup
½ cup butter
⅔ cup light brown sugar

Into a medium bowl sift the flour and combine it with the pecans. In a small saucepan over medium heat bring the Karo syrup, butter, and sugar to the boiling point, stirring constantly. DO NOT BOIL. Remove the mixture from the heat immediately and stir in the flour and pecan mixture. Drop the batter by scant teaspoonfuls onto lightly greased cookie sheets 3 inches apart. Bake at 350°F for 7 minutes. Let the cookies stand a few minutes. When the cookies are crisp enough to remove with a spatula, transfer them to a wire rack to continue cooling. Store the cookies in a tightly covered tin. Makes 48 cookies.

Pecan Crisps

1¾ cups sifted flour
¾ teaspoon baking powder
¼ teaspoon salt
1 cup sugar
¾ cup butter or margarine
2 teaspoons grated lemon rind
2 egg whites
1 cup chopped pecans

Into a medium bowl sift together the flour, baking powder, salt, and sugar. Cut in the butter until grainy. Add the lemon rind and egg whites and mix well. Stir in the pecans. Tightly pack the dough into empty frozen fruit juice concentrate cans and cover them tightly with plastic wrap. Place the dough in the refrigerator overnight. Remove the bottoms from the cans and push the dough out. Slice the dough ⅛ inch thick and arrange the slices on greased cookie sheets. Bake the cookies at 375°F for 8 to 10 minutes, or until the edges are brown. Let the cookies cool on the cookie sheets for 1 minute. Transfer them to racks to complete cooling. Store in a tightly covered tin. Makes 36 cookies.

Gingerbread Boys

½ cup margarine
½ cup sugar
½ cup cane syrup
1 egg, separated
2 cups sifted flour
½ teaspoon salt
½ teaspoon baking soda
1 teaspoon baking powder
1 teaspoon ground cloves
1 teaspoon ginger
1½ teaspoons cinnamon
½ teaspoon nutmeg
Raisins or nuts (optional)
Icing (optional)

In a large bowl cream together the margarine, sugar, and syrup. Add the egg yolk and mix well. Into a separate bowl sift together the flour, salt, baking soda, baking powder, and spices. Stir the flour mixture into the creamed mixture and mix well. Refrigerate the dough overnight. On a lightly floured board roll out the dough ¼ inch thick. With a 5-inch gingerbread boy cookie cutter cut out the cookies and place them on ungreased cookie sheets. Decorate the cookies with raisins or nuts and bake them at 350°F for 8 to 10 minutes, or until they are firm but not browned. Transfer the cookies to racks to cool and decorate them with icing, if desired. Makes 24 gingerbread boys.

Scotch Shortbread

1 pound butter
1 cup sugar
4 cups flour
Pinch of salt

In a bowl cream together by hand the butter and sugar. Into another bowl sift together the flour and salt. Cut the flour and salt into the creamed mixture. Press the mixture firmly into a 9″ pie pan. With a fork flute the edges and prick the surface. Bake the shortbread at 350°F for 15 minutes. LOWER OVEN TEMPERATURE to 300°F and bake for 30 to 45 minutes or until light golden brown. The shortbread will puff. To test for doneness, touch the center. If it springs back immediately, it is done. Remove the shortbread from the pan and transfer it to a rack to cool. Serve the shortbread by breaking off pieces rather than cutting.

Store soft cookies in a tightly covered container. An apple slice will mellow cookies and keep them moist.

Salt-Free Brownies

1 cup unsalted butter
2 cups sugar
4 eggs
4 tablespoons cocoa
1½ cups flour
1 teaspoon vanilla
Pecans (optional)
1 (10½ ounce) package miniature marshmallows
FROSTING:
1⅔ cups confectioners' sugar
4 tablespoons milk
½ teaspoon vanilla
3 tablespoons shortening
3 tablespoons cocoa

In the large bowl of an electric mixer cream together the butter
and sugar. Add the eggs, 1 at a time, beating after each addition.
Mix in the cocoa and flour. Add the vanilla and nuts and mix
only until blended. Pour the batter into a greased 9″ x 13″ pan
and bake at 350°F for 30 minutes. In a bowl blend all of the
frosting ingredients. Frost the brownies, sprinkle the
marshmallows on top, and brown under the broiler. Makes
30 brownies.

Chocolatines

¾ cup butter (at room temperature)
1¼ cups sugar
½ cup cocoa
1 egg
1 tablespoon rum
1½ cups sifted flour
1¼ teaspoons baking powder
⅛ teaspoon salt

In a bowl with an electric mixer combine the butter, sugar, and
cocoa. Add the egg and rum, blending thoroughly. Gradually add
all the dry ingredients. Form the dough into a ball and chill
it for 30 minutes. Roll ½ of the dough into a round ⅛ inch thick
on a scantly floured board. With a biscuit cutter cut out rounds.
Repeat this step with the remaining dough. Using a spatula
place the rounds on ungreased cookie sheets and bake them
at 350°F for 5 minutes or until firm, but not brown. Makes 36
cookies.

Melt-In-Your-Mouth Butter Cookies

½ cup butter
½ cup margarine
2 tablespoons Crisco shortening
1 cup sifted confectioners' sugar
2¼ cups sifted cake flour
2 teaspoons vanilla
1 cup finely chopped pecans

In the large bowl of an electric mixer cream the butter, margarine, and shortening. Gradually add the confectioners' sugar to the creamed mixture. Add the flour and vanilla to the butter-sugar mixture and blend well. When the mixture is thoroughly blended, stir in the pecans by hand. Drop the dough by teaspoonfuls on ungreased cookie sheets. Bake the cookies at 325°F for 15 to 20 minutes, or until a faint line of brown is around the edge. Let them cool on the cookie sheets briefly. Transfer the cookies to wire racks to continue cooling. Store in an airtight container. Makes 48 cookies.

A "parade" standby
Ranger Cookies

1 cup shortening or margarine
1 cup sugar
1 cup brown sugar
2 eggs, well beaten
1 teaspoon vanilla
2 cups flour
1 teaspoon soda
½ teaspoon salt
½ teaspoon baking powder
2 cups uncooked oatmeal
2 cups Rice Krispies
1 cup grated coconut

In a bowl with an electric mixer cream together the shortening, sugar, and brown sugar. Add the eggs and vanilla. Into a large bowl sift together the flour, soda, salt, and baking powder. Add the flour mixture to the creamed mixture. Stir in the oatmeal, Rice Krispies, and coconut and mix well. Shape the mixture into small balls, arrange them on greased cookie sheets, and press them with the bottom of a glass that has been oiled and dipped in sugar. Bake the cookies at 350°F for 10 to 12 minutes. Transfer the cookies to a rack to cool. Makes 60 cookies.

Shiny pans are best for baking cookies.

Peanut Butter Cookies

½ cup margarine
¼ teaspoon salt
1 cup crunchy peanut butter
¾ cup sugar
¾ cup brown sugar
2 eggs, well beaten
1 tablespoon milk
1 cup sifted flour
¼ teaspoon soda
¼ teaspoon ginger

In the large bowl of an electric mixer combine the margarine, salt, and peanut butter and blend well. Add the sugar, brown sugar, eggs, and milk and continue mixing until the mixture is creamed. Into a separate bowl sift together the flour, soda, and ginger. Gradually stir the dry ingredients into the creamed mixture. Roll the dough in small balls and place on ungreased cookie sheets. Press the centers with a fork. Bake the cookies at 325°F for 15 to 20 minutes. Transfer them to wire racks to cool. Makes 60-72 cookies.

Ginger Snaps

¾ cup shortening
1 cup sugar
4 tablespoons molasses
1 egg, beaten
2 teaspoons soda
1 teaspoon ginger
1 teaspoon cinnamon
2 cups flour
Sugar

In a bowl with an electric mixer cream together the shortening and 1 cup sugar. Add the molasses and blend thoroughly. Add the egg and mix well. Into a bowl sift together the soda, spices, and flour. Add the flour mixture to the creamed mixture, a little at a time, and blend thoroughly. Form the mixture into very small balls, roll them in a small bowl of sugar, and place them on greased cookie sheets. Bake the cookies at 350°F for 8 to 10 minutes. Transfer the cookies to racks to cool completely. Makes 75 cookies.

Date Chewies

1 cup chopped dates
½ cup water
1 cup shortening
1 cup firmly packed brown sugar
1 egg
1 teaspoon vanilla
1¾ cups flour
2 teaspoons baking powder
½ teaspoon salt
1½ cups grated coconut
Pecan halves

In a small saucepan cook the dates in the water for 5 minutes,
or until they are soft. Remove them from the heat, cool, and set
aside. In a bowl cream together the shortening and brown
sugar. Add the egg and vanilla and mix thoroughly. To the creamed
mixture blend in the flour, baking powder, and salt, mixing
well. Stir in the dates and coconut. Drop the mixture by
teaspoonfuls onto ungreased cookie sheets. Top each with
a pecan half and bake at 375°F for 12 to 15 minutes. Makes
48 cookies.

Delta Bars

½ cup margarine
1 cup sugar
1 egg
1 egg, separated
1 teaspoon vanilla
1¼ cups self-rising flour
1 cup packed light brown sugar
Chopped nuts

In the large bowl of an electric mixer cream together the margarine
and sugar. Beat in the egg, egg yolk, and vanilla. Add the flour,
folding in by hand. Spread the dough into a greased and floured
9″ x 13″ baking pan. Set aside and prepare the frosting. Beat
the egg white until it is stiff. Fold in the brown sugar. Spread
the frosting over the cookie dough. Top it with the chopped nuts.
Bake at 350°F for 30 minutes. Let the bars cool in the pan, cut
into squares, and serve. Makes 12 bars.

Surfer Bars

1 cup butterscotch chips
¼ cup brown sugar
¼ cup butter
1 egg
¾ cup flour
1 teaspoon baking powder
¼ teaspoon salt
1 cup chocolate chips
½ cup chopped nuts
1 teaspoon vanilla

In a medium saucepan melt the butterscotch chips, brown sugar, and butter, stirring constantly. Remove from the heat and cool slightly. Add the egg and beat well. Stir in the flour, baking powder, and salt and blend well. Stir in the remaining ingredients. Spread the mixture into a greased 8″ x 8″ baking pan and bake on the center rack of the oven at 350°F for 20 to 25 minutes. Let cool slightly before cutting into 2-inch squares. Makes 16 squares.

Grandma's Jelly Cookies

2 cups butter or margarine
1 cup sugar
3 egg yolks
2 teaspoons vanilla
5 cups flour
Red currant jelly

In the large bowl of an electric mixer cream the butter and sugar until light and fluffy. Add the egg yolks and vanilla and mix until well blended. Gradually add the flour until the mixture holds together and can be rolled into balls. Form the dough into walnut-size balls and arrange them 2 inches apart on cookie sheets. Make a depression in the center of each and fill with ¼ teaspoon of the jelly. Bake them at 375°F for 15 minutes. Transfer the cookies to wire racks to cool. Makes 96 cookies.

Pecan-Orange Snowballs

1 cup butter
⅓ cup sugar
2 cups flour
2 cups finely chopped pecans
2 tablespoons grated orange rind
1 teaspoon vanilla
1 cup sifted confectioners' sugar

In the large bowl of an electric mixer cream together the butter and sugar. Stir in the flour, pecans, orange rind, and vanilla. Shape the dough into walnut-size balls. Bake the balls on ungreased cookie sheets on the center rack of the oven at 300°F for 20 to 30 minutes. Cool the balls slightly and roll them in the confectioners' sugar. Makes 36 snowballs.

English Fruit Cake Drops

½ cup butter
½ cup sugar
2 eggs
1½ cups flour
1 teaspoon soda
1 teaspoon cinnamon
½ teaspoon allspice
½ teaspoon cloves
⅓ cup fruit juice
1 pound raisins
1 pound mixed candied fruit, chopped
1 pound pecans, chopped

In the large bowl of an electric mixer cream together the butter, sugar, and eggs. Into a separate bowl sift together the flour, soda, cinnamon, allspice, and cloves. Beat the dry mixture into the creamed mixture alternately with the fruit juice. Stir in the fruits and nuts. Drop the batter by teaspoonfuls onto greased cookie sheets. Bake the cookies at 350°F for 12 to 15 minutes. Transfer the cookies to wire racks to cool and store them in tightly sealed tins. Makes 120 cookies.

An excellent refrigerator or freezer cookie

Butterscotch Cookies

1 cup butter
2 eggs
2 cups brown sugar
4 cups flour
1 teaspoon cream of tartar
1 teaspoon soda
1 teaspoon salt
1 teaspoon vanilla
1 cup chopped nuts

In the large bowl of an electric mixer cream together the butter, eggs, and brown sugar. Into another bowl sift together all of the dry ingredients and gradually add the flour mixture to the egg mixture. Stir in the vanilla and chopped nuts. Drop the dough by tablespoonfuls on a cookie sheet, pressing into the center of each mound with the thumb. Bake the cookies at 350°F for 8 to 10 minutes. If the dough is to be frozen, divide it into thirds, wrap it in wax paper, and freeze it. Makes 60 cookies.

Old-Fashioned Bourbon Balls

1 cup pecans, crushed
½ cup 100-proof bourbon
6½ tablespoons butter
1 (1 pound) box confectioners' sugar
8 (1 ounce) squares semi-sweet chocolate
1 square paraffin
Small pecan pieces

In a jar soak the nuts in the bourbon, covered, for 24 hours, shaking occasionally. In the bowl of an electric mixer cream the butter until it is smooth. Add the sugar and continue beating until thoroughly blended. Add the nut and bourbon mixture to the creamed mixture and stir until stiff. Continue working the dough with your hands until it forms a small ball. In a double boiler melt the chocolate and paraffin together. Form the dough into small balls and freeze them for 3 to 5 minutes. Place a large piece of aluminum foil on a flat surface. Insert a toothpick in each ball and dip them into the chocolate, coating them completely. Transfer the balls to the foil and remove the toothpick. Place a small piece of pecan where the toothpick was inserted. Arrange the bourbon balls on a platter and refrigerate them.

To soften brown sugar place it in a dish with a slice of apple and microwave for 15 seconds.

Candy

Humidity must be low to successfully make Divinity

Divinity

3 cups sugar
⅔ cup light Karo syrup
⅓ cup water
3 egg whites
Dash of salt
2 cups pecans, broken

Spread wax paper on a large surface. In a saucepan combine
the sugar, Karo, and water. Stir the mixture until it is thoroughly
blended and bring it to a boil. Continue boiling until a candy
thermometer registers 238°F, or the syrup reaches the soft ball
stage. While the syrup is boiling, in a large bowl beat the egg
whites and salt until stiff peaks form. When the syrup has reached
the soft ball stage, pour ½ of it into the beaten egg whites in
a VERY SLOW, STEADY STREAM, beating the mixture
with an electric mixer. Return the remaining syrup to the heat.
Continue cooking the syrup until a candy thermometer registers
250°F, or the syrup reaches the hard ball stage. Remove the syrup
from the heat and add it to the egg white mixture in a slow, steady
stream, beating constantly, with the mixer. With a strong, wooden
spoon stir the pecans into the divinity. Continue stirring for
1 minute, or until the candy is stiff enough to drop by teaspoonfuls
onto the wax paper. Makes 24-36 pieces.

Pecan Pralines

1½ cups dark brown sugar
1 cup sugar
1 cup condensed milk
3 tablespoons butter
1 teaspoon vanilla
2 cups pecan halves and pieces

Butter a jelly-roll pan. In a large heavy saucepan combine the
brown sugar, sugar, milk, butter, and vanilla and stir until
blended. Bring the mixture to a boil over moderate heat. Continue
boiling until a candy thermometer registers 238°F, or the candy
reaches the soft ball stage. Remove from the heat, add the pecans,
and beat well with a wooden spoon for no more than 1 minute.
Immediately pour the candy onto the buttered jelly-roll pan.
Let the candy stand for 1 hour, or until it is cool. Break the
candy in pieces and store the pralines in an airtight container.

A large wooden paddle or spoon is ideal for stirring and beating
candy.

Sweet Popcorn

8 quarts popped corn
GLAZE:
½ cup light Karo syrup
2 cups brown sugar
1 cup margarine
1 teaspoon vanilla
½ teaspoon baking soda

Place the popped corn in a large roaster. In a saucepan combine the syrup, brown sugar, and margarine and boil the mixture over low heat for 5 minutes. Remove from the heat. Add the vanilla and baking soda. Stir the mixture and pour it over the popcorn, mixing well. Bake the popcorn at 250°F for 45 minutes, stirring every 15 minutes.

Chocolate Turtles

1 pound Kraft vanilla caramels
2 tablespoons water
3 cups pecan halves
1 (12 ounce) plain chocolate candy bar

In the top of a double boiler melt the caramels. Add the water and pecans, stirring, until the nuts are evenly distributed. Using a teaspoon, drop the candy on wax paper and let it cool. In a double boiler melt the candy bar. Dip the candy pieces in the chocolate or spoon the chocolate over them. Let the turtles stand until the candy is hardened.

Date Loaf

1½ cups milk
3 cups sugar
1 tablespoon light Karo syrup
1 (8 ounce) package dates, chopped
2 tablespoons butter
2 cups chopped pecans
½ teaspoon vanilla

Combine the milk, sugar, and Karo syrup in a saucepan and bring the mixture to a boil. Add the dates and cook until a firm ball forms when dropped into a cup of water. (It will look curdled while cooking.) Stir in the butter and remove the mixture from the heat. Let the candy stand until it is nearly cold, beat until almost stiff, and stir in the nuts and vanilla. Beat until the mixture is real creamy and rather firm. With dampened hands place the mixture on a damp cloth and form it into a roll. Cover the roll with a cloth and refrigerate it overnight. Slice the roll the next day. This can be frozen.

Candy

Creamy Creole Pralines

1 cup sugar
1 cup dark brown sugar
2 tablespoons light Karo syrup
½ cup whipping cream
2 tablespoons butter
1 teaspoon vanilla
1 cup pecan halves or pieces

In a saucepan dissolve the sugars and Karo syrup in the cream over medium heat. Bring the mixture to a boil and continue cooking until a candy thermometer registers 228°F, stirring occasionally. Add the butter, vanilla, and pecans and cook to 236°F and remove from the heat. Cool the candy to 225°F and beat just until thickened. (This happens almost instantly.) Drop the candy by tablespoonfuls on wax paper, working rapidly. The candy will flatten out. When cool, wrap in wax paper, individually, and store in a covered container. Makes 10-15 pralines.

Glazed Nuts

1 cup water
1 cup sugar
2 cups pecans, walnuts, or peanuts

Place the water, sugar, and pecans into a heavy skillet. Stir the ingredients constantly over medium heat for 20 minutes. Reduce the heat and continue cooking, stirring constantly, until the mixture returns to a liquid state. Take care that the sugar does not burn. Pour the nuts onto an ungreased baking sheet, separating them carefully. Cool and place in a tin or jar. Makes 1 pound.

Pineapple Fudge

2 cups sugar
½ cup evaporated milk
½ cup crushed pineapple
1 tablespoon butter
Green food coloring
¼ cup chopped nuts

In a large saucepan combine the sugar, milk, pineapple, and butter. Cook the mixture until a candy thermometer registers 238°F, or until the candy reaches the soft ball stage. Remove the candy from the heat and tint it with a few drops of food coloring. Add the nuts and beat, vigorously by hand, with a wooden spoon, for a maximum of 1 minute. The candy should be thick and creamy. Pour the candy into a buttered 8″ x 8″ pan, allow it to cool, and cut it in squares. Makes 24 pieces.

Peanut or Pecan Brittle

2 cups raw Spanish peanuts or pecans
½ cup light Karo syrup
½ cup water
1 cup sugar
½ teaspoon soda
1 teaspoon vanilla

Have all ingredients measured and ready to use. In a heavy skillet over medium heat, stir the nuts, syrup, water, and sugar with a wooden spoon until a thread forms when the spoon is lifted from the syrup (293° on a candy thermometer). Remove the mixture from the heat and immediately add the soda and vanilla, stirring briskly. As soon as the mixture is clear, IMMEDIATELY SPREAD AS THINLY AS POSSIBLE on a well-buttered cookie sheet and set aside to cool. When the brittle is cool, break into pieces and store in an airtight container. DO NOT ATTEMPT THIS RECIPE ON A HUMID DAY.

Fudge

⅔ cup cocoa
3 cups sugar
1½ cups milk
1 tablespoon vanilla
1 tablespoon butter
1-2 cups pecans, broken (optional)

In a large saucepan combine the cocoa, sugar, and milk. Bring the mixture to the rolling bubble stage, stirring constantly. Reduce the heat and cook the mixture until a candy thermometer registers 238°F, or until the candy reaches the soft ball stage. Remove the mixture from the heat and add the vanilla and butter. Set aside to cool. While the fudge is still slightly warm, beat it until it is creamy and just begins to hold its shape. Add the pecans and quickly pour the fudge into a buttered 8″ x 8″ pan to set. Cut the fudge into squares. Makes 24 pieces.

COLD WATER TEST:
Use a fresh cup of cold water for each sample. Drop 1 teaspoon of syrup into the water. Shape it into a ball to test the degree of doneness.

Soft ball:	Can be picked up but flattens.
Firm ball:	Holds its shape until pressed.
Hard ball:	Holds its shape but is pliable.
Soft crack:	Separates into hard but not brittle threads.
Hard crack:	Separates into hard brittle threads.

New Orleans Pralines

1 (1 pound) box dark brown sugar
1 cup sugar
½ teaspoon salt
¾ cup milk
2-3 cups whole pecan halves
2 tablespoons butter
½ teaspoon vanilla

In a saucepan cook the sugars, salt, and milk until a candy thermometer registers 238°F, or the mixture reaches the soft ball stage. Add the pecans and bring the mixture to a rolling boil. Remove the mixture from the heat and add the butter and vanilla. Let the mixture cool in the saucepan for 20 minutes. Spread newspapers on a table or countertop and cover the newspapers with wax paper. Beat the mixture slightly, just until glossy (30 to 45 seconds at the most). Drop by spoonfuls on the wax paper. Let the candy cool on the paper for 15 to 20 minutes. Lift the pralines gently from the wax paper and wrap them individually in wax paper or plastic wrap. Store the pralines in an airtight container. Makes 20-30 (2-inch) pralines.

Buttermilk Candy

2 cups sugar
¼ teaspoon salt
1 teaspoon baking soda
1 cup buttermilk
1 teaspoon butter
1 teaspoon vanilla
1 cup chopped pecans

In a large saucepan combine the sugar and salt. In a bowl stir the soda into the buttermilk, mix well, and pour over the sugar and salt mixture. Cook the mixture, stirring, until a candy thermometer registers 238°F, or the candy reaches the soft ball stage. Remove the candy from the heat and cool. Add the butter and vanilla. Beat the mixture in the same direction for 1 minute. Stir in the pecans. Line a 8″ x 8″ pan with wax paper. Transfer the candy to the pan and spread it out evenly. Cut the candy in squares. Makes 24 pieces.

Heavy metal pots are best for cooking candy, because the syrup will not stick as easily as in thin ones.

A special occasion cake
Louisiana Cream Cake

1 cup butter
2 cups sugar
3½ cups cake flour
3 teaspoons baking powder
½ teaspoon salt
1 cup milk
6 egg whites
1 teaspoon vanilla

In a large bowl cream the butter and gradually mix in the sugar.
Into another bowl sift together the flour, baking powder, and salt.
Add the flour mixture alternately with the milk to the sugar and
butter mixture. In a separate bowl beat the egg whites and vanilla
with an electric mixer until they are stiff and fold them into the
batter. Divide the batter into 3 greased and floured 9″ cake pans.
Bake the layers at 350°F for 30 minutes. Let the layers cool in the
pans for 10 minutes and turn them out onto wire racks to complete
cooling. Using a long serrated knife, slice each layer horizontally
to create 6 thin layers. Prepare the Cream Filling.

CREAM FILLING:
1½ cups sugar
4 tablespoons flour
1 cup evaporated milk
4 egg yolks
1 cup water
1 cup butter (do not substitute)

In a medium saucepan combine the sugar and flour until evenly
blended and set aside. In a bowl briskly beat the milk and egg
yolks with a fork, drawing the fork out frequently and throwing
away any white pigment. Add the water and when well blended,
add to the sugar and flour mixture. Cook over medium heat,
stirring constantly, until thick. Remove the pan from the heat, add
the butter and cool completely. Beat the mixture with a wooden
spoon until it is completely blended. Spread the filling between
the 6 cooled layers of cake and assemble them. Spread filling
on the top, not on the sides, of the cake. Refrigerate the cake
covered. Before serving, prepare the Seven Minute Frosting and
frost the sides, leaving the top covered only with the cream filling.
Serves 14-16.

SEVEN MINUTE FROSTING:
¼ cup egg whites
1½ cups sugar
⅓ cup water
1 tablespoon light corn syrup
1 teaspoon vanilla extract

In the top of a double boiler combine the egg whites, sugar,
water, and syrup. Beat the mixture for 1 minute with a portable
electric mixer on high speed until all the ingredients are thoroughly
blended. Place the pot in boiling water. Beat the frosting constantly
with the mixer for 7 minutes, at high speed, until stiff peaks form.
Remove the top portion of the double boiler, add the vanilla,
and continue beating for 2 minutes. Frost the cake immediately.

Cakes

Jam Cake

½ cup butter or margarine
1 cup sugar
1 teaspoon baking soda
8 tablespoons cold water
4 eggs
2 cups flour
1 teaspoon each ground cloves, cinnamon, and nutmeg
1 cup thick jam

In a large bowl cream together the butter and sugar. In a measuring cup dissolve the soda in the water. Add the eggs, 1 at a time, alternating with the soda and water mixture and beat well. Into another bowl sift together the flour and spices and gradually beat the dry mixture into the egg mixture. Add the jam and beat vigorously for 1 minute. Pour the batter into 3 greased and floured 8″ or 9″ cake pans. Bake the layers at 375°F for 20 to 25 minutes. Let the layers cool and frost the cake with Penuche Icing. Serves 14-16.

PENUCHE ICING:
3 cups brown sugar
1 cup sugar
1½ cups milk
6 tablespoons butter
2 teaspoons vanilla

In a heavy pan thoroughly combine the brown sugar, sugar, milk, and butter. Cook the mixture over medium heat, stirring constantly, with a wooden spoon until a candy thermometer registers 242°F to 248°F, or a firm ball forms when a small amount of the syrup is dropped into ice water. Remove the mixture from the heat, add the vanilla, and beat with an electric mixer until the icing is of spreading consistency. If the mixture starts to harden while being mixed, add a small amount of milk to thin it.

Honey Yogurt Cake

2¼ cups sifted flour
1 teaspoon baking soda
½ teaspoon salt
1 teaspoon ground cinnamon
1 teaspoon ground allspice
1 teaspoon ground cloves
½ cup butter
1 cup firmly packed brown sugar
½ cup honey
2 eggs
1 (8 ounce) carton plain yogurt

Sift the first 6 ingredients into a bowl. In the large bowl of an electric mixer beat the butter, sugar, and honey until it is fluffy. To the sugar mixture add the eggs, 1 at a time, beating well after each addition. Add the flour mixture alternately with the yogurt, beating after each addition on low speed. Continue beating the mixture for 2 minutes and pour the batter into a greased and floured 9" x 9" pan. Bake the cake at 350°F for 45 minutes, or until the cake springs back when lightly touched. Serves 8-10.

Sheathe Cake

2 cups sugar
2 cups flour
1 teaspoon baking soda
1 teaspoon cinnamon
1 cup water
½ cup butter
½ cup oil
4 tablespoons cocoa
½ cup buttermilk
2 eggs, beaten
1 teaspoon vanilla

Into a large bowl sift together the sugar, flour, baking soda, and cinnamon and set aside. In a saucepan combine the water, butter, oil, and cocoa. Bring the mixture to a boil and pour it over the dry ingredients, mixing well, and set aside. In another bowl mix together the buttermilk, eggs, and vanilla and add the mixture to the chocolate batter. Pour the batter into a greased and floured 9" x 13" pan and bake the cake at 400°F for 20 to 30 minutes. Begin preparing Chocolate Sheathe Frosting 5 minutes after placing the cake in the oven.

CHOCOLATE SHEATHE FROSTING:
½ cup butter
4 tablespoons cocoa
6 tablespoons milk
1 (1 pound) box confectioners' sugar
1 teaspoon vanilla
1 cup chopped pecans

In a saucepan combine the butter, cocoa, and milk. Bring the mixture to a boil, being careful not to scorch it. Add the sugar, vanilla, and pecans and spread the frosting on the hot cake. Liquid may be slightly increased to obtain spreading consistency. Serves 12-14.

Have all cake ingredients at room temperature, assemble utensils, prepare pans, and set oven temperature before starting to mix.

Chewy Chocolate Fudge Cake

2 cups self-rising flour
2 cups sugar
1 cup water
½ cup oil
6 tablespoons margarine
4 tablespoons cocoa
½ cup buttermilk
1 teaspoon baking soda
1 egg
1 teaspoon vanilla

In a large bowl mix together the flour and sugar. In a saucepan combine the water, oil, margarine, and cocoa and bring the mixture to a rapid boil. Add the cocoa mixture to the flour mixture. In a measuring cup mix together the buttermilk and soda and add it to the batter. Add the egg and vanilla and stir until well blended. Pour the batter into a greased and floured 9″ x 13″ pan and bake at 325°F for 60 minutes. Spread the cake with Buttermilk Frosting while it is still warm. Serves 12-14.

BUTTERMILK FROSTING:
½ cup margarine
4 tablespoons cocoa
6 tablespoons buttermilk
1 (1 pound) box confectioners' sugar
1 teaspoon vanilla
½ cup chopped pecans

In a small saucepan melt the margarine. Using a wooden spoon, stir in the cocoa and buttermilk. Blend in the sugar and vanilla, stirring, until smooth. Spread the frosting on the warm cake. Sprinkle the top of the cake with the pecans.

Buttermilk Pound Cake

1 cup margarine
2 cups sugar
4 eggs
3½ cups cake flour
¼ teaspoon salt
1 cup buttermilk
1 teaspoon lemon extract
½ teaspoon baking soda

In a large bowl cream together the margarine and sugar. Add the eggs, 1 at a time, beating after each addition. Add the flour and salt alternately with the buttermilk and flavoring. Dissolve the baking soda in 1 tablespoon boiling water and slowly stir it into the batter. Pour the batter into a greased and floured 10″ tube pan and bake at 325°F for 1 hour and 20 minutes. Serves 14-16.

Spicy Pumpkin Cake

1½ cups corn oil
2 cups sugar
3⅛ cups flour
2 teaspoons cinnamon
2 teaspoons allspice
2 teaspoons baking powder
1 teaspoon salt
2 teaspoons baking soda
2 cups mashed pumpkin
4 eggs
2 teaspoons vanilla
1 cup chopped nuts
1 cup raisins

In a large bowl mix the oil, sugar, 3 cups of the flour, spices, baking powder, salt, soda, and pumpkin. Add the eggs, 1 at a time, beating well after each addition. Add the vanilla, nuts, and raisins which have been mixed with the remaining flour. Pour the batter into a greased tube pan and bake the cake at 350°F for 1 hour. Spread the cake with Raisin Frosting. Serves 14-16.

RAISIN FROSTING:
1 cup evaporated milk
1 cup sugar
3 egg yolks, slightly beaten
½ cup butter
1 teaspoon vanilla
Coconut to taste
1 cup raisins

In a saucepan combine the first 5 ingredients. Cook the mixture over medium heat for 12 minutes, stirring. Stir in the coconut and raisins and frost the cake.

Angel Food Orange Sauce

1 cup sugar
2 egg yolks
1 tablespoon flour
1 large orange, juiced, rind grated
1 cup whipping cream

In a saucepan beat together the sugar, egg yolks, and flour with a wire whisk. Add the orange juice and rind and mix well. Cook the mixture over low heat until it thickens. Set aside to cool. In a bowl with an electric mixer whip the cream and fold in the cooled orange mixture. Refrigerate the sauce. Serve the sauce by heaping spoonfuls over large slices of angel food cake.

Cakes

Orange Cake

¾ cup shortening (Crisco preferred)
¾ teaspoon salt
grated rind of 1 orange
1½ cups sugar
3 eggs
3 cups flour (sift before measuring)
3 teaspoons baking powder
2 tablespoons lemon juice
Juice of 1 orange + enough water to make 1 cup

In large mixing bowl, combine shortening, salt, orange rind and sugar. Cream until light and fluffy. Add eggs, one at a time, beating well after each addition. Sift flour, measure, sift again with baking powder. Add lemon juice to orange juice/water mixture. Add flour mixture to creamed mixture alternately with the orange juice/water and lemon juice mixture, beginning and ending with flour. Beat until well mixed. Pour into 2 greased and floured 9″ cake pans. Bake the layers at 350°F for 25 to 30 minutes. Let layers cool in pan for 5 minutes, then turn out on wire racks to cool. Frost with Orange Frosting. Serves 12-14.

ORANGE FROSTING:
½ cup butter
3 tablespoons grated orange rind
1 box (1 lb.) confectioner's sugar
3 tablespoons frozen orange juice concentrate (thawed)
1 to 2 tablespoons cream

In small mixing bowl, combine butter, grated orange rind, ½ box of confectioner's sugar and orange juice concentrate. Beat until smooth. Add remaining sugar and 1 tablespoon cream. Beat until smooth and creamy, adding more cream if necessary until frosting is of good spreading consistency. Frosts one 9-inch layer cake.

Whipping Cream Pound Cake

1 cup butter
3 cups sugar
6 large or 7 small eggs
3 cups sifted flour
2 teaspoons vanilla
1 cup whipping cream

In the large bowl of an electric mixer cream the butter and sugar for 10 minutes on high speed. Add the eggs, 1 at a time, beating well after each addition. Slowly add the flour beating at medium speed. Add the vanilla. Beating at low speed, add the whipping cream, beating only until it is blended in. Pour the batter into a well-greased bundt pan. Place the cake in a COLD OVEN, set the oven temperature at 325°F, and bake the cake for 1 hour and 25 minutes. Serves 14-16.

Polynesian Banana Sheet Cake

1½ cups sugar
½ cup margarine
2 eggs
1 teaspoon vanilla
1 cup mashed ripe banana
1 teaspoon salt
1½ cups flour
1 teaspoon baking soda
4 tablespoons milk
½ cup coarsely chopped nuts

In a large bowl cream the sugar and margarine. Add the eggs, vanilla, and banana. Into another bowl sift together the salt, flour, and baking soda. To the banana mixture add the milk and flour mixture, alternately, mixing between additions. Stir in the nuts. Pour the batter into a greased and floured 9″ x 13″ pan and bake at 325°F for 45 minutes. Let the cake cool in the pan.

TOPPING:
3 tablespoons butter
5 tablespoons brown sugar
2 tablespoons cream
½ cup coarsely chopped nuts
½ cup coconut

In a small saucepan melt the butter. Stir in the brown sugar and cream. Cream the mixture until it is blended. Sprinkle the nuts over the cake in the pan and sprinkle it with the coconut. Pour the brown sugar topping over the cake. Place the cake 3 to 5 inches below the broiler and broil it until the coconut is lightly browned and the sugar is bubbling. Serves 12-14.

Date-Nut Cake

2 cups chopped dates
1½ cups hot water
1 teaspoon baking soda
1½ cups sugar
¾ cup shortening
2 large eggs
1 teaspoon vanilla
1¾ cups flour
⅔ cup chopped nuts

In a bowl cover the dates with the hot water and soda. In another bowl cream together the sugar and shortening. Add the eggs and vanilla. Alternately add the flour and date mixture. Stir in the nuts. Pour the batter into 2 greased and floured 9″ cake pans and bake the layers at 350°F for 30 to 40 minutes, or until the cake tests done. Frost with Brown Sugar Frosting (see Index). Serves 12-14.

Italian Cream Cake

2 cups brown sugar
1 cup butter
5 eggs
1 teaspoon baking soda
1 cup sour milk or buttermilk (see hint on page 262)
2 cups flour
5 tablespoons cocoa
1 teaspoon cinnamon
2 cups sweetened, flaked coconut
½ cup raisins
1½ teaspoons vanilla
½ cup chopped pecans or walnuts

In the large bowl of an electric mixer cream the sugar and butter. Add the eggs, 1 at a time, beating well after each addition. In a 2-cup measuring cup stir the soda into the milk. Into another bowl sift the flour, cocoa, and cinnamon together and add alternately with the milk to the creamed butter and sugar. Fold in the coconut, raisins, vanilla, and nuts. Pour the batter into 3 greased and floured 8″ cake pans. Place the layers in a COLD OVEN, set the oven temperature at 375°F, and bake the cake for 1 hour. Frost the cake with Cream Cheese Icing (see Index). Serves 10-12.

Jewish Apple Cake

3-4 apples, peeled, cored, and sliced
1 teaspoon cinnamon and 2 tablespoons sugar, mixed
4 eggs
1 cup cooking oil
2 cups sugar
3 cups flour
3 teaspoons baking powder
3 teaspoons vanilla
¼ cup orange juice

In a bowl combine the apples and cinnamon-sugar mixture. In a large bowl mix together the eggs, oil, and sugar. Add the remaining ingredients, mixing well. Spoon ½ of the batter into a well-greased and lightly floured tube pan. Cover it with ½ of the apple mixture. Spoon the remaining batter into the pan and cover it with the remaining apples. Bake the cake at 350°F for 1½ hours, or until the batter puffs around the apples on top and is golden brown and spongy. Serves 12-14.

Do not grease and flour pans for classic angel food and chiffon cakes.

Uptown Chocolate Layer Cake

1½ cups butter
2 cups sugar
2 eggs
2 eggs, separated
3½ squares unsweetened chocolate
3 cups sifted cake flour
3 teaspoons baking powder
¾ teaspoon salt
½ teaspoon baking soda
1¼ cups milk
1 teaspoon vanilla
2 egg whites

In a large bowl cream together the butter and 1 cup of the sugar. Add the 2 whole eggs, 1 at a time, beating well after each addition. Add the 2 yolks to the mixture and blend thoroughly. In a double boiler melt the chocolate and add it to the sugar mixture, blending well. In another bowl combine the flour, baking powder, salt, and soda. Add the flour mixture to the sugar mixture alternately with the milk and vanilla. In the large bowl of an electric mixer combine the 4 egg whites. Beat the egg whites until stiff, gradually adding the remaining sugar. Add the egg whites to the batter. Pour the batter into 3 greased and floured 9″ cake pans and bake the layers at 325°F for 20 to 25 minutes. Let the cake cool. Frost the cake with Basic White Frosting. Serves 14-16.

BASIC WHITE FROSTING:
2 cups sugar
¾ cup water
¼ teaspoon cream of tartar
2 egg whites
1 teaspoon vanilla
½ cup finely chopped nuts (optional)
½ cup finely chopped cherries (optional)

In a saucepan over medium heat combine the sugar and water. Cook the mixture until a candy thermometer registers 238°F or to the soft ball stage. In the small bowl of an electric mixer combine the cream of tartar and egg whites and beat the mixture on high until stiff peaks form. Stir the syrup and vanilla into the egg whites and beat until spreading consistency is reached. Frost the cake and decorate it with the nuts and cherries.

Shiny metal or heatproof glass pans are preferred for cake baking, because they reflect heat away from the cake which produces a tender crust. When using glass pans, reduce the oven temperature 25°F.

Coconut Pound Cake

1 cup butter
½ cup margarine
3¾ cups sugar
6 eggs
3 cups sifted flour
¼ teaspoon baking soda
1 (8 ounce) carton sour cream
1 cup Angel Flake coconut
½ teaspoon coconut flavoring
¾ cup water
1 teaspoon almond flavoring

In the large bowl of an electric mixer cream the butter and margarine. Add 3 cups of the sugar gradually and cream the mixture at high speed for 10 minutes. Add the eggs, 1 at a time, beating well after each addition. Sift the flour with the baking soda. Add the flour mixture to the sugar mixture alternately with the sour cream and beat well. Fold in the coconut and the coconut flavoring. Pour the batter into a greased and floured 10″ tube pan and bake the cake at 325°F for 1½ hours. In a saucepan combine the remaining sugar, water, and almond flavoring and boil the glaze for 5 minutes. With a two-pronged fork, pierce holes in the hot cake and pour the glaze over it. Serves 12-14.

Cranberry Cake

2½ cups flour
1 cup sugar
¼ teaspoon salt
1 teaspoon baking powder
1 teaspoon baking soda
2 eggs
1 cup buttermilk
¾ cup Wesson oil
2 orange rinds, grated
1 cup cranberries
1 cup chopped nuts
1 cup chopped dates
1 cup orange juice
1 cup confectioners' sugar

Into a large bowl sift together the first 5 ingredients. In another bowl mix together the eggs, buttermilk, and oil, and add the mixture to the dry ingredients. Fold in the orange rind, cranberries, nuts, and dates. Pour the batter into a greased and floured bundt pan and bake the cake at 325°F for 60 to 75 minutes. In a small bowl mix the orange juice and confectioners' sugar together. While the cake is hot, pierce holes in the top with a two-pronged fork. Pour the glaze over the top of the cake. Serves 14-16.

Cotton Pickin' Good Cake

1 (18½ ounce) package butter cake mix

4 eggs

½ cup Wesson oil

1 cup finely chopped pecans

1 (11 ounce) can mandarin orange slices (reserve juice)

In a large bowl mix the first 4 ingredients together. Add the mandarin orange slices and juice and stir by hand. Pour the batter into 3 greased 9″ cake pans and bake at 350°F for 25 minutes. Let the layers cool well. Ice the cake with Cotton Pickin' Frosting. Serves 14-16.

COTTON PICKIN' FROSTING:

1 (20 ounce) can crushed pineapple (including juice)

1 (6 ounce) package instant vanilla pudding mix

1 (9 ounce) carton whipped topping

In a large bowl mix all ingredients together with a fork. Spread the frosting between the layers and on the top and sides of the cake. Refrigerate the iced cake.

Candied Fruit Cake

1½ pounds dates, chopped

1 pound candied pineapple, coarsely chopped

1 pound whole candied cherries

2 cups sifted flour

2 teaspoons baking powder

½ teaspoon salt

4 eggs

1 cup sugar

8 cups pecan halves

Grease 2 (9″ x 5″ x 3″) loaf pans with margarine. Line the sides and bottom of each pan with brown paper and grease the paper. Place the fruit in a large bowl and sift the dry ingredients over it. Using your fingers coat each piece of fruit with the dry mixture. In another bowl beat the eggs until they are frothy, gradually add the sugar, add to the fruit mixture, and stir well with a large spoon. Add the nuts and mix the ingredients together with your fingers. Pack the batter into the loaf pans, pressing it down with the palm of your hand. Bake the fruit cakes at 275°F for 1½ hours. The tops should look dry but not brown. Serves 20-24.

For even distribution of raisins in cake batter, heat them in the oven before adding to the batter.

Carrot-Nut Cake

1 cup butter (at room temperature)
1½ cups sugar
½ cup packed brown sugar
½ teaspoon cinnamon
1 lemon rind, grated
¼ teaspoon nutmeg
4 eggs (at room temperature)
3 cups sifted flour
3 teaspoons baking powder
½ teaspoon salt
½ cup fresh orange juice (at room temperature)
2 cups finely grated carrots (at room temperature)
½ cup finely chopped pecans
1 teaspoon vanilla

In the large bowl of an electric mixer cream together the butter, sugar, and brown sugar for 10 minutes or until the mixture is light and fluffy. Add the cinnamon, lemon rind, and nutmeg. Beat in the eggs, 1 at a time. Into a large bowl sift together the flour, baking powder, and salt. Add the flour mixture alternately with the orange juice, beginning and ending with the flour mixture. Stir in the carrots, pecans, and vanilla. Pour the batter into a greased and floured 10″ tube pan and bake at 350°F for 60 to 65 minutes, or until the cake tests done. Let the cake cool and ice it with Cream Cheese Icing. Serves 14-16.

CREAM CHEESE ICING:
4 ounces cream cheese (at room temperature)
½ cup butter (at room temperature)
2½ cups sifted confectioners' sugar
½ teaspoon vanilla

In a bowl cream together the cream cheese and butter. Slowly add the confectioners' sugar and vanilla and blend until the mixture is smooth. Spread the icing on a cooled cake.

Cake Pan Coat: Combine and blend thoroughly with a spoon 1 cup shortening and 1 cup flour. This is an easy alternative to greasing and flouring cake pans. Coat the cake pans thoroughly with the pan coat.

Brown Sugar Pound Cake

3 cups flour
½ teaspoon baking powder
¼ teaspoon salt
¾ cup butter (at room temperature)
¾ cup vegetable shortening
1 (1 pound) box light brown sugar
1 cup sugar
5 large eggs
1 cup milk
1½ teaspoons vanilla
1 cup chopped pecans

Into a large bowl sift together the flour, baking powder, and salt. In another large bowl cream the butter and shortening until light and creamy. Gradually add the brown sugar and sugar, mixing, until light and creamy. Beat in the eggs, 1 at a time. To the sugar mixture add the dry ingredients alternately with the milk, ending with the dry ingredients, and beat each addition just until blended. Stir in the vanilla and nuts. Pour the batter into a greased and floured 10″ tube pan. Bake at 325°F for 1¾ to 2 hours, or until the cake begins to pull away from the sides of the pan. Cool the cake upright for 10 minutes on a wire rack. Invert it on the rack and let cool. Serve unfrosted or with Brown Sugar Frosting. Serves 12-14.

BROWN SUGAR FROSTING:
½ cup butter or margarine
2½ tablespoons flour
½ cup milk
½ cup brown sugar
2 cups confectioners' sugar

In a saucepan melt the butter. Blend in the flour. Add the milk and cook for 1 minute, stirring constantly. Mix the sugars together in the medium bowl of an electric mixer. Add the milk mixture, a little at a time, blending at medium speed. Continue beating until the sugar is dissolved. Frosts a 2-layer (8-inch) cake.

Delicious on toast or biscuits
Lemon Cake Filling

6 tablespoons butter
3 whole eggs, beaten
1⅛ cups sugar
3 lemons, juiced

In a small saucepan melt the butter, cool it, and mix it with the eggs. Add the sugar and lemon juice. Cook the mixture slowly in a double boiler until thickened. Makes 1 cup.

Heavenly Hash Cake

1 cup margarine
2 cups sugar
2½ tablespoons cocoa
3 eggs
1½ cups sifted flour
½ teaspoon salt
1 teaspoon baking powder
1 teaspoon vanilla
1 cup chopped pecans
24 large marshmallows

In a large bowl mix all ingredients together except the marshmallows and pour the batter into a well-greased and floured 9″ x 13″ pan. Bake the cake at 325°F for 35 to 40 minutes. As soon as the cake is done, cut each marshmallow in half and place them on the hot cake. Let the cake cool for 10 minutes and cover with Icing. Serves 12-14.

ICING:
2 tablespoons cocoa
2 tablespoons butter, melted
2 cups confectioners' sugar
4 tablespoons evaporated milk
1 teaspoon vanilla

Mix all ingredients together in the large bowl of an electric mixer and beat the mixture until it is smooth. Spread the icing on top of the cake. Let the cake cool completely before cutting it into squares.

An excellent accompaniment for pound cake

Hard Sauce

1¼ cups milk
3 egg yolks
¼ cup sifted flour
1 teaspoon vanilla
½ cup sugar
½ teaspoon salt
3 tablespoons butter

In a bowl beat the milk into the egg yolks thoroughly by hand. Draw a fork through the liquid several times, removing any white pigment from the mixture. In a heavy saucepan over medium heat combine the milk mixture with the flour, vanilla, sugar, and salt, stirring constantly, until it is well blended and thickened. Remove the pan from the heat and stir in the butter. Let the sauce cool. Store the sauce in a jar, refrigerated, or serve it warm on slices of plain cake. Makes 2 cups.

Chess Cake

1 (18½ ounce) box yellow cake mix
2 eggs
1 cup butter, melted
1 (8 ounce) package cream cheese
2 eggs
1 (1 pound) box confectioners' sugar

In a large bowl mix together by hand the cake mix, 2 eggs, and ½ cup of the butter. Press the mixture into a lightly greased and floured 9" x 13" glass baking dish. In the bowl of an electric mixer blend the cream cheese, 2 eggs, remaining butter, and confectioners' sugar and pour the mixture over the pressed cake batter. Bake the cake at 350°F for a maximum of 45 minutes. Serves 12-14.

Pineapple Cake Filling

½ cup cornstarch
1 (20 ounce) can crushed pineapple
1¼ cups packed light brown sugar
¼ cup sugar
¼ teaspoon salt
¼ cup butter
1 teaspoon vanilla

In a heavy saucepan blend the cornstarch with the pineapple. Add the brown sugar, sugar, salt, and butter and cook over low heat, stirring constantly. When the filling is thick, remove it from the heat and add the vanilla. Let the filling cool and cover it with wax paper to keep a film from forming. The filling will be very thick. Fills a 2-layer (9-inch) cake.

Cooked Coconut Icing

1 cup milk
5 tablespoons flour
1 cup butter
1 cup confectioners' sugar
1 teaspoon vanilla or almond flavoring
3 ounces coconut

In a small saucepan combine the milk and flour and cook the mixture, stirring constantly, over low heat until it reaches the consistency of a thick paste. Set the mixture aside to cool and refrigerate it. In a bowl cream together the butter, sugar, and vanilla until the mixture is light and fluffy. Fold in the flour paste until thoroughly blended. Spread the icing on a cake and sprinkle it with the coconut. Frosts a 2-layer (9-inch) cake.

Prune Cake

2 cups flour
1 scant teaspoon salt
½ teaspoon nutmeg
½ teaspoon cinnamon
1½ cups sugar
3 eggs
1 cup Wesson oil
1 teaspoon baking soda
1 cup buttermilk
1 teaspoon vanilla
1 cup chopped, pecans
1 cup pitted, cooked prunes

Into a large bowl sift together the flour, salt, nutmeg, and cinnamon
and set aside. In the large bowl of an electric mixer beat the
sugar, eggs, and oil at medium speed until the mixture is fluffy.
In a 2-cup measuring cup combine the soda, buttermilk, and
vanilla. Stir to dissolve the soda and add to the sugar
mixture. Add the dry ingredients, all at once, and stir by hand until
well blended. Add the pecans and prunes and stir just until
they are well distributed throughout the batter. The batter will
be thin. Pour into a well buttered 9″ x 13″ pan and bake at 350°F
for 35 minutes. Check with a straw for doneness. While still hot,
spoon the Sauce over the cake. Cool the cake in the pan before
cutting it into squares for serving. Serves 12-14.

SAUCE:
½ teaspoon baking soda
½ cup buttermilk
1 tablespoon light Karo syrup
1 cup sugar
½ cup butter or margarine

In a medium saucepan over medium heat dissolve the soda in the
buttermilk. Add the syrup, sugar, and butter. Bring the mixture
to a boil and remove it from the heat. The sauce will be thin. Spoon
the sauce over the cake.

Orange Blossom Glaze

2 lemons, juiced, rinds grated
2 oranges, juiced, rinds grated
1 (1 pound) box confectioners' sugar, sifted

In a bowl combine the juices, rinds, and sugar. Cream together
all of the ingredients until very smooth. Frost immediately while
the cake or cupcakes are hot. Frosts a 2-layer (9-inch) cake.

To make sour or buttermilk from whole milk, use 1 tablespoon
vinegar or lemon juice PLUS enough whole milk to make 1 cup. Stir.

Fruit Cakes

4½ cups flour
1 (1 pound) box brown sugar
1 teaspoon salt
3 tablespoons baking powder
1 tablespoon cinnamon
1 tablespoon nutmeg
1 tablespoon ground cloves
1 tablespoon allspice
3 cups cane syrup
2 cups whiskey
1 pound pecans, chopped
3 pounds crystallized fruit, coarsely chopped
2 pounds dates, chopped
2 (9 ounce) boxes raisins
Bourbon or brandy to taste

Into a large bowl sift together all the dry ingredients. Gradually add the syrup and whiskey and mix well. Fold in the nuts and fruit. Pour the batter into paper-lined muffin tins. Bake at 350°F for 35 minutes. Test for doneness. Remove from the oven and cool completely. Store in an airtight container and baste the cakes with bourbon or brandy. Makes 30 cakes.

Stay-Soft Chocolate Frosting

⅓ cup cocoa
3 tablespoons cornstarch
1⅓ cups sugar
¼ teaspoon salt
1½ cups milk
1 teaspoon butter
1 teaspoon vanilla

In a saucepan combine the cocoa, cornstarch, sugar, salt, and milk. Cook the mixture over medium heat until thick, stirring often. Remove the pan from the heat and add the butter and vanilla. Let the frosting cool before spreading it. Frosts a 2-layer (9-inch) cake.

Lightly dust cake pans with cocoa instead of flour when making chocolate cake.

Apple Pie

5 *large apples, peeled and sliced*
½ *teaspoon cinnamon*
½ *teaspoon nutmeg*
2 *tablespoons flour*
1 *tablespoon lemon juice*
1 *(9 inch) pie shell, unbaked*
½ *cup butter or margarine*
½ *cup sugar*
½ *cup flour*

In a bowl mix the apples with the cinnamon, nutmeg, and 2 tablespoons flour and sprinkle the mixture with the lemon juice. Transfer the apple mixture to the pie shell. In another bowl mix the butter, sugar, and ½ cup flour until the mixture is crumbly. Pat the sugar mixture on top of the apple mixture. Place the pie in a large brown bag on a baking sheet and bake it at 425°F for 55 minutes. CAUTION: When using an electric oven, be especially careful that paper bag does not come in contact with heating elements. Serves 6.

Black Bottom Pie

½ *cup sugar*
1¼ *tablespoons cornstarch*
4 *eggs, separated*
2 *cups milk*
1¼ *ounces unsweetened chocolate squares, melted*
1 *teaspoon vanilla*
1 *(9 inch) chocolate wafer pie crust*
1¼ *tablespoons unflavored gelatin*
¼ *cup cold water*
4 *tablespoons rum*
4 *tablespoons sugar*
Whipped cream
Chocolate curls

In a bowl combine the sugar, cornstarch, and egg yolks. In a double boiler combine the milk and the egg yolk mixture. Cook, stirring, until the custard coats the spoon. Remove one cup of the custard, add the chocolate and vanilla, and pour the mixture into the chocolate wafer crust. Dissolve the gelatin in the water. Add the gelatin to the remaining custard, cool, and add the rum. In the large bowl of an electric mixer beat the egg whites, adding the sugar slowly, fold into the gelatin-custard mixture, and pile the filling on top of the chocolate custard in the crust. Refrigerate the pie for at least 8 hours. Decorate the pie with whipped cream and chocolate curls. Serves 8.

When rolling pie crust dough out, keep it in a circle by occasionally pushing the edge in gently with cupped hands.

Chocolate Pie

1 cup sugar
½ cup flour
4 tablespoons cocoa
1 teaspoon salt
3 eggs, separated
2 cups milk
1 teaspoon vanilla
2 tablespoons butter
1 (8 inch) pie shell, baked

In a heavy saucepan combine the sugar, flour, cocoa, and salt, stir until the ingredients are thoroughly combined, and add the egg yolks. Beat the yolks into the flour mixture until a paste is formed. Add the milk and stir until the paste has completely dissolved. Cook the mixture over medium heat, stirring constantly, until very thick and shiny. Remove from the heat and stir in the vanilla and butter. Pour the filling into the baked pie shell and prepare the meringue.

MERINGUE:
3 egg whites
1 teaspoon vanilla
¼ teaspoon cream of tartar
8 tablespoons sugar

In the large bowl of an electric mixer beat the egg whites, vanilla, and cream of tartar until stiff. Gradually add 1 tablespoon of sugar at a time continuing to beat until stiff peaks form. Spread the meringue over the top of the pie being sure to seal the edges to the crust. Bake the pie at 350°F on the middle rack for 12 to 15 minutes, or until the meringue is light golden brown. Cool the pie before cutting. Serves 8.

Coconut Pie

4 eggs, beaten
1¾ cups sugar
½ cup self-rising flour
2 cups milk
¼ cup margarine or butter, melted
Pinch of salt
1 tablespoon vanilla
1 cup Angel Flake coconut

Place all the ingredients except the coconut in a blender and blend well. Add the coconut and transfer the mixture to a well-buttered 9″ pie plate. Bake the pie at 350°F for 30 to 35 minutes, or until the custard is set. Serves 6-8.

Chocolate Fudge Pecan Pie

3 (1 ounce) squares unsweetened chocolate
3 tablespoons margarine
4 eggs
2 cups sugar
Pinch of salt
1 teaspoon lemon juice
1 cup broken pecans
1 (10 inch) pie shell, unbaked
1 cup whipping cream, whipped

In the top of a double boiler combine and melt the chocolate
and margarine. In the bowl of an electric mixer beat the eggs
slightly. Gradually add the sugar, salt, and lemon juice. Slowly add
the chocolate mixture until thoroughly blended. Stir in the
pecans. Pour the mixture into the unbaked pie shell. Bake at
350°F for 35 minutes, or until the pie is flaky. DO NOT CHILL.
Cool the pie completely and serve it topped with the whipped
cream. Serves 6-8.

Crème de Menthe Pie

1 box chocolate wafer cookies
1 tablespoon sugar
¼ cup butter, melted
20 marshmallows
½ cup milk
1 pint whipping cream
3 tablespoons crème de menthe
Fresh strawberries

Into a bowl finely crumble the cookies and stir in the sugar. Add
the butter and mix well. Press the mixture into a pie plate to form a
crust. In a saucepan combine the marshmallows and milk, cook
until the marshmallows melt, and cool completely. In a chilled
bowl beat the whipping cream with an electric mixer and add
the crème de menthe. Reserve ½ cup of the mixture for garnish
and fold the remainder into the cooled marshmallow mixture.
Pour the filling into the crust and chill the pie for at least 3 hours.
Serve the pie garnished with strawberries around the outer
edge and dollops of the reserved whipped cream. Serves 8.

When using self-rising flour, omit the salt.

Flaky Pie Crust

1¾ cups flour
1 teaspoon salt
5 tablespoons Crisco shortening
5 tablespoons water

Into a mixing bowl sift the flour. Add the salt and shortening.
With a fork or cutting knife begin cutting in the shortening
until it is well worked into the flour. This must be done thoroughly
before adding the water, or the dough will be tough. Add the
water and work it in briefly. DO NOT OVERWORK. Flour a
cloth or other surface and divide the dough into portions:
⅔ and ⅓, the larger for the bottom of a 2-crust pie. Lightly
flour the larger ball of dough and roll it out. Transfer the dough
to line a pie plate. Bake a fruit-filled pie, covered with the top
crust, at 350°F for 45 minutes. If the crust is to be filled after
it is baked, prick the bottom with a fork, and bake it at 350°F for
20 minutes.

Variation: When making crust for meat pie, add to the dough
pepper to taste and ¼ cup grated cheddar cheese.

Meringue Tips

Always have egg whites at room temperature before beating
them. Use at least 3 egg whites for meringue for 1 pie. Add ¼
teaspoon cream of tartar or salt when the meringue starts to get
frothy to stabilize it. Slowly add 3 tablespoons sugar for each
egg white after adding the cream of tartar or salt. The
meringue should always be sealed to the edges of the pie crust
to avoid shrinkage. Spread the meringue on the pie while the filling
is hot to prevent the meringue from weeping. If the pie is placed on
the middle shelf of the oven, it will brown evenly without burning.
When the meringue is almost the desired color, turn the oven
off and open the door slightly, and the meringe will cool slowly and
not crack or split. For ease in cutting through the meringue,
dip the knife in warm water.

Lemon Frozen Pie

1 (13 ounce) can evaporated milk, chilled
3 lemons, juiced
¾ cup sugar
2 cups graham cracker crumbs

In the bowl of an electric mixer beat the milk for several minutes.
Add the lemon juice and beat until very thick. Add the sugar and
beat until the sugar is dissolved. Line a 10″ pie pan with the cracker
crumbs. Pour the milk mixture into the pie pan and freeze.
Serves 8.

Crunchy Chocolate Pie

CRUST:

3 egg whites

1 teaspoon vanilla

1 cup sugar

¾ cup chopped pecans

1 teaspoon baking powder

¼ teaspoon salt

½ cup saltine cracker crumbs

In the large bowl of an electric mixer beat the egg whites until
they are stiff. To the egg whites, gradually add the vanilla
and sugar and beat until stiff. In a separate bowl combine the
pecans, baking powder, salt, and cracker crumbs. Fold this
mixture into the sugar mixture. Transfer the mixture to a
greased 9″ pie pan. Bake the crust at 300°F for 40 minutes, cool,
and pour in the Filling.

FILLING:

1 cup sugar

⅓ cup cocoa

⅓ cup flour

3 egg yolks

1¾ cups milk

1 teaspoon vanilla

2 tablespoons butter

1 pint whipping cream, whipped

In a medium saucepan combine the sugar, cocoa, flour, egg
yolks, and milk and cook for 20 minutes, stirring frequently,
or until the mixture is thick. Stir in the vanilla and butter and
cool. Transfer the filling to the pie crust. Top with the whipped
cream. Serves 6-8.

Million Dollar Pie

1 (14 ounce) can condensed milk

⅓ cup lemon juice

⅓ cup crushed pineapple, drained

⅓ cup chopped cherries, drained

½ cup chopped pecans

1 (8 ounce) container whipped topping

½ teaspoon vanilla or lemon flavoring

1 graham cracker crust

Pecan halves or cherry slices

In a large bowl combine the first 7 ingredients. Pour the mixture
into the crust and chill the pie for 1 hour. Serve the pie garnished
with pecan halves or cherry slices. Serves 8.

The best apples for pies are tart, firm, and juicy.

Frozen Coffee Pie

1½ cups ground pecans
¼ cup sugar
⅛ teaspoon salt
1 egg, separated
1 tablespoon instant coffee
½ cup milk
16 marshmallows
1 cup whipping cream, whipped
¼ teaspoon almond extract

Butter a 9″ pie plate. Line the bottom with foil and butter the foil. In a bowl mix the pecans, sugar and salt. In another bowl with an electric mixer beat the egg white until soft peaks form. Add the beaten egg white to the nut mixture and stir. Press the mixture into the pie plate and bake the crust at 375°F for 12 to 15 minutes or until light brown. Let the crust cool and slip it out of the foil onto a serving plate. In a saucepan combine the coffee, milk, and marshmallows and cook the mixture over low heat until the marshmallows melt. In a small bowl beat the egg yolk lightly. Stir in a small amount of the hot mixture and return to the saucepan. Cook 1 minute longer, stirring. Refrigerate, stirring occasionally, until thickened but not set. Fold in the whipped cream with the extract and transfer the mixture to the cooled crust. Place the pie in the refrigerator until time to serve. Serves 6-8.

Pecan Pie

½ cup butter or margarine
¾ cup light brown sugar
2 tablespoons flour
3 eggs, slightly beaten
1 cup light Karo syrup
Dash of salt
1 teaspoon vanilla
1 cup pecans
1 (9 inch) pie shell, unbaked

In a large bowl cream together the butter, brown sugar, and flour. Add the eggs and beat the mixture until it is smooth. Mix in the syrup, salt, and vanilla. Spread the pecans in the bottom of the unbaked pie shell and pour the mixture over them. Bake the pie at 350°F for 45 minutes. Cool the pie for 1 hour. Serves 6-8.

Frozen baked pie shells will keep for 4 months, unbaked shells for 2 months.

Pumpkin Pie

6 eggs
1 cup light brown sugar
1 cup sugar
1 teaspoon cinnamon
1/2 teaspoon ginger
1/4 teaspoon nutmeg
1/8 teaspoon ground cloves
2 (16 ounce) cans pumpkin
1 1/2 cups milk
1 cup whipping cream
3 (9 inch) pie shells, unbaked
1 cup whipped cream

In a large bowl beat the eggs slightly. Add the sugars, spices, and pumpkin and beat until well blended. Slowly add the milk and whipping cream. Divide the filling among the 3 pie shells and bake at 350°F for 60 to 70 minutes, or until a knife comes out clean when inserted in the center of the pie. Let the pies cool at least 2 hours and serve them garnished with whipped cream. Serves 18-24.

Strawberry Pie

1 1/2 cups flour
1 tablespoon sugar
1/2 teaspoon salt
2 tablespoons milk
1/2 cup oil
2 pints whole strawberries, washed and stemmed
1 cup sugar
3/4 cup water
3 tablespoons cornstarch
3 tablespoons light Karo syrup
3 tablespoons strawberry gelatin
1 pint whipping cream, whipped

In a large bowl combine the flour, 1 tablespoon sugar, salt, milk, and oil and press the mixture into a pie pan. Bake the crust at 400°F for 15 to 18 minutes. Cool the crust before filling it with whole strawberries stem side down. Fill the spaces with cut strawberries. In a saucepan bring 1 cup sugar, water, cornstarch, and Karo syrup to a boil, stirring often. Boil until the mixture is thick and clear. Stir in the gelatin. When cool, cover the strawberries with the glaze. Refrigerate the pie for 6 to 8 hours. Serve topped with whipped cream. Serves 6-8.

Bake fruit pies before freezing them. Do not freeze custard, cream, or meringue pies. Custard and cream fillings separate.

Strawberry Pie Delight

2-3 pints fresh strawberries
1 (10 inch) pie crust, unbaked
1¼ cups sugar
1 tablespoon lemon juice
4 tablespoons cornstarch
Whipped cream

Remove the stems from the strawberries, wash, and drain them. Sprinkle the pie crust with 2 tablespoons of the sugar, prick it with a fork, and bake it at 350°F for 10 to 15 minutes. Reserve 1 pint of the most perfect berries, dip them in the remaining sugar, and refrigerate them. In a saucepan mash the remaining berries. Add the remaining sugar, stirring well. Add enough water to make the mixture 2 cups. Add the lemon juice. Cook the mashed berries over low heat until the mixture simmers. In a cup mix the cornstarch in a small amount of cold water until it is dissolved and add it to the simmering mixture, stirring, until it is clear and thick. Cool the mixture until it is quite firm. Arrange a layer of ½ of the whole berries over the bottom of the pie crust. Pour the thickened sauce over the berries, top it with the remaining whole berries, and chill the pie for 2 hours. Serve the pie topped with whipped cream. Serves 8-10.

Pumpkin Chiffon Pie

1 cup brown sugar
3 egg yolks, slightly beaten
1½ cups pumpkin
½ cup milk
½ teaspoon salt
½ teaspoon ginger
¼ teaspoon allspice
2 teaspoons cinnamon
2 tablespoons unflavored gelatin
3 tablespoons cold water
3 egg whites, stiffly beaten
2 tablespoons sugar
1 (9 inch) pie shell, baked
Whipped cream

In a saucepan combine the brown sugar, egg yolks, pumpkin, milk, salt, and spices. Cook the mixture over low heat for 20 minutes, or until it is thick. In a cup soak the gelatin in the cold water until it is softened and add it to the hot mixture. Cool the mixture until it has thickened. In the bowl of an electric mixer beat the egg whites with the sugar until stiff and fold them into the pumpkin mixture. Pour the filling into the baked pie crust and chill the pie for 1 hour. Serve the pie topped with whipped cream. Serves 6-8.

Caramel Pie

CARAMEL SYRUP:

CARAMEL SYRUP:

1 cup sugar

½ cup boiling water

Sprinkle the sugar over the bottom of an iron or heavy aluminum skillet. Heat the sugar slowly over low heat, stirring constantly, with a long handled wooden spoon until light brown syrup forms. (It will form hard crystals and lumps before the syrup forms. This is normal.) Add the boiling water very slowly. It may form a hot, sticky mass at this point, but just keep cooking and it will melt down. Cook only until the water and sugar are well blended into a syrup. Remove the syrup from the heat and cool. Pour the syrup into a jar and store it at room temperature for several days.

PIE:

1 cup sugar

7-8 tablespoons flour

¼ teaspoon salt

1½ cups milk

3 eggs, separated

½ cup caramel syrup

1 tablespoon butter

1 teaspoon vanilla

¼ cup toasted pecans (optional)

2 (9 inch) pie shells, baked

3 egg whites

12 tablespoons sugar

1 teaspoon vanilla

In the top of a double boiler mix the sugar, flour, and salt. Add the milk slowly, stirring constantly. Cook over medium heat, stirring constantly, until the mixture is hot. Add the beaten egg yolks to the mixture. Stir in the caramel syrup. Stir often with a wire whisk to keep lumps from forming. When the mixture is thick, about 15 minutes, set it aside to cool for 5 minutes. Add the butter, vanilla, and pecans, mix, and pour the filling into the pie shells. In the large bowl of an electric mixer combine the 6 egg whites and beat until stiff, gradually adding the sugar. Fold in the vanilla and spread the meringue on the top of each pie. Bake at 400°F for 6 to 8 minutes or until golden brown. Cool and store the pies in the refrigerator. Serves 14-16.

New Orleans Chocolate Pie

1 cup sugar
2½-3 tablespoons cocoa
2½ tablespoons flour
Pinch of salt
¼ cup butter
2 egg yolks, beaten
2 cups milk
1½ teaspoons vanilla
1 (10 inch) pie crust, baked
Meringue

In a large saucepan combine the sugar, cocoa, flour, and salt.
Add the butter, egg yolks, and milk and cook the mixture over
low heat until it is thick. Stir in the vanilla, pour the filling into
the pie crust, cover with meringue, and bake it at 350°F for 12 to
15 minutes. Cool the pie before cutting it. Serves 8-10.

Strawberry Snowbank Pie

1 (9 inch) pastry shell, baked
2 cups strawberries
1½ cups sugar
½ cup water
Pinch of salt
½ teaspoon cream of tartar
3 egg whites
½ teaspoon almond extract
½ teaspoon vanilla

Fill the pastry shell with the berries. In a saucepan combine
the sugar, water, salt, and cream of tartar and boil the mixture until
it spins double threads. In the large bowl of an electric mixer,
beat the egg whites until stiff. Add the syrup mixture,
almond extract, and vanilla and continue beating until peaks
form. Pour the mixture over the berries and chill the pie for
1 hour. Serves 6-8.

Brownie Pie

1 (1 ounce) square unsweetened chocolate
1 cup butter
1 cup sugar
½ cup flour
2 eggs
1 teaspoon vanilla
½ cup chopped pecans
1 pint whipping cream, whipped or 1 pint vanilla ice cream

In the top of a double boiler melt the chocolate. In the bowl of an electric mixer cream the butter and sugar. Blend in the flour, eggs, vanilla, and chocolate. Stir in the pecans. Pour the mixture into a greased 9″ pie pan. Bake the pie at 375°F for 25 minutes. Cool the pie thoroughly and serve it topped with whipped cream. Serves 6-8.

Pecan Cream Cheese Pie

1 (8 ounce) package cream cheese
4 eggs
1/3 cup sugar
¼ teaspoon salt
2 teaspoons vanilla
1 (10 inch) pie shell, unbaked
1¼ cups coarsely chopped pecans
1 cup light or dark corn syrup
1 cup light brown sugar

In the bowl of an electric mixer beat the cream cheese, 1 of the eggs, 1/3 cup sugar, salt, and 1 teaspoon of the vanilla until light and fluffy. Spread the mixture on the bottom of the pie shell. Sprinkle the pecans on top. Beat the remaining eggs until they are light and fluffy. Add the syrup, remaining vanilla, and brown sugar and blend well. Pour the mixture into the pie shell. Bake the pie at 375°F for 45 minutes. Serves 8.

Strawberry Batter Pudding

9 tablespoons butter
⅓ cup flour
¼ teaspoon salt
2 cups milk
4 eggs, separated
1 cup sugar
1 pint fresh strawberries, crushed

In a bowl cream 3 tablespoons of the butter. Add the flour, salt, and milk and mix well. Beat the egg whites until they are stiff and set them aside. To the flour mixture add the egg yolks and beat well. Fold in the egg whites. Pour the batter into a greased 2-quart baking dish. Place the baking dish in a pan with hot water and bake it at 350°F for 45 minutes. In a bowl cream together the remaining butter and sugar. Add the strawberries, mix well, and refrigerate the sauce. Serve the pudding warm topped with the sauce. Serves 6-8.

Summer Delight

1 cup grated coconut
1 cup light brown sugar
½ cup slivered almonds
¼ cup butter, melted
¾ cup whole grape preserves
½ cup crushed pineapple, drained
¼ teaspoon lemon juice
1 quart vanilla ice cream, softened

In a bowl combine the coconut, sugar, almonds, and butter. Pack the mixture in a 9″ x 5″ x 3″ loaf pan to form the crust. In a separate bowl combine the preserves, pineapple, and lemon juice. Layer the ice cream and preserve mixture alternately in the pan, ending with the ice cream. Wrap the pan with plastic wrap and freeze it. Serves 6-8.

Fresh Fruit Cobbler

½ cup margarine
1 cup flour
1 cup sugar
¾ cup milk
1 teaspoon baking powder
½ teaspoon salt
3 cups fresh fruit, peeled

In a 3-quart baking dish melt the margarine in the oven. In a large bowl combine the flour, sugar, milk, baking powder, and salt and add the mixture to the melted margarine, mixing well. Top the batter with the fruit. Bake the cobbler at 350°F for 45 minutes, or until the top is browned. The batter will rise to the top.

Top Hat Bread Pudding

12 large eggs
3 (13 ounce) cans evaporated milk
1 quart skim milk
2 cups sugar
1 tablespoon vanilla
1 cup raisins
12 whole slices fresh sandwich bread
¼ cup confectioners' sugar
1 teaspoon cream of tartar

In 2 large bowls separate the yolks and whites of 9 of the eggs and add the remaining 3 whole eggs to the 9 yolks. With an electric mixer beat the yolks until they are creamy. Gradually add the evaporated milk, beating constantly, until creamy. Stir in the skim milk, sugar, vanilla, and raisins. Break the bread into small pieces and stir them into the custard. Let the bread soak in the custard mixture for 30 minutes. Pour the mixture into a 10″ x 14″ baking pan. Bake the pudding at 350°F for 1 ½ hours, or until it is set, stirring occasionally. Do not let the pudding get too dry. Beat the egg whites until soft peaks form. Combine the confectioners' sugar and cream of tartar and gradually add it to the meringue. Continue beating the meringue until stiff peaks form. Spread the meringue over the top of the pudding, return it to the oven, and bake it for 15 minutes, or until the meringue is golden brown. Serves 14.

Joseph Conrad Pudding

12 macaroons, crushed
6 tablespoons sugar
6 egg yolks
1½ teaspoons vanilla
2 cups half-and-half cream
Apricot or strawberry preserves
3 egg whites
¼ cup sugar

Into a 7″ x 11″ pan distribute the macaroon crumbs. In a bowl combine the sugar, egg yolks, and vanilla. Scald the cream, add it to the sugar mixture, and mix well. Pour the mixture over the macaroons. Place the pan in a pan of water and bake the pudding at 325°F for 1 hour or until set. Cover the hot pudding with scoops of preserves. In a bowl beat the egg whites, gradually adding the sugar, until the meringue is stiff. Cover the preserves with the meringue and return the pudding to the oven for 15 minutes. Serve the pudding hot or cold. Serves 8-10.

Line serving dishes for pudding with crushed chocolate or mint cookies for a taste treat. Save a few to sprinkle on top.

Soufflé Froid au Grand Marnier

1 (4 inch) slice sponge cake or 5 ladyfingers
5 ounces Grand Marnier
9 eggs, chilled
2 orange rinds, finely grated
1½ pints whipping cream, chilled
1½ cups confectioners' sugar, sifted
Pinch of salt
Chocolate curls or grated chocolate
Crisp sugar cookies

Surround a 2-quart soufflé dish with a strip of aluminum foil tied or pinned in place to make a collar that stands at least 3 inches above the rim of the dish. In a small bowl soak the cake in 3 ounces of the Grand Marnier to saturate it. Separate the eggs while they are still chilled and let them come to room temperature. The whites should contain no trace of yolk. In a chilled bowl whip the cream with chilled beaters and refrigerate it. In a small mixing bowl gradually combine the egg yolks, orange rinds, and ½ cup of the confectioners' sugar and continue beating at high speed for 5 minutes, or until the mixture is thick and lemon colored. When the yolks are sufficiently beaten, they will flow in a thick stream from the lifted beaters. With the electric mixer stir in the remaining Grand Marnier. Fold by hand the egg yolk mixture into the whipped cream. Fold in the saturated sponge cake. With clean dry beaters in a large mixing bowl (NOT PLASTIC) beat the egg whites with the pinch of salt until stiff peaks form. The egg whites should appear moist and glossy, not dry. Continue beating the egg whites for 1½ minutes, or until stiff peaks form. To the beaten egg whites add the remaining confectioners' sugar and continue blending the mixture gently. Blend together by hand the egg yolk mixture and the beaten egg whites. Transfer the mixture to the soufflé dish, letting it rise part way up the collar. Freeze the soufflé for at least 12 hours, but not more than 24 hours. Remove the foil collar and decorate the top of the soufflé with the chocolate curls. Serve the soufflé in the dish on a silver tray surrounded by the sugar cookies.

Test bread puddings and baked custards for doneness with a silver knife. Insert the knife in the center and if it comes out clean, it's ready.

Pecan Tarts

---

1 (3 ounce) package cream cheese
½ cup butter (at room temperature)
1 cup flour

In a bowl cream together the cream cheese and butter until smooth. Stir in the flour and mix well. Refrigerate the dough for 1 hour. Shape the dough into 24 balls. Make pastry shells by molding the dough balls on the outside of small muffin tins. Bake the shells on the inverted muffin tins at 350°F for 15 minutes. Prepare the Filling and fill each pastry shell with 1 teaspoon of the filling. Bake the tarts at 350°F for 17 minutes. Makes 24.

FILLING:
1 tablespoon butter
¾ cup brown sugar
1 egg, beaten
1 teaspoon vanilla
⅔ cup chopped pecans

In a saucepan melt the butter. Stir in the sugar and egg and blend thoroughly. Stir in the vanilla and pecans.

Saints' Reward

12-16 ladyfingers
½ cup apricot brandy
1 gallon strawberry royale or vanilla ice cream, slightly softened
1 cup strawberry jam

Line the bottom and sides of an 8″ springform pan with the ladyfingers. Sprinkle the ladyfingers with ⅔ of the brandy. Spoon ½ of the ice cream into the pan and pack it down. Pour the remaining brandy over the ice cream, turning the dish so that it runs down the sides. Fill the pan with the remaining ice cream to within ½ inch of the top of ladyfingers. Cover the top with the jam. Freeze the dish for 6 to 8 hours. Apply a small amount of warm water to the bottom and lower sides of the pan and unmold it on a serving plate. Return to the freezer until serving time. Serve the dessert cut in wedges. Serves 12.

Pour 3 tablespoons amaretto over individual servings of vanilla ice cream and garnish each with a sprig of mint.

Pavé au Chocolat

| French Buttercream Frosting |
| 2 tablespoons cherry brandy |
| ½ cup cold water |
| 2 dozen ladyfingers |
| Whipped cream |

Prepare the French Buttercream Frosting. Line the bottom of a 9″ loose bottom cake pan with wax paper. In a bowl combine the brandy and water and dip the ladyfingers, 1 at a time, in the liquid. (DO NOT SOAK.) Split the ladyfingers in halves lengthwise (many are already split for your convenience when purchased). Arrange 6 ladyfingers (12 half pieces), pinwheel fashion, in the pan. Cover with ½ of the frosting. Add another layer of 6 ladyfingers (12 half pieces) and top with remaining frosting. Arrange the remaining 12 ladyfingers (24 half pieces) on top, also in pinwheel fashion. Refrigerate for at least 2 hours. TO UNMOLD: Run a knife around the sides of the pan and INVERT onto a cake plate (what has been the top, with the most ladyfingers, now becomes the sturdy dessert bottom). Discard the wax paper and decorate the dish with rosettes of whipped cream. Serves 8.

| FRENCH BUTTER CREAM FROSTING: |
| 1 (6 ounce) package semi-sweet chocolate pieces |
| ¼ cup boiling water |
| ¼ cup confectioners' sugar |
| 4 egg yolks |
| ½ cup butter (at room temperature) |
| 2 tablespoons rum |

In the top of a double boiler melt the chocolate over boiling water. Remove from the heat and blend in the water. Add the sugar, egg yolks, butter, and rum and mix until smooth. Chill the frosting until it is of spreading consistency.

Lemon Dessert

| 1/3 cup lemon juice |
| 2 egg yolks |
| 1 tablespoon grated lemon rind |
| 1½ cups sugar |
| Dash of salt |
| 1 (13 ounce) can evaporated milk, chilled |
| 2 egg whites |
| 6 ounces vanilla wafers, crushed |

In a saucepan combine the lemon juice, egg yolks, lemon rind, ½ cup of the sugar, and salt and cook until just thickened. Remove from the heat and cool. In a bowl whip the milk and ½ cup of the sugar together. In a separate large bowl beat the egg whites and remaining sugar until stiff. Into the egg whites fold the whipped milk and cooked mixture. Sprinkle ½ of the wafers in the bottom of a 9″ x 13″ pan, pour the folded mixture into the pan, sprinkle the remaining crumbs on top, and freeze the dessert. Serves 12.

Chocolate Sundae Crunch

1 cup self-rising flour
¼ cup firmly packed brown sugar
½ cup butter or margarine
¾ cup chopped walnuts or pecans
1 (3 ¾ ounce) package instant French vanilla pudding
1 cup milk
1 pint vanilla ice cream, slightly softened
3 tablespoons milk
½ cup miniature marshmallows
½ cup semi-sweet chocolate bits

In a large mixing bowl combine the flour and brown sugar. Cut in
the butter until the mixture is crumbly and stir in the nuts. Spread
the crumb mixture in an ungreased 8" x 8" pan. Bake at 350°F for
25 to 30 minutes or until light golden brown and cool. In the large
bowl of an electric mixer combine the pudding mix with 1 cup
milk. Beat for 2 minutes at low speed, scraping the bowl
occasionally. Add the ice cream and blend at low speed just until
the mixture is smooth and creamy. In a double boiler combine the
3 tablespoons milk, marshmallows, and chocolate bits and
cook until melted. Remove the crust from the pan and crumble it.
Press the crumbs back into the pan, reserving ½ cup for the
topping. Pour the pudding mixture into the pan and sprinkle it with
the reserved crumbs. Drizzle the chocolate mixture over the
top and refrigerate the dessert for 2 hours, or until it is set. Serves 8.

Cup Custard

4 eggs
1 cup sugar
1 quart milk
1 teaspoon vanilla
Nutmeg

Preheat the oven to 450°F. In a large bowl mix the eggs and sugar
together until the eggs are well broken. Add the milk and vanilla;
stir until well blended. DO NOT BEAT. Fill 4 oz. custard cups.
Sprinkle with nutmeg. Place cups in a pan of water. Place in
preheated oven and turn oven down to 325°F. Bake
approximately 1 hour. Tops of custard will be a light golden
brown. To test for doneness, insert a knife blade. When it comes
out clean, the custards are done. Serve chilled. Serves 10.

Most puddings and custards are enhanced by a garnish of whole
berries or cherries, mandarin orange section, toasted coconut,
or chopped nuts.

Baked Lemon Custard Surprise

1 teaspoon water

4 egg yolks

1 cup sugar

⅓ cup lemon juice

3 tablespoons melted butter

1½ cups milk

¼ cup sifted flour

Pinch of salt

4 egg whites

In a large bowl combine the water and egg yolks and beat until frothy. Gradually beat in the sugar, lemon juice, and butter. Into a separate bowl sift together the flour and salt. To the egg yolk mixture stir in the milk alternately with the flour. In a separate bowl beat the egg whites until stiff and fold them into the egg yolk mixture. Pour the mixture into a 9″ x 5″ x 3″ loaf pan and set it in a pan of water. Bake the dessert at 350°F for 30 to 40 minutes. Serves 6-8.

Angel Chocolate Drop Cake

2 (6 ounce) packages chocolate chips

4 eggs, separated

½ pint whipping cream

3 tablespoons sugar

½ angel food cake

Pecans (optional)

Marshmallows (optional)

Chocolate curls (optional)

In a double boiler melt the chocolate chips and cool slightly. In a small bowl beat the egg yolks and fold them into chocolate. In a separate bowl with an electric mixer whip the cream. In the small bowl of an electric mixer beat the egg whites, gradually adding the sugar, until stiff. Transfer the chocolate to a large bowl and fold in ½ of the beaten egg whites. When thoroughly blended, gently fold in the whipped cream and remaining egg whites. Break the angel food cake in bite-size pieces into a 3-quart serving dish. Pour the chocolate-whipped cream mixture over the cake and fold it in gently, coating the cake pieces thoroughly, being careful not to break them. Gently fold in the pecans and marshmallows and decorate the dessert with chocolate curls. Refrigerate the dish overnight. Serves 8-10.

Rinse the pan in cold water before scalding milk to avoid coating.

Heavenly Chocolate Dessert

1 cup flour
½ cup butter (at room temperature)
¾ cup chopped walnuts or pecans
¾ cup Angel Flake coconut
1 (8 ounce) package cream cheese (at room temperature)
2 (8 ounce) containers whipped topping
¼ cup confectioners' sugar
1¾ cups milk
1 (4½ ounce) box instant chocolate pudding

In a medium bowl combine the flour, butter, ½ cup of the
nuts, and ½ cup of the coconut with a pastry cutter or a fork.
Mix until well blended and press the mixture into a well greased
10″ x 10″ x 2″ baking dish. Bake the crust at 350°F for 30 minutes or
until golden brown and cool. In a small bowl combine the cream
cheese, 1 container of the whipped topping and confectioners'
sugar, blend well, and spread the mixture evenly over the crust.
In a bowl blend together the milk and pudding mix for 2 minutes,
spread the pudding evenly over the filling, and chill until set.
Spread the remaining whipped topping evenly over the pudding
and sprinkle the top with the remaining nuts and coconut.
Refrigerate for at least 4 hours. Serves 8.

Mocha Mousse

1 tablespoon instant coffee
1 (1 ounce) square unsweetened chocolate
⅔ cup condensed milk
⅓ cup milk
½ teaspoon vanilla
1 cup whipping cream
Chocolate curls

In the top of a double boiler combine the coffee, chocolate,
and condensed milk. Heat the mixture, stirring constantly, until
the sauce is thick and smooth. Remove from the heat. Add the
milk and vanilla, stirring constantly. Put the saucepan into
the refrigerator along with an additional mixing bowl and chill
for 2 hours. Just before removing the sauce from the refrigerator,
in the chilled bowl beat the whipping cream until very thick and
gently fold in the mocha sauce. Chill the mousse, covered,
overnight. Before serving, beat the mocha mixture until it is
fluffy and spoon it into saucer champagne glasses. Serve the
mousse garnished with chocolate curls. Serves 6-8.

Jam Sauce for Ice Cream: In a saucepan combine ½ cup jam,
2 tablespoons hot water, and 2 teaspoons lemon juice and heat
thoroughly.

Apricot Mousse

1 (6 ounce) package dried apricots
1¼ cups sugar
1 envelope unflavored gelatin
4 egg whites (at room temperature)
Dash of salt
2½ cups whipping cream
½ teaspoon vanilla
½ teaspoon almond extract
1 tablespoon confectioners' sugar

In a 2-quart saucepan combine the apricots and 2½ cups water, bring to a boil, and simmer, covered, for 30 minutes. Liquid will be almost gone. Place ⅓ of the cooked apricots in a blender with ¼ cup water, cover, and blend until very smooth. Add the remaining apricots, ⅓ at a time, blending after each addition until very smooth. Stir in ¾ cup of the sugar and set aside. In a medium saucepan sprinkle the gelatin over ½ cup cold water and cook it over low heat, stirring until the gelatin is completely dissolved. Gradually add the gelatin to the apricots in the blender and purée until well combined. In a large bowl combine the egg whites and salt and beat with an electric mixer until soft peaks form. Gradually add the remaining sugar, beating after each addition. Continue beating until stiff peaks form. In a separate chilled bowl beat 2 cups of the whipping cream until stiff. Stir in the vanilla and almond extracts. With a large wire whisk gently fold the apricot purée into the whipped cream. Add the beaten whites in thirds, folding gently, until combined. Pour the apricot mousse mixture into a 2½-quart serving dish or 10 parfait glasses, cover with plastic wrap, and refrigerate. Chill the mousse for 6 hours or overnight. Just before serving, beat the remaining heavy cream with the confectioners' sugar until it forms soft peaks. Spoon a ring of whipped cream onto the surface of the mousse. Serves 10.

Only 85 calories per ½ cup serving
Chocolate Sherbet

½ cup sugar
¼ cup cocoa
1 (¼ ounce) envelope unflavored gelatin
⅓ teaspoon salt
2½ cups skim milk
1½ teaspoons vanilla

In a medium saucepan stir together the sugar, cocoa, gelatin, and salt. With a wire whisk beat in the milk. Cook the mixture over low heat, stirring, until the gelatin and sugar are dissolved. Stir in the vanilla. Freeze the sherbet for 4 hours or until firm but not hard. Transfer the sherbet to a large bowl and beat it until it is smooth. Transfer the mixture to a freezer container and freeze it, covered, for 4 hours. Serves 8.

Glazed Pears

6 large pears with stems
4 tablespoons lemon juice
3 cups water
¾ cup sugar
4 whole cloves
1 (12 ounce) jar orange marmalade
3 tablespoons orange liqueur
1 small bunch grapes
1 (16 ounce) can apricot halves, drained
Mint leaves

Pare and core the pears and rub them with 1 tablespoon of the lemon juice. In a Dutch oven combine the water, sugar, remaining lemon juice, and cloves and boil the mixture for 5 minutes. Reduce the heat and add the pears. Simmer the pears, covered, over low heat, turning frequently, for 20 to 30 minutes. Remove the pears and discard the cloves. Simmer the liquid until it is reduced to 1¼ cups. Stir in the marmalade, remove the syrup from heat, and let it cool. Add the liqueur. In a serving dish arrange the grapes and apricot halves around the pears. Pour the syrup over the fruit and garnish with mint leaves. Serves 6.

Orange Mousse

1 cup sugar
⅓ cup water
2 tablespoons grated orange rind
6 egg yolks
2 cups whipping cream

Surround a 2-quart soufflé dish with a strip of aluminum foil tied or pinned in place to make a collar that stands 3 inches above the rim of the dish. In a heavy saucepan combine the sugar, water, and orange rind and bring the mixture to a boil over moderately high heat. Cook the syrup until a candy thermometer registers 220°F. In a large mixing bowl beat the egg yolks until they are very thick. When the syrup is 220°F, begin pouring it in a very slow stream into the yolk mixture, beating constantly, until it is cool and thick. In a separate chilled bowl beat the whipping cream until it is stiff and fold it gently into the cooled egg yolk mixture. Transfer the mousse to the soufflé dish and freeze it for at least 6 hours. Serves 10-12.
VARIATION: Layer the mousse with ladyfingers drizzled with ½ cup orange liqueur before serving.

Party Pineapple Chantilly

1 *fresh pineapple*
1 *tablespoon brown sugar*
1 *tablespoon rum*
1 *tablespoon butter*
2 *tablespoons toasted slivered almonds*

Cut ⅓ of the pineapple off lengthwise, leaving the crown attached to the large portion. With a metal spoon remove the fruit from both pieces, leaving the shells and crown intact. Remove the core and dice the fruit. Mix the fruit with the brown sugar and rum. Pile the fruit back into the larger shell and dot it with the butter, reserving the small shell. Cover the crown with foil. Broil the pineapple about 6 inches from the heat for 10 minutes, or until it is thoroughly heated. Sprinkle with almonds and serve the fruit in the shell with Chantilly Sauce. Serves 4-6.

CHANTILLY SAUCE:
1 *cup half-and-half cream*
2 *egg yolks*
¼ *cup sugar*
¼ *teaspoon salt*
1 *tablespoon grated orange peel*
1 *tablespoon rum*
1 *cup whipping cream*

In a double boiler heat the cream over simmering water until tiny bubbles form around the sides of the pan. In a bowl beat the egg yolks slightly. Stir in the sugar and salt. Add the hot cream very slowly to the egg yolks, stirring constantly. Transfer the mixture to the double boiler and cook it over simmering water until it thickens enough to thinly coat a metal spoon. Remove the sauce from the heat and stir in the orange peel and rum. Cool the sauce completely and chill it. In a chilled bowl whip the cream until stiff and fold it into the chilled sauce. Serve the sauce chilled in the small pineapple shell.

Creamy Vanilla Ice Cream

1 *quart half-and-half cream*
1 *(6 ounce) package vanilla instant pudding*
4 *eggs*
1 *quart milk*
1 *(14 ounce) can condensed milk*
2 *tablespoons vanilla*

In the large bowl of an electric mixer combine all of the ingredients and mix thoroughly. Refrigerate the mixture overnight. Transfer the mixture to an ice cream freezer and proceed according to the manufacturer's directions. Allow 1 hour when using an electric ice cream freezer. Makes ½ gallon.
Variation: Add 2 cups mashed peaches and 2 teaspoons lemon juice.

Baklava

2 cups walnuts, ground
1 cup sugar
1 teaspoon cinnamon
1 pound phyllo dough
1½ cups melted butter
SYRUP:
1 cup water
1 teaspoon lemon juice
2 cups sugar or 1½ cups honey, heated

In a small bowl combine the nuts, sugar, and cinnamon and set aside. Butter a 9″ x 13″ baking pan. Place the phyllo sheets, 1 at a time, in the pan. Butter each phyllo sheet. After every third sheet spread a layer of the walnut mixture. Continue this procedure, ending with phyllo. Place the baklava pan in the freezer for 10 minutes. With a very sharp knife cut ¾ through the baklava in a diamond pattern (6 down, 4 across). Bake the baklava at 275°F for 1½ hours, or until it is golden brown. In a saucepan combine the water, lemon juice, and sugar and boil until syrupy. If you use honey, heat it. Pour the syrup evenly over the baklava while it is hot. Cool in the pan for at least 1 hour. When cool, cover. Serve the baklava at room temperature, being sure to complete cutting through the layers.
NOTE: This dessert may be made up to 2 days before serving. Serves 24.

Meringue Tarts

2 egg whites
Pinch of salt
1 teaspoon lemon juice
½ cup sugar

In the bowl of an electric mixer beat the egg whites with the salt until foamy. Add the lemon juice and beat until stiff. Gradually add the sugar and continue beating until glossy. Cover a large baking sheet with heavy brown paper. (Part of a grocery bag will do.) Heap 6-9 mounds of meringue on the paper, leaving equal distance between the mounds, and shape each into a shell with the back of a spoon. Bake the tarts at 275°F for 60 minutes. Turn off the heat and let the tarts stand in the oven until cool or overnight. Peel off the paper and store the tarts in a tight fitting container. Makes 6-9 tarts.
NOTE: Tarts may be filled with ice-cream, custard, fruits, etc.

European Cheesecake

1½ cups cinnamon graham cracker crumbs
1 cup very finely chopped nuts
⅓ cup butter, melted
1⅝ cups sugar
2½ (8 ounce) packages cream cheese
Pinch of salt
1½ teaspoons vanilla
4 eggs, separated
1 cup whipping cream, whipped
½ cup flour
1 cup fresh strawberries or blueberries
2 tablespoons cornstarch

In a bowl combine the crumbs, nuts, butter, and 2 tablespoons of the sugar and mix by hand until the ingredients are well blended. Spread the crumbs on the bottom of a thoroughly greased 9″ springform pan. Firmly press the mixture into the pan until the mixture holds together. In a large bowl with an electric mixer combine the cream cheese, ½ cup of the sugar, salt, and vanilla. Beat in the egg yolks. In a separate bowl beat the egg whites until they form soft peaks. Begin adding ½ cup of the sugar, 1 tablespoon at a time, beating after each addition. When the egg whites are stiff, add the whipped cream and the cream cheese mixture and sprinkle the flour on top. Gently fold all of the ingredients together. Pour the batter into the prepared pan and bake it at 300°F for 1½ hours, or until it is golden brown. Do not open the oven for 1 hour. Turn the oven off and let the cheesecake remain in it for 3 to 4 hours to cool. The cake may crack slightly, but this is expected. In a small pan combine the berries, remaining ½ cup sugar, and cornstarch. Cook the mixture over medium-high heat, stirring, until thick and bubbly. Remove the mixture from the heat when it becomes clear. Let the topping cool slightly and spread it on the cake. Serves 10-12.

A typical French dessert that Creoles serve to accompany a rich meal

Fresh Fruit with Vermouth

Whole fresh figs
Mandarin oranges
Peach halves or pineapple slices
Sweet vermouth
Unsweetened whipped cream
Fresh nutmeg

In a bowl marinate the fruit for 3 hours in enough vermouth to half cover the fruit. Turn the fruit 2 or 3 times while it is marinating. Cover the fruit completely with the whipped cream and turn it over once to blend the vermouth and cream. Refrigerate the mixture for 1 hour. Serve the dish with nutmeg grated over the top.

Orleans Cheese Pie

1½ rows Lorna Doone cookies, crumbled

½ cup margarine, melted

1 (8 ounce) package cream cheese

2 eggs

½ cup sugar

2 teaspoons vanilla

2 tablespoons lemon juice

1 (8 ounce) carton sour cream

¼ cup sugar

In a bowl combine the cookie crumbs and margarine. Press the
mixture into a 10″ pie pan or 9″ springform pan. In another bowl
combine the cream cheese, eggs, sugar, 1 teaspoon of the vanilla,
and 1 tablespoon of the lemon juice and stir until creamy. Transfer
the filling to the pie shell. Bake the pie at 350°F for 20 minutes.
Let the pie cool completely. In another bowl combine thoroughly
the sour cream, remaining vanilla, remaining lemon juice, and
sugar. Pour the mixture on top of the pie and return it to the oven
for 15 minutes. Refrigerate the pie overnight. Serves 8.

Jelly Roll with Assorted Fillings

---

1 cup flour

1 teaspoon baking powder

¼ teaspoon salt

3 large eggs

1 cup sugar

⅓ cup water

1 teaspoon vanilla

Confectioners' sugar, sifted

Prepare the filling before beginning to prepare the cake. Line a
jelly-roll pan with wax paper. Into a bowl sift the flour. Add the
baking powder and salt and blend well. In a medium bowl beat
the eggs with an electric mixer until they are very thick and lemon
colored. Continue beating while adding the sugar slowly. Turn
the mixer to low and gradually add the water and vanilla. Slowly
mix in the dry ingredients until the batter is smooth. Pour the
batter into the paper-lined pan and bake it at 375°F for 12 to 15
minutes, or until the cake just starts to leave the sides of the wax
paper. Turn the cake onto a sheet of wax paper that has been coated
with confectioners' sugar and let cool for 1 to 2 minutes. Peel the
wax paper away from the bottom of the cake. If the edges are
crisp, trim them with a bread knife. Spread the hot cake with the
filling. To roll it, tuck in the long edge of the cake and roll it
to the other end using the wax paper under cake to wrap the roll.
Twist the ends and place the roll on a wire rack to cool.

CHOCOLATE JELLY ROLL:

Add 1 tablespoon cocoa to the Jelly Roll ingredients if using chocolate filling. Add 4 tablespoons cocoa to the Jelly Roll ingredients if using vanilla filling.

CARAMEL FILLING:

1 (14 ounce) can condensed milk
½ cup chopped pecans (optional)

Place the unopened can of milk in a pot of boiling water and boil it for 2½ hours, always keeping the top of the can covered with water. Spread the caramel on the cake, sprinkle it with the pecans, and roll it.

CHOCOLATE FILLING:

4 tablespoons flour
½ cup sugar
1 teaspoon salt
4 tablespoons cocoa
3 egg yolks
1½ cups half-and-half cream
1 teaspoon vanilla
2 tablespoons butter

In a medium heavy pot combine the flour, sugar, salt, and cocoa until thoroughly blended. Stir the egg yolks into the flour mixture with wooden spoon to form a paste. Stir in the cream until the paste is completely dissolved. Place the pot over medium heat and stir the mixture constantly until it is very thick. Remove the filling from the heat. Add the vanilla and butter and stir until the butter melts. Spread the filling on the cake and roll it.

VANILLA FILLING:

1 cup whipping cream
⅓ cup confectioners' sugar
½ teaspoon vanilla
Cherries, minced (optional)
Nuts, finely chopped (optional)
Coconut (optional)

In a bowl combine the cream, sugar, and vanilla. With an electric mixer beat the mixture until it is stiff. Spread the filling over a cooled jelly roll that has been rolled in a towel to cool.

Cream Puffs

1 cup water
½ cup butter
2 teaspoons sugar
¼ teaspoon salt
1 cup sifted flour
4 large eggs
FILLING:
1 cup milk
¼ cup sugar
4 egg yolks
2 tablespoons cornstarch
Pinch of salt
1 tablespoon vanilla
Confectioners' sugar

In a heavy saucepan bring the water to a boil. Stir in the butter, sugar, and salt. When the butter is melted, add the flour, stirring hard, until the paste no longer clings to the sides of the pan. Remove the mixture from the heat. Add the eggs, 1 at a time, beating thoroughly, with a wooden spoon. Drop the mixture by spoonfuls on a jelly-roll pan, or use a pastry bag without the tip. Bake the puffs at 400°F for 12 minutes, REDUCE OVEN TEMPERATURE to 375°F, and bake them for 15 minutes, or until they are puffed and golden. Transfer them to a rack to cool. In a heavy saucepan with a wire whisk combine and beat the milk, sugar, egg yolks, cornstarch, and salt. Cook the filling over moderate heat, stirring constantly. Bring the filling to a boil and continue boiling, stirring constantly, until it is very thick. Remove the filling from the heat and stir in the vanilla. With a small knife slit the side of each puff. Fill a pastry bag with the filling and press the filling into the puffs. Sprinkle the filled puffs with confectioners' sugar. Makes 24.

Apple-Pecan Delight

2 eggs, well beaten
1 cup sugar
½ cup sifted flour
2 teaspoons baking powder
¼ teaspoon salt
½ cup chopped apples
1 cup chopped pecans or walnuts
1 teaspoon vanilla
½ cup whipping cream, whipped
Cherries

In a large bowl cream together the eggs and sugar until light and fluffy. Into a separate bowl sift together all of the dry ingredients and gradually add to the sugar mixture, beating only until thoroughly combined. Fold in the apples and nuts. Add the vanilla. Pour the mixture into a 9″ pie pan. Bake the dessert at 350°F for 30 minutes. Serve the dessert warm or chilled, garnished with whipped cream and cherries.

Big Apple Bake

PASTRY:
2 cups flour
1 teaspoon salt
⅔ cup plus 2 tablespoons shortening
4-5 tablespoons cold water
30 inches heavy-duty foil
FILLING:
7 medium tart apples
½ cup sugar
1 teaspoon cinnamon
¼ teaspoon nutmeg
TOPPING:
¾ cup flour
½ cup sugar
½ cup butter or margarine

To prepare the pastry, in a bowl combine the flour and salt.
Add the shortening and cut it in until the mixture is crumbly.
Blend in the water and form the dough into a ball. Cut 2 (15 inch)
circles of foil. Place each on a baking sheet. Place ½ of the pastry
dough on each circle. Roll out the pastry to the size of the
foil and trim. Core, peel, and slice the apples in thin slices.
Beginning ¾ inch from the edge of the pastry overlap the apple
slices making 2 circles on each pastry. Combine the sugar and
spices. Sprinkle this mixture over the apples. To make the
topping combine the flour and sugar. Cut in the butter until
crumbly. Sprinkle ½ of the topping over each pastry round. Turn
up the ¾ inch rim of the pastry and foil. Use your fingers to
flute the edges. Bake at 450°F for 20 to 25 minutes, or until
the crust is brown and the apples are done. Serve each cut in
10 wedges.
NOTE: If apples aren't tart, sprinkle with 1 ½ tablespoons lemon
juice.

Tipsy Dessert

1 package unflavored gelatin
¼ cup cold water
2 cups hot milk
2 egg yolks, slightly beaten
½ cup sugar
½ cup sherry
2 egg whites, stiffly beaten
1 cup whipping cream, whipped
2 dozen ladyfingers, split

In a bowl soften the gelatin in the water. Stir in the milk, egg
yolks, sugar, and sherry. Chill the mixture until it begins to
congeal. Fold in the beaten egg whites and whipped cream. Line
a 2-quart mold or bowl with ladyfingers. Add alternate layers
of the gelatin mixture and ladyfingers. Chill the dish for at least
8 hours. Serves 8.

Old Time Bread Pudding

4 slices buttered toast, quartered
½ cup seedless raisins
2 eggs, slightly beaten
¼ cup sugar
⅛ teaspoon salt
1 cup evaportated milk
1 cup boiling water
1 teaspoon vanilla
4 teaspoons sugar
¼ teaspoon cinnamon

Arrange the toast in a buttered 1½-quart baking dish. Sprinkle the raisins over the toast. In a bowl combine the eggs, sugar, salt, milk, water, and vanilla. Pour the mixture over the toast and let it stand for 10 minutes. In a cup combine the sugar and cinnamon and sprinkle the mixture over the dish. Bake the pudding at 350°F for 30 minutes, or until a knife inserted in the center comes out clean. Serve the pudding topped with the Sauce. Serves 4.

SAUCE:
½ cup butter or margarine
1 cup sugar
1 egg, beaten
Whiskey or rum to taste

In a double boiler combine the butter and sugar and cook until the mixture is very hot and the sugar is well dissolved. Add the egg and beat the mixture with a wire whisk, briskly. Let the sauce cool and add the whiskey. Serve the sauce warm.

Blueberry Delight

1 cup margarine
½ cup light brown sugar
1 cup flour
¾ cup chopped pecans
1 (8 ounce) package Philadelphia cream cheese (at room temperature)
1 cup confectioners' sugar
2 envelopes Dream Whip
1 cup cold milk
1 teaspoon vanilla
1 (21 ounce) can blueberry pie filling, chilled

In a bowl with an electric mixer cream together the margarine and brown sugar. Add the flour and pecans and mix well. Press the mixture into the bottom of a 9″ x 13″ pan. Bake the crust at 350°F for 12 minutes and let it cool. In a large bowl combine the cream cheese and sugar. In a separate bowl whip the Dream Whip with the milk and vanilla and add it to the cream cheese mixture. Spoon the filling over the crust and top it with the pie filling. Chill the dessert and serve it cut in squares. Serves 20.

RESTAURANT RECIPES

One of the glories of New Orleans is its restaurants.
Some are grand, some simple. Some are internationally
known, while others cater mostly to the inhabitants
of a particular neighborhood. Most serve a version of
the local cooking, and each has something it makes
especially well. Together, they help make New Orleans
still what Thackeray once said it was, "the old
Franco-Spanish city on the banks of the Mississippi,
where, of all the cities in the world, you can eat the most
and suffer the least . . . "

NEW ORLEANS RESTAURANTS

Courtyards, fountains, beautiful flourishing greenery—these have been painted for decades as typical scenes of New Orleans. And they are typical—not only of a distant past culture in a romantic city, but still typical of a viable, active city; where beauty is as necessary as good food to the existence of its inhabitants.

From: Andrew Jackson Restaurant
Red Snapper Beluche

4 filets of red snapper (5 to 6 ounce)
16 medium size raw shrimp
1 cup flour
1 small white onion
3 green onions
1 pound oleo
4 potatoes (Snowflake)
1 cup milk
⅛ pound butter
Salt
1 oak plank or saucer (about 6 inches in diameter)

Melt oleo, place peeled, deveined, butterfly shrimp together
with chopped white and green onions. Cook on medium fire until
shrimp are done. Salt red snapper, pass through flour, grill
on greased pan, cook on both sides until golden brown. Boil potatoes,
mash, add milk, and butter. Spoon into pastry bag. Line outer
edge of board or plate with approximately ½ inch wall. Place filet
of fish in center of board. Spoon shrimp and sauce generously.
Yields 4 servings.

From: Andrew Jackson Restaurant
Lobster Savannah

5 whole lobsters
½ pound oleo
1 bell pepper
1 small white onion
1 ounce pimento
1 quart milk
5 ounces flour
½ pound mushrooms
5 ounces sherry

Sauté pepper, onion in margarine, add mushrooms, flour.
Heat milk separately and add stirring to keep consistency smooth.
Add pimento, salt and white pepper to taste, while simmering
add sherry. Lobster should be cut in half and meat removed.
Add meat from lobster to sauce and heat through and through. Stuff
lobster shell with above ingredients, top with grated cheddar
cheese and put in oven to brown. Serves 10 persons.

From: Andrew Jackson Restaurant
Caesar Salad

1 dash salt
3 pieces garlic
3 anchovies
4 dashes Worcestershire sauce
1 egg
1 squeeze of ½ lemon
2 tablespoons wine vinegar
6 tablespoons oil
1 dash dry mustard
¼ cup Parmesan cheese
Romain lettuce
Cracked pepper
¼ cup croutons

Add dash salt to dry salad bowl. Crush garlic pieces and anchovies
in bottom of bowl. Add Worcestershire and coddled egg, blend
mixture. Add wine vinegar and oil; add dry mustard and dash
of Parmesan; blend mixture, add lemon juice. Place Romain into
bowl containing salad dressing. Add croutons; toss salad until lettuce
leaves are coated with dressing. Serve salad on ice cold plates;
add dash of cracked pepper per serving. Top each serving with
healthy sprinkling of Parmesan cheese. For 6.

From: Alzina Pierce
of the Bon Ton Restaurant

Shrimp and Oyster Jambalaya

4 dozen medium shrimp
4 dozen oysters
3 large white onions
3 bell peppers
3 stems of celery
½ cup shortening
1 teaspoon chopped garlic
2 small cans tomato paste

Melt shortening, add chopped onions, chopped garlic, bell
pepper, tomato paste and cook about 2 hours. Add shrimp and
cook about 10 minutes. Add oysters and cook about 15 minutes.
Add 2 cups cooked rice and serve. Serving for 10.

From: Alzina Pierce
of the Bon Ton Restaurant

12 Stuffed Eggplant (Halves)

6 medium eggplants
1 pound small shrimp
1 pound white lump crab meat
4 bell peppers
4 medium onions
½ cup parsley
3 pods garlic
Salt and pepper to taste
½ cup celery
Bread crumbs

Boil eggplants till soft; then dig out meat. Save eggplant shells. While you are doing this, fry bell peppers, onion, celery and garlic together till limp, then add eggplant meat. Let smother on medium fire till most water is cooked out, then add shrimp. Cook for another 20 minutes, then put all of this in another bowl and fold in crab meat and parsley. Let cool a little, then add enough bread crumbs to be firm enough to stuff shells. Sprinkle a little bread crumbs on top and paprika. Then sprinkle a little oil or oleo on top. Bake till done or brown in 350°F oven.

From: Alzina Pierce
of the Bon Ton Restaurant

Bread Pudding

1 loaf French bread
1 quart milk
3 eggs
2 cups sugar
2 tablespoons vanilla
3 tablespoons oleo
1 cup raisins

Soak bread in milk; crush with hands till well mixed. Then add eggs, sugar, vanilla and raisins and stir well. Pour oleo in bottom of thick pan and bake till very firm. Let cool; then cube pudding and put in individual dessert dish; when ready to serve, add sauce and heat under broiler. Serve with Whiskey Sauce.

WHISKEY SAUCE:
1 stick of butter or oleo
1 cup sugar - cream sugar
1 egg

Cook sugar and butter in double boiler till very hot and well dissolved. Then add well beaten egg and whip real fast so egg doesn't curdle. Let cool and add whiskey to taste.

From: Alzina Pierce
of the Bon Ton Restaurant

Crab Meat Imperial

1 pound crab meat
½ pound butter
1 bunch green onions
1 tablespoon chopped pimento
1 cup olive oil
Few sliced mushrooms
1 tablespoon sherry

Sauté green onions in ½ pound butter about 5 minutes. Add olive oil, pimento, crab meat, mushrooms, dash of salt and pepper, sauté about 5 minutes. Add 1 tablespoon sherry, serve on toast points. 4 servings.

From: Alzina Pierce
of the Bon Ton Restaurant

Shrimp Etouffee

1 tablespoon butter
1 cup small shrimp
¼ teaspoon chopped garlic
Dash of salt and pepper
1 teaspoon chopped parsley

Melt butter, add shrimp, salt and pepper and garlic. Cook about 10 minutes, add parsley. Serve with parsley buttered rice. 1 serving.

From: Brennan's

Veal Jason

Pound 2 (3 ounce) medallions of veal until thin. Lightly salt and pepper. Dip in beaten egg and thoroughly cover with Progresso Italian bread crumbs. Sauté in butter until golden brown.

SAUCE:
½ cup sour cream
3 tablespoons ketchup
Juice from ¼ lemon
2 dashes Lea and Perrins
1 tablespoon butter

Blend ingredients together and heat.

From: Brennan's
Shrimp Creole

½ cup vegetable oil
1 cup coarsely chopped green pepper
2 cups coarsely chopped onion
1 cup coarsely chopped celery
2 tablespoons minced garlic
2 cups whole tomatoes
1 tablespoon paprika
¼ teaspoon cayenne
1 teaspoon salt
1 teaspoon white pepper
3 cups water
1 bay leaf
2 tablespoons cornstarch
3 pounds raw shrimp, peeled and deveined

Heat vegetable oil and sauté first four ingredients until tender, add tomatoes and cook 3-4 more minutes. Stir in paprika, cayenne, salt, pepper, water and bay leaf. Simmer 15 minutes. Add shrimp and continue to cook an additional 15 minutes. Thicken with cornstarch mixed in cold water. Serve with hot fluffy rice.

From: Brennan's
Brennan's Oyster Soup

1 cup butter
2 cups celery, finely chopped
2 cups green onions, finely chopped
2 tablespoons flour
2 tablespoons garlic, finely chopped
4 dozen large, freshly shucked oysters
12 cups oyster water (the oyster liquor plus sufficient water to make up to 12 cups)
2 bay leaves
2 teaspoons salt
1 teaspoon white pepper

Melt the butter over medium heat in a 6-quart heavy saucepan, then sauté the celery and green onions until tender but not browned, stirring frequently. Gradually stir in the flour and cook 5 minutes longer, stirring constantly, over low heat. Add the remaining ingredients and simmer for 20 minutes. Remove the pan from the heat and scoop out the bay leaves with a slotted spoon or a long fork; discard. Serve immediately. For eight.

From: Brennan's
Eggs Hussarde

2 thin slices of Canadian Bacon, grilled
2 Holland Rusks
¼ cup Marchand de Vin Sauce
1 Grilled Tomato
2 poached eggs
¼ cup Hollandaise Sauce

On a dinner plate, lay slices of Canadian Bacon on 2 Holland
Rusks, then cover each with Marchand de Vin Sauce. Top now each
rusk with a poached egg and top with the Hollandaise Sauce.
Garnish with Grilled Tomato. For eye appeal, you may sprinkle
paprika and chopped parsley on eggs.

MARCHAND DE VIN SAUCE:

¾ cup butter
¾ cup finely chopped mushrooms
½ cup minced ham
⅓ cup finely chopped shallots
½ cup finely chopped onions
2 tablespoons minced garlic
2 tablespoons flour
1 teaspoon salt
1 teaspoon white pepper
½ teaspoon cayenne
¾ cup beef stock
½ cup red wine

Melt butter in a medium saucepan and lightly saute mushrooms,
ham, shallots, onions and garlic. When onion is golden brown,
add the flour, salt, pepper and cayenne, then brown well,
about 7-10 minutes. Blend in the stock and wine and simmer
over low heat for 35 minutes.

HOLLANDAISE SAUCE:

4 egg yolks
2 tablespoons lemon juice
½ pound of melted butter
¼ teaspoon salt

In the top half of double boiler, heat egg yolks and lemon
juice. Cook very slowly in double boiler over low heat, never
allowing water in bottom pan to come to a boil. Add butter,
a little at a time, stirring constantly with a wooden spoon. When
mixture thickens, add salt and pepper.

From: Broussard's Restaurant

Crepes Brulatour

1 pound cream cheese
1 cup sugar
2 tablespoons vanilla
½ cup chopped pecans
1 ounce half-and-half

Let cream cheese get room temperature, mix with sugar, half-and-half, vanilla and chopped pecans, mix thoroughly. Set in box and chill.

CRÊPES:
1 cup milk
3 eggs
1 teaspoon vanilla
½ cup flour
2 ounces vegetable oil

Put all ingredients in mixing machine and mix at high speed for five minutes. Let set at least thirty minutes. Cook in greased 8 inch saute pan. Roll one tablespoon of the above filling in each crepe.

TOPPINGS:
1 quart strawberries
4 ounces cherry brandy liqueur
2 ounces strawberry liqueur
4 ounces butter
1 pint whipping cream
4 ounces powdered sugar
1 tablespoon vanilla
1 jar of prepared Melba sauce

Put four ounces of butter in chafing pan, add strawberries, cook until thick, add cherry brandy and flame with strawberry liqueur, put crepes in strawberries, simmer, place on plate and top with strawberries, rosette of whipped cream and Melba sauce.

From: Broussard's Restaurant

Shrimp Ernie

1 pound (15-20 count) shrimp
Egg wash
Corn flour
Deep fat to fry shrimp

SAUCE FOR DIP:
1 pint mayonnaise
2 green onions, cut fine
2 tablespoons horseradish
¼ cup creole mustard
2 tablespoons chopped parsley
1 clove of garlic minced very finely

In a mixing bowl add ingredients, stir well with wire whip. Let stand at least one hour before serving. Clean shrimp, let fan tail remain on, split and devein. Season yellow corn flour with salt and pepper. Dip shrimp in egg wash and roll in corn flour. Drop in deep fat at 325°F and cook about five minutes. Serves 5.

From: Broussard's Restaurant

Crab Bisque

4 hard crabs, cleaned and cut
¼ cup onion, diced
½ pound lump crab meat
2 celery ribs, diced
1 quart half-and-half
8 ounces butter
¾ cup flour
1 gallon chicken stock

Melt butter in soup pot, add crabs, cook until crabs are dry. Add onion and celery, cook until tender add flour and blend the roux, add chicken stock, let simmer at least thirty minutes. Heat half-and-half and blend in soup. Strain soup, add lump crab meat and serve. Serves 6 or 8.

From: Broussard's Restaurant

Redfish Bonaparte

2 (8 ounce) redfish
½ pound lump crab meat
4 ounces lemon juice
8 ounces butter
12 large shrimp
Salt
Pepper
2 eggs
1 cup milk
1 cup flour

Dip redfish in egg wash (2 eggs and 1 cup milk) and flour.
Saute in 2 ounces butter in pan until golden brown. Remove from
pan, place on hot platter. Saute crab meat and butter (2 ounces)
with 2 ounces of lemon juice, add salt and pepper to taste.
Place redfish on platter, cover with crab meat, and shrimp, 3
shrimp per serving. Glaze under broiler. Serve immediately.
Serves 4.

From: The Caribbean Room
of the Pontchartrain Hotel

Crab Meat Remick

1 pound lump crab meat
6 small pieces cooked bacon

SAUCE:
½ teaspoon dry mustard
½ teaspoon paprika
½ teaspoon celery salt
½ teaspoon Tabasco
½ cup chili sauce
½ cup mayonnaise
1 teaspoon Tarragon vinegar

Divide the crab meat into 6 portions, pile into individual remekins.
Heat in oven. While waiting for crab meat to heat, proceed
with making sauce. Blend together all dry ingredients and
Tabasco Sauce. Add chili sauce and Tarragon vinegar, mix well.
Then blend in mayonnaise. When crab meat is very hot, place a
piece of crisp bacon in the middle of each ramekin and on top
spread the Remick Sauce, just enough to cover. Return ramekin
to oven just for a few seconds and serve immediately. (The
Remick Sauce will separate if dish is left inside oven too long.)

From: The Caribbean Room of the Pontchartrain Hotel

Oysters en Brochette

½ pound bacon (strips, cut into 2-inch lengths)
3 dozen fresh, select oysters
2 cups flour
4-6 tablespoons solid shortening

In a skillet, fry bacon until transparent, but not crisp. Remove and drain. On a 10-inch skewer, alternate pieces of bacon and oysters, using approximately 9 oysters per skewer. Dredge skewered oysters and bacon in flour until well coated. Shake off excess flour and sauté in shortening until crisp on the outside and golden brown. Remove from sauté pan, slide skewer out. Garnish with half broiled tomato, parsley and slice of lemon. 4 servings.

From: The Caribbean Room of the Pontchartrain Hotel

The Pontchartrain's Tenderloin of Trout Veronique

4 trout fillets from 1 ½ pound trout
½ pint sauterne wine
1 lemon
1 ½ pints Hollandaise Sauce
½ pound white grapes

Poach trout in equal parts water and sauterne wine and juice of one lemon. Place trout on plate. Cover with four split grapes and Hollandaise Sauce. Brown under broiler and serve. Serves 4.

From: Christian's Restaurant

Chocolate Mousse

2 egg whites
125 grams sugar
½ quart whipping cream
170 grams vanilla sweet chocolate, combined with
3 tablespoons water

Combine the egg whites and sugar and make a genoise meringue.
Melt the chocolate in a double boiler until just melted, then
stir until smooth. Fold the chocolate into the meringue then chill.
Meanwhile chill the whipping cream and beat until stiff. Fold
the whipped cream into the previously prepared mixture and chill.

From: Christian's Restaurant

Redfish Froid
Served with Horseradish Sauce

6 (3 ounce) filets of redfish

"Redfish" is a specialty fish of the region, but any boneless
filet of fish will work for this formula. Poach the fish and cool
it in the court bouillon, possibly overnight in refrigerator.
Next day, drain and mask with the Horseradish Sauce. Serve on beds
of shredded lettuce, garnish with finely minced parsley. Serves
6 as an appetizer.

COURT BOUILLON:
1 stalk celery, sliced
3 sprigs parsley
1 bay leaf
2 carrots, coarsely chopped
1 lemon, sliced
1 teaspoon salt
2 quarts water
10 peppercorns, bruised
1 pinch thyme
1 large white onion, sliced
1 cup dry white wine
¼ cup cider vinegar

Combine all ingredients in a deep saucepan, and simmer uncovered
for 20 minutes. Strain the liquid through a fine sieve. About 1 quart.

HORSERADISH SAUCE:

2 cups commercial sour cream, blended judiciously with 1½
cups horseradish, drained thoroughly, ⅓ cup chopped pecans
and salt and pepper to taste.

From: Christian's Restaurant

Bouillabaisse

Heat ⅛ cup olive oil in very large skillet and add 1 finely sliced onion. Saute onion slices for a few minutes on medium fire until transparent. Then add:

3 cloves garlic, chopped
½ bay leaf
¼ teaspoon thyme
⅛ teaspoon powdered anise
1 tomato, peeled, seeds removed and crushed
½ cup white wine
1 ½ quarts fish stock

and simmer uncovered until onions are tender (about 15-20 minutes). Then add:

16 shrimp (pre-cooked if frozen) peeled
12 oysters
¼ pound crab meat or gumbo crabs
8 fish fillets (trout, redfish, etc.)

and continue to simmer until the fish fillets are tender. Do not overcook the fish fillets! Add ¼ teaspoon powered saffron. Serve the bouillabaisse immediately, very hot, in large soup plates with toasted garlic bread rounds and Rouille in separate plates. Add some Rouille to enhance the flavor of the Bouillabaisse.

GARLIC BREAD ROUNDS:

Cut some French bread into ¼ inch rounds (about 6 pieces per person) baste with olive oil and finely chopped garlic and toast on a tray under broiler until light brown.

ROUILLE:

Make a regular mayonnaise using 3 egg yolks (room temperature) and ½ quart olive oil and add 1 heaping teaspoon chopped garlic and ¾ teaspoon cayenne pepper. For 4 to 6 persons. Bon appetit!

From: Christian's Restaurant
Shrimp Madeleine

2 tablespoons dry English mustard
4 tablespoons butter
3 pounds raw shrimp, medium size
⅓ cup brandy
2 cups heavy cream
Salt and pepper

Mix the dry mustard with a little water to make a light paste.
Melt the butter over high heat and saute the shrimp until all water
has evaporated. Then pour over brandy and ignite. When the
flames subside, add the cream and cook, stirring all the time, till
a smooth sauce is obtained. Add the mustard paste and season
to taste with salt and pepper. Serve in individual casserole
dishes or on a platter; garnish with parsley. Serves 8.

From: Christian's Restaurant
Oysters Roland

1 bunch parsley
1 pound butter, softened
1 teaspoon black pepper
1 teaspoon salt
2 cloves garlic
1 (12 ounce) can mushrooms, stems and pieces with juice
1 cup bread crumbs
¼ teaspoon nutmeg
5 dozen parboiled oysters

Blend in high speed food processor such as "Cuisinart" in this
order: parsley, garlic, mushrooms, blend well until parsley
is finely chopped; then add butter, spices and blend again; now
add mushroom juice, bread crumbs and blend well. If this
type of food processor is not available, a meat grinder may be
substituted using the smallest plate for grinding parsley, garlic
and mushrooms and blending after with a mixer. Place 6 par-
boiled oysters each in 4 ½ inch au gratin dishes, smooth butter
mixture over it and put under broiler until brown and bubbly.
Makes about 10 servings.

From: Christian's Restaurant

Stuffed Trout

4 ounces trout
4 ounces Trout Stuffing
Flour
Egg wash
Bread crumbs
Fried parsley

Slit trout in half and place log of stuffing on it and roll. Dust in flour, dip in egg wash and coat with bread crumbs. Deep fry till brown and bake in 350°F oven for 10 minutes or until hot in center. Garnish with fried parsley.

TROUT STUFFING:
1 cup heavy cream sauce
8 ounces crab meat
6 ounces chopped boiled shrimp
2 tablespoons thinly sliced green onions
Salt and pepper

Mix well. Makes 6 to 8 portions.

GARLIC SAUCE:
2 egg yolks
¾ cup olive oil
¾ cup cottonseed oil
2 tablespoons ketchup
½ teaspoon chopped garlic
Salt and pepper
Add chopped parsley for color

Proceed as per mayonnaise recipe and add remaining ingredients near end.

From: Commander's Palace
Commander's Salad

3 cups each Iceberg lettuce and Romaine lettuce, washed, dried and torn into bite size pieces
2 grated hard-cooked eggs
8 strips bacon, fried crisp, drained and crumbled
½ cup croutons
Commander's House Dressing

Combine lettuces with the hard-cooked eggs, bacon and croutons — reserving 2 to 3 croutons per serving to toss on top of salad — with Commander's House Dressing until all ingredients are well coated. Heap on small salad plates, top with reserved croutons. Serves 6.

COMMANDER'S HOUSE DRESSING:
½ cup onions, diced
1 egg
1 cup salad oil
3 tablespoons vinegar
Pinch of garlic powder
Pinch of black pepper

In blender, puree onion, add whole egg and blend two minutes more. Switching blender on and off, add oil in a steady stream until mixture thickens to the consistency of heavy mayonnaise. On medium speed, blend in vinegar. Add seasonings and blend 10 seconds more. Chill. Makes 1 ½ cups.

From: Commander's Palace
Crab Meat Lausanne

½ cup butter
3 tablespoons blanched sliced almonds
½ cup finely chopped green onion tops
½ teaspoon salt
¼ teaspoon black pepper
⅛ teaspoon cayenne pepper
⅛ teaspoon garlic powder
2 tablespoons chopped parsley
1 tablespoon lemon juice
1 pound lump crab meat, gently remove any shells
2-3 cups steamed rice

Melt butter in a large skillet and saute almonds until golden brown. Add the green onion tops and seasoning and saute for 3 minutes. Add parsley, lemon juice and crab meat; toss well. Heat thoroughly. Serve over steamed rice. Serves 4.

From: Commander's Palace
Crab Meat Imperial

2 tablespoons butter	
¼ cup onions, minced	
2 tablespoons green pepper, minced	
2 tablespoons celery, minced	
¼ cup green onions, tops only, minced	
½ teaspoon freshly ground black pepper	
1 teaspoon powdered garlic	
1 cup mayonnaise	
½ cup pimiento, minced and well drained	
¼ cup Creole mustard	
1 tablespoon Worcestershire sauce	
1 tablespoon Tabasco sauce	
2 tablespoons parsley, chopped	
2 pounds cooked, fresh lump crab meat — pick out any shells	

TOPPING:
Mayonnaise
Paprika

In a large skillet, melt butter; add onions, green peppers, celery, green onions, and seasonings, saute for 15 minutes. Remove from heat; add mayonnaise, pimiento, mustard, Worcestershire sauce, Tabasco sauce and parsley. Mix well. Let cool for about 20 minutes. Place crab meat in large mixing bowl and pick out any shells, being careful not to break up lumps. Ladle the sauce over the crabmeat and mix gently to coat the crab meat without breaking up lumps. Using your hands, fill individual casserole dishes, or ramekins, or large flat sea shells, with ¾ cup of crab meat mixture. Coat each casserole with 1 tablespoon mayonnaise, sprinkle paprika over top. Heat in 350°F oven for 8-10 minutes, or until it bubbles. Yields 8 servings.

From: Corinne Dunbar's
Red Bean Soup

½ pound red kidney beans
1 small onion, chopped
2 cloves garlic, chopped
2 strips celery, chopped
2 bay leaves
2 sprigs thyme
¼ stick butter
1 teaspoon Worcestershire sauce
½ pound ham, ground fine
Water
Salt and pepper to taste
Claret wine, sieved hard boiled egg, lemon slice — garnish

Brown onion in butter. Simmer beans for about 3 hours in water
with seasoning. Strain mixture through coarse strainer — mash
with large spoon. Add ham. Add salt and pepper. Place 1 tablespoon
claret wine in bottom of each bouillon cup. Pour soup. Garnish
with sieved egg and lemon slice. Serves 8.

From: Corinne Dunbar's
Filet of Trout Dunbar

1 (6 ounce) filet per person (2 pounds, gives 2 (6 ounce) filets)
2 tablespoons butter
Water to cover trout

SAUCE FOR 15:
1 pound butter
3 hard boiled eggs, sieved
1 can anchovy filets, mashed
1 bottle capers
Juice of 2 lemons
1 tablespoon horseradish mustard
1 tablespoon Worcestershire sauce
1 pod garlic, crushed-minced
1 tablespoon onion juice

Wash filets well, bake submerged in water and butter in 350°F
oven about 10 minutes or until done. Melt butter in saucepan. Add
all ingredients and simmer very slowly for 15 minutes. Remove
trout from water and shortening, allow to drain, place on
heated plate. Pour sauce over trout. Decorate with parsley,
pimiento strips and lemon quarters.

From: Corinne Dunbar's
Baked Crab Meat and Avocado

1 pound lump crab meat
2 cans cream of mushroom soup
2 avocados
1 cup evaporated milk
Salt and pepper to taste
2 teaspoons bread crumbs
1 can anchovy filets
¼ pound butter

Melt butter. Add soup and simmer 5 minutes. Add crab meat.
Add milk, salt and pepper, simmer 5 minutes longer. Peel
and slice avocados, line baking dish with slices. Pour crab meat
mixture over slices of avocado. Sprinkle with bread crumbs
and brush with melted butter. Heat until brown in 350°F oven,
approximately 15 minutes. Before serving, sprinkle a few
drops of anchovy oil on top and garnish with anchovy strips.
Serves 4 to 6.

From: Delmonico
Turtle Soup au Sherry

1½-2 pounds turtle meat
2 ribs celery
1 whole garlic
1 onion
Salt
3-4 tablespoons flour
½ cup mixed olive and cooking oil
1½ cups chopped leeks and onions
1 cup chopped tomatoes
Chopped hard-boiled egg
Sherry

Combine turtle meat, celery, garlic, onion, and salt and cook
in approximately ½ gallon water about 30 minutes. Skim if
necessary. Brown flour in oil; add onions and tomato. Simmer until
onions are brown, stirring. Cut up turtle meat and add to
broth. Add flour mixture to broth. Add more water and salt
if necessary. Just before serving add chopped egg and sherry.

From: Delmonico
Trout Elmere

½ cup celery
1 tablespoon olive oil
4 strips anchovies
1 cup seasoned bread crumbs
3 tablespoons Romano cheese
½ tomato

Mince celery. Saute in small amount of olive oil. Melt anchovies and add seasoned bread crumbs to mixture. Simmer until almost dry. Add grated Romano cheese. This is the Elmere dressing. Salt and pepper trout fillet. Spread Elmere dressing on trout, roll, broil in lemon butter sauce, adding minced tomato.

From: Delmonico
Baked Creole Eggplant

2 eggplants, diced
1 onion
1 cup raw peeled shrimp
1 piece celery
½ cup butter or oil

Boil eggplants until soft. Saute onion, chopped shrimp, and celery in butter or oil; combine with eggplant. Put in baking pan and sprinkle with bread crumbs. Bake approximately 30 minutes at 350°F.

From: The Fairmont Hotel
Bananas Foster

Vanilla ice cream
3 large bananas
½ cup brown sugar
½ cup butter
1 pinch clove
½ teaspoon cinnamon
1 ounce each rum and brandy

Split and slice bananas into small pieces. Melt butter over low heat, add sugar and spices and bring to a boil. Heat bananas in sauce and pour brandy and rum over mixture, then ignite. Serve over vanilla ice cream. Serves 6.

From: The Fairmont Hotel

Stuffed Eggplant

3 eggplants
1 tablespoon salt
3 eggs
9 tablespoons olive oil
1 pound Mozzarella cheese
½ cup grated Parmesan cheese
⅛ tablespoon pepper
¼ tablespoon basil
1 (6 ounce) can tomato paste
2 small onions, chopped
½ cup bread crumbs
1 cup water

Slice eggplant in half and scoop out meat. Saute onions in 2 tablespoons olive oil. Add meat of eggplant plus all other ingredients. Add flour to thicken to proper consistency. Cook over moderate heat for 10 minutes. Let cool. Stuff eggplant mixture back into shells. Bake in 350°F oven for 30 minutes. Serves 6.

From: The Fairmont Hotel

Filet of Redfish with Crayfish Tails

6 (7 ounce) redfish filets
1 pound crayfish tails
2 ounces butter
1 cup white wine
1 onion, sliced
1 quart heavy cream
1½ ounces cognac
Salt
White pepper
Thyme
Bay leaves
Roux (½ teaspoon melted butter, ½ teaspoon flour)

Poach filets in fish stock with white wine, onions, salt, thyme and bay leaves. In skillet, melt butter and saute crayfish tails. Add cognac and ignite. Pour in heavy cream, bring to a boil and add roux to thicken. Season to taste. Serve on platter garnished with parsley.

From: The Fairmont Hotel
Imperial Salad

2 heads bibb lettuce
12 artichoke hearts
1 cup sliced radishes
1 cucumber, peeled and sliced
12 cherry tomatoes
Chopped parsley

Prepare dressing and toss with above in large bowl.

SALAD DRESSING:
2 eggs
1 ounce vinegar or red wine
1 teaspoon Dijon mustard
1 cup salad oil
½ teaspoon garlic
½ teaspoon dill weed
1 teaspoon sugar
2 tablespoons whipped cream

Combine all ingredients except whipped cream and blend until
creamy. Fold in whipped cream and toss with salad. Serves 6.

From: Galatoire's
Crêpes Maison

8 six inch dessert crêpes
8 tablespoons grape jelly
6 tablespoons toasted, sliced almonds
Peel of one orange and one lemon, slivered
Powdered sugar
4 jiggers Grand Marnier

Roll one tablespoon grape jelly in each crêpe. Place 2 crêpes on
each of four ovenproof plates. Top with sliced almonds,
orange and lemon peel and sprinkle with powdered sugar. Pass
under broiler until hot. Pour 1 jigger of Grand Marnier over
each serving. Serves 4.

From: Galatoire's
Oysters en Brochette

2 dozen raw oysters
12 strips bacon cut in half
4 (8 inch) skewers
1 egg
¾ cup milk
Flour
Salt and pepper to taste
Oil for deep frying

Fry bacon until not quite crisp. Alternate 6 oysters and 6 half
strips of bacon (folded) on each skewer. Make a batter with
egg and milk and season well with salt and pepper. Dip each skewer
in batter, roll in flour and deep fry until golden. Serve on
toast points with lemon wedges. Serves four as appetizer or
two as main course.

From: Galatoire's
French Fried Eggplant

1 large, long eggplant
1 egg
¾ cup milk
Flour
Salt and white pepper to taste
Oil for deep frying
Powdered sugar

Peel eggplant and cut to size of large French fries. Soak 30
minutes in salted water. Rinse and pat dry. Make a batter with
egg and milk and season well with salt and pepper. Dip eggplant into
batter, roll in flour and deep fry until golden. Sprinkle with
additional salt and serve with powdered sugar. Serves 4 as hors
d'oeuvre with cocktails, or as vegetable with entrée.

From: Galatoire's
Trout Meunière Amandine

4 (6 to 8 ounce) fillets of speckled trout
½ pound butter
Juice of 1 lemon
Oil for frying
4 ounces sliced, toasted almonds
½ tablespoon chopped parsley
Salt, pepper, flour, milk

Dip salted and peppered fillets in milk then roll in flour. Fry in hot oil in shallow pan until golden on both sides. In a separate pan melt and continuously whip butter until brown and frothy. Add sliced almonds and lemon juice and pour over trout. Garnish with chopped parsley. Serves 4.

From: Joe Marcello, Jr. and Nick Mosca, Owners La Louisiane Restaurant
Shrimp Mosca

2 pounds whole fresh shrimp (15 to 20 count suggested)
6-8 buds of garlic
2 whole bay leaves
1 teaspoon crushed whole black pepper
1 teaspoon salt
1 teaspoon rosemary
1 teaspoon oregano
2 ounces olive oil
1 ounce sauterne wine

Heat oil in fry pan and add shrimp and spices, sauté for 15 to 20 minutes, or until shrimp turn pink. Add wine and simmer for 10 to 15 minutes more. Shrimp are to be peeled at table and served with hot crisp bread for dunking into sauce. Serves 2.

From: Joe Marcello, Jr. and Nick Mosca, Owners La Louisiane Restaurant

Trout Meuniere

2 pieces of trout, fileted (8 ounces each)
¼ pound butter
Juice of 1 large lemon
1 tablespoon Lea & Perrin sauce
Flour for dredging
Salt and pepper to taste

Salt and pepper fish pieces, dredge in flour and deep fry until golden brown. Place fish on serving plate and keep warm. Melt butter in sauté pan, add lemon juice and Lea & Perrin sauce, stir well and simmer until thoroughly heated. Pour Meuniere sauce over fish, garnish with sprigs of parsley and lemon wedges. Serves 2.

From: La Provence

Salad Dressing a La Provence

Blend together:

1 ounce garlic
3 ounces anchovies — then add:
3 ounces prepared mustard
4 eggs
2 tablespoons oregano

Mix well — then add:

½ cup wine vinegar
½ cup lemon juice
Salt and pepper

Slowly add:

4 cups salad oil

From: La Provence

Pepper Steak

4 steaks
1 tablespoon green peppercorn
2 tablespoons shallots
1 pint heavy cream
2 tablespoons lemon juice
Salt and pepper
Brandy

This dish features prime filet of beef, cut into 8 ounce steaks. Cook steaks as desired in pan, and add to sauce, when almost done. Saute in butter, green peppercorn, and shallots. Flame with brandy. Add heavy cream, lemon juice, salt and pepper. Remove steaks, reduce liquid until thickened. Pour sauce over steaks.

From: La Provence

Poulet Fromage

Chicken, cut into serving pieces
2 teaspoons chopped shallots
½ cup dry vermouth
¾ cup heavy cream
Salt and pepper
2 tablespoons grated Swiss cheese
1 tablespoon bleu cheese
1 tablespoon softened butter
1 teaspoon Dijon mustard

Saute chicken in butter, but do not brown! Add chopped shallots, dry vermouth. Reduce liquid slightly. Add heavy cream, (enough to almost cover), salt and pepper. Bring to a boil. Put in oven and cover with oiled waxed paper. Cook approximately 15 minutes. Remove, and strain sauce, reduce. Whip Swiss cheese, bleu cheese and butter and mustard. Pour over chicken and serve.

From: La Provence

Coq au Vin

Chicken, cut into serving pieces
Red wine
¼ cup chopped shallots
½ teaspoon black pepper
½ teaspoon thyme
2 bay leaves
2 tablespoons butter
Pearl onions and sliced fresh mushrooms

Saute chicken, but do not brown. Add red wine to cover. Add shallots, black pepper, thyme, bay leaves. Cover pan and bake in oven for 15 minutes. Remove chicken (keep warm). Reduce liquid. Whip in butter and pour over chicken. Place pearl onions and sauteed fresh mushrooms on top.

From: La Provence

Crepes Gallant

1 pound country ham
2 cups chopped fresh mushrooms
1 cup dry sherry
2 bay leaves
¼ cup diced tomatoes
1 cup cream sauce
½ cup grated Swiss cheese

Dice ham, blanch in water for 10 minutes. Drain. Cook mushrooms and shallots in butter until dry (about 10 minutes). Combine mushrooms, ham and sherry, simmer and reduce with bay leaves until most of liquid is gone, then add diced tomatoes, cream sauce and grated Swiss cheese. Roll into thin crepes, and top with Mornay Sauce.

MORNAY SAUCE:
1 cup cream sauce with ¼ cup Swiss cheese

From: La Provence
Baked Oysters Jean Batiste Reboul

3 pounds fresh mushrooms
4 ounces garlic
2 ounces shallots or white of green onion
3 cups dry white wine
1-2 bay leaves
Pinch of thyme
Salt and pepper

Saute chopped fresh mushrooms in butter, add garlic and shallots, chopped fine. Then add white wine and reduce, with bay leaves and thyme. Salt and pepper. Cover fresh oysters in a casserole dish with mushroom sauce. Cook in oven until oysters are done 450°F. Cover with Hollandaise sauce and brown under broiler.

From: Le Ruth's Restaurant
Russian Dressing

⅔ cup mayonnaise
⅓ cup chili sauce
1½ tablespoons chopped green pepper
1 tablespoon chopped pimento
1 tablespoon chopped onion
1 tablespoon sugar
1 tablespoon vinegar
¼ teaspoon Lea & Perrin sauce

Mix well and refrigerate.

From: Le Ruth's Restaurant
Sweet and Sour Celery Seed Dressing

3 tablespoons catsup
2 tablespoons white vinegar
1 tablespoon sugar
¼ teaspoon salt
¼ cup light corn syrup
2 teaspoons steak sauce
2 tablespoons water
1 teaspoon onion juice
¼ teaspoon whole celery seeds
3 tablespoons corn oil

Mix well and refrigerate.

From: Le Ruth's Restaurant
Avocado Dressing

1 mashed ripe avocado
1½ cups mayonnaise
1 lemon, juice only
1 toe garlic, chopped
1 teaspoon salt
¼ teaspoon crushed black pepper
½ teaspoon anchovy paste
¼ cup whipping cream

Mix well and refrigerate.

From: Le Ruth's Restaurant
Tartar Sauce

1 cup mayonnaise
½ cup chopped dill pickle
¼ cup chopped onion
2 tablespoons chopped parsley
Tabasco to taste

Mix well and refrigerate.

From: Le Ruth's Restaurant
Roquefort Dressing

1 cup mayonnaise
2 tablespoons sour cream
2 tablespoons buttermilk
¼ teaspoon Lea & Perrin sauce
¼ teaspoon white pepper
⅛ teaspoon M.S.G.
½ teaspoon salt
2-3 ounces Roquefort cheese, crumbled

Mix well and refrigerate.

From: Le Ruth's Restaurant
Remoulade Sauce

¾ cup Creole mustard
2 tablespoons paprika
1 cup corn oil
¼ cup chopped onion
½ cup chopped celery
2 tablespoons chopped parsley
½ teaspoon sugar (optional)
Tabasco to taste

Mix well and refrigerate.

From: Masson's
Frog Legs Belle Meuniere

8 pair medium frog legs
¼ pound butter
¼ cup chopped green onions
¼ cup sliced mushrooms
¼ cup white wine
3 teaspoons cognac
Juice of 1 lemon

Cut frogs into individual legs. Salt and pepper. Saute slowly
in butter until brown. Add onions and mushrooms. Simmer 5
minutes. Add wine and lemon. Cook 5 minutes. Finish with
cognac and chopped parsley.

From: Masson's
Sabayon

6 eggs, separated
¾ cup sugar
¾ cup cream sherry
¾ cup heavy cream
1 teaspoon vanilla

Beat yolks with sugar until creamy, add sherry and cook in
double boiler until thick. Cool in bowl for 10-15 minutes. Add
whipped cream and vanilla. Fold in stiffly beaten whites.
Divide into 4 small ramekins and chill for 2-3 hours.

From: Masson's
Bayou Oysters en Brochette

6 dozen oysters
½ pound butter
¼ cup white wine
⅛ cup chopped parsley
6 cherry tomatoes
Salt, pepper and paprika
1 can (12 count) artichoke hearts
12 fresh large mushroom caps
1 cup flour
½ cup cooking oil
¼ cup lemon juice
6 (10 inch) skewers

Make six skewers by alternating a mushroom, three oysters
(through eye), one artichoke heart, three oysters, one tomato,
three oysters, one artichoke heart, three oysters and one
mushroom cap. Sprinkle with salt, pepper and paprika. Dredge
with flour, pan fry in ½ cup oil til brown and place brochettes
on side plate. Pour oil out of pan and brown ½ pound butter,
add lemon and wine. Pour sauce over oysters, sprinkle with
parsley and serve. Six servings. Bon Appetit.

From: Masson's
Lobster Marinade

2 teaspoons salt
¼ teaspoon pepper
1 clove garlic
¼ cup wine vinegar
1 cup olive oil
½ cup chopped green onions
2 tablespoons chopped parsley
1 pound cooked lobster meat

Mash garlic in wooden bowl with salt and pepper. Add vinegar
and mix well. Add oil, green onions, and parsley. Mix well.
Pour over lobster meat and toss lightly. Refrigerate for 2-3 hours
before serving.

From: Masson's
Tomato Florentine

4 medium tomatoes
½ pound frozen spinach
1 medium onion, chopped fine
⅛ pound butter
Romano cheese, grated

Saute onion in butter. Salt and pepper to taste. Add spinach. Cut top and bottom off tomatoes. Scoop out to ½ of depth. Fill cavity with spinach. Top with cheese and bake 10-12 minutes at 300°F.

From: Tchoupitoulas Plantation
Bananas Tchoupitoulas

1 cup sugar
1 tablespoon honey
1 orange
6 sliced bananas
1 teaspoon vanilla extract
1 stick butter
2 ounces rum
½ cup cornstarch

Take a small pot of water put in sugar, honey, vanilla and a sliced orange; cook until it all comes to a boil. Then mix cornstarch diluted with water and let thicken, cook together for about 15 minutes. Simmer, add bananas and rum when ready to serve.

From: Tchoupitoulas Plantation
Egg Custard

½ dozen eggs
1 stick butter
1½ cups sugar
1 teaspoon vanilla extract
1 quart milk
1 cup evaporated milk

Beat eggs, milk, butter and sugar until thick, add vanilla. Beat well, pour into cups and place in a pan of water one inch deep. Bake in 375°F oven for about 45 minutes. Serves 6.

From: Tchoupitoulas Plantation
Bread Pudding

1 small French bread
2 eggs
2 cups of sugar
1 tablespoon vanilla extract
1 cup fruit cocktail
1 cup raisins
1 stick butter
1 large can evaporated milk

Beat well eggs, milk, butter and vanilla. Add raisins, fruit cocktail when all ingredients are well blended, then dice French bread and add to all the ingredients. Let ingredients soak for about 5 minutes. Then pour into a 10 x 6½ x 1½ inch baking pan and let bake 30 to 40 minutes in a 350°F oven. Serves 6.

BUTTER SAUCE FOR BREAD PUDDING:
1 stick butter
1 cup sugar
1 cup of rum

Melt butter, rum and sugar and blend well.

From: Tchoupitoulas Plantation
Shrimp Imperial

1 pound peeled shrimp
1 medium onion
½ dozen mushrooms, sliced
1 cup grated American cheese
½ cup chopped parsley
2 cups of mushroom soup
1 cup Italian bread crumbs
1 teaspoon pepper

Saute onion, parsley in butter, add soup, mushrooms and cheese. Then add all other ingredients top with bread crumbs. Bake in 375°F oven for about 20 minutes. Serves 6-8 guests.

From: Tchoupitoulas Plantation
Oysters Tchoupitoulas

1 quart oysters
2 quarts water
1 bunch of green onions
1 (5 ounce) bottle of A-1 sauce
3 bay leaves
½ cup of chicken base

Boil oysters in water until firm. Add base, bay leaves and A-1 sauce.
On a low flame cook green onions in butter until tender. Make
a roux medium brown in color and mix all ingredients and
cook for about 20 minutes. If you need to add color add Kitchen
Bouquet. Serves 6.

From: Tchoupitoulas Plantation
Veal Cordon Bleu

12 (4 ounce) veal cutlets
6 slices of ham
6 slices Swiss cheese

Lay cutlets out flat. Then lay one slice of ham and one slice
of cheese and add another cutlet. (It will look like a sandwich.)
Bread the veal very lightly and fry until golden in color.

CHAMPAGNE SAUCE:

Make a light brown gravy and add Burgundy wine to your
taste. Pour over veal and serve.

From: Vieux Carre Restaurant
Almond Tort

Blend 1 pound butter and ¾ pound powdered sugar in blender.
Separate yolks from 4 eggs and beat egg whites separately into
a meringue. Add the 4 yolks, meringue, ½ cup almonds (chopped
fine), and ½ pound coconut macaroon cookies (chopped fine)
to blender. Blend until completely mixed. Place mixture into
baking pan and refrigerate until it hardens. Then cut into
desired squares. Top tort with whipped cream and sprinkle
with chopped almonds. Serves 12.

From: Vieux Carre Restaurant
Bouillabaisse à la Creole

1 bunch celery
2 medium white onions
2 bunches green onions
6 medium green peppers
3 cloves garlic
4 cups canned tomatoes with juice
1 bunch parsley
1 teaspoon thyme
2 bay leaves
2 pounds redfish
¼ pound shrimp
4 oysters per person including oyster water
Crab meat (optional)
1 pinch saffron
¾ cup white wine

Very thinly slice celery, onions, peppers, and garlic. Saute lightly in margarine in large pot. Break up tomatoes and add with juice. Finely chop parsley, add with thyme and bay leaves. Add 8 cups water, bring to a boil, and simmer about 1 hour. Slice redfish into thin steaks. Bake lightly to seal in juices. Add redfish and shrimp to vegetables and simmer another ½ hour. Add oysters (including water) and saffron and leave on 5 more minutes. Add wine and remove from heat. Should be approximate consistency of vegetable soup. Garnish with croutons.

From: Vieux Carre Restaurant
Sweetbreads Richelieu

1 ½ pounds sweetbreads, (sliced to desired thickness) sauteed in ¼ pound of butter or margarine for 2 minutes. Remove braised sweetbreads from skillet and add ¼ cup of flour to butter essence and brown roux until shade of brown desired. Add 6 whole shallots (chopped fine) and 12 large mushrooms (sliced) to roux in skillet. Let cook for 10 minutes and stir constantly. (6 cèpes (sliced) may be used instead of mushrooms). Add 1 (10 ounce) can of consomme and 3 peeled tomatoes (pre-chopped fine) to skillet and let simmer for 10 minutes. Return braised sweetbreads to skillet and let simmer for 4 minutes. Then add 2 ounces dry white wine, 1 ounce brandy to skillet and let simmer for 2 minutes and remove. Serves 4.

Table of Measurements
and Equivalents in U.S. and Metric

U.S.	Equivalents	Metric* Volume-milliliters
Dash	less than 1/8 teaspoon	
1 teaspoon	60 drops	5 ml.
1 tablespoon	3 teaspoons	15 ml.
2 tablespoons	1 fluid ounce	30 ml.
4 tablespoons	1/4 cup	60 ml.
5 1/3 tablespoons	1/3 cup	80 ml.
6 tablespoons	3/8 cup	90 ml.
8 tablespoons	1/2 cup	120 ml.
10 2/3 tablespoons	2/3 cup	160 ml.
12 tablespoons	3/4 cup	180 ml.
16 tablespoons	1 cup or 8 ounces	240 ml.
1 cup	1/2 pint or 8 fluid ounces	240 ml.
2 cups	1 pint	480 ml.
1 pint	16 ounces	480 ml. or .473 liter
1 quart	2 pints	960 ml. or .95 liter
2.1 pints	1.05 quarts or .26 gallons	1 liter
2 quarts	1/2 gallon	
4 quarts	1 gallon	3.8 liters

		Weight-grams
1 ounce	16 drams	28 grams
1 pound	16 ounces	454 grams
1 pound	2 cups liquid	
1 kilo	2.20 pounds	

Temperature Conversion Fahrenheit to Celsius*

Fahrenheit	200	225	250	275	300	325
Celsius	93	106	121	135	149	163

Fahrenheit	350	375	400	425	450	475
Celsius	176	191	205	218	231	246

Fahrenheit	500	550
Celsius	260	288

*These are round figures. The important thing to remember in cooking
is to use relative amounts in measuring.

Index—Alphabetical

Index—Alphabetical

Index—Category

Index—Category

Index—Category

Index — Category

Index—Category

LA BONNE CUISINE

TOLL FREE 1-800-375-1416
100 REX DRIVE • 504-737-1416
RIVER RIDGE, LA 70123

Please send

_____ copies **La Bonne Cuisine** .... @ $12.95 each $ _____

_____ copies **Cooking New Orleans Style** ...... @ $ 6.95 each $ _____

_____ copies **LBC Lagniappe** .... @ $ 3.00 each $ _____

Total for Books $ _____

POSTAGE AND HANDLING—within Continental U.S.

For **Cooking New Orleans Style** or
La Bonne Cuisine:
1 Book only .... Add $3.00
2 or more to same address, shipping is free.

For 1–5 **Lagniappe** books .... Add $1.00
6 or more to same address, shipping is free.

Order **Lagniappe** with **La Bonne Cuisine**
or **Cooking New Orleans Style**
and add no shipping for **Lagniappe** books!

Sales Tax (La. residents 4%) _____

Postage and Handling _____

TOTAL $ _____

☐ Payment Enclosed — Make check or money order payable to
La Bonne Cuisine

Charge to:
☐ VISA
☐ MASTERCARD

Credit Cards Welcome!

Exp. Date _____

Acct. No. _____

Signature _____

Order with VISA or MASTERCARD by phone:
1-800-375-1416 or **Fax 504-738-7829**

Daytime Phone (In Case of Problem) (_____) _____

Ship to:

Please show Street Address
and indicate type of address:
☐ Commercial ☐ Residence

Name _____

Address _____

Prices are subject to change.

City/State/Zip _____

LA BONNE CUISINE

TOLL FREE 1-800-375-1416
100 REX DRIVE • 504-737-1416
RIVER RIDGE, LA 70123

Please send

_____ copies **La Bonne Cuisine** .... @ $12.95 each $ _____

_____ copies **Cooking New Orleans Style** ...... @ $ 6.95 each $ _____

_____ copies **LBC Lagniappe** .... @ $ 3.00 each $ _____

Total for Books $ _____

POSTAGE AND HANDLING—within Continental U.S.

For **Cooking New Orleans Style** or
La Bonne Cuisine:
1 Book only .... Add $3.00
2 or more to same address, shipping is free.

For 1–5 **Lagniappe** books .... Add $1.00
6 or more to same address, shipping is free.

Order **Lagniappe** with **La Bonne Cuisine**
or **Cooking New Orleans Style**
and add no shipping for **Lagniappe** books!

Sales Tax (La. residents 4%) _____

Postage and Handling _____

TOTAL $ _____

☐ Payment Enclosed — Make check or money order payable to
La Bonne Cuisine

Charge to:
☐ VISA
☐ MASTERCARD

Credit Cards Welcome!

Exp. Date _____

Acct. No. _____

Signature _____

Order with VISA or MASTERCARD by phone:
1-800-375-1416 or **Fax 504-738-7829**

Daytime Phone (In Case of Problem) (_____) _____

Ship to:

Please show Street Address
and indicate type of address:
☐ Commercial ☐ Residence

Name _____

Address _____

Prices are subject to change.

City/State/Zip _____

LA BONNE CUISINE

TOLL FREE 1-800-375-1416
100 REX DRIVE • 504-737-1416
RIVER RIDGE, LA 70123

Please send

_____ copies **La Bonne Cuisine** .... @ $12.95 each $ _____

_____ copies **Cooking New Orleans Style** ...... @ $ 6.95 each $ _____

_____ copies **LBC Lagniappe** .... @ $ 3.00 each $ _____

Total for Books $ _____

POSTAGE AND HANDLING—within Continental U.S.

For **Cooking New Orleans Style** or
La Bonne Cuisine:
1 Book only .... Add $3.00
2 or more to same address, shipping is free.

For 1–5 **Lagniappe** books .... Add $1.00
6 or more to same address, shipping is free.

Order **Lagniappe** with **La Bonne Cuisine**
or **Cooking New Orleans Style**
and add no shipping for **Lagniappe** books!

Sales Tax (La. residents 4%) _____

Postage and Handling _____

TOTAL $ _____

☐ Payment Enclosed — Make check or money order payable to
La Bonne Cuisine

Charge to:
☐ VISA
☐ MASTERCARD

Credit Cards Welcome!

Exp. Date _____

Acct. No. _____

Signature _____

Order with VISA or MASTERCARD by phone:
1-800-375-1416 or **Fax 504-738-7829**

Daytime Phone (In Case of Problem) (_____) _____

Ship to:

Please show Street Address
and indicate type of address:
☐ Commercial ☐ Residence

Name _____

Address _____

Prices are subject to change.

City/State/Zip _____

Names and addresses of bookstores, gift shops, etc., in your area would be appreciated.

_____

_____

_____

_____

_____

_____

_____

_____

_____

_____

Names and addresses of bookstores, gift shops, etc., in your area would be appreciated.

_____

_____

_____

_____

_____

_____

_____

_____

_____

_____

Names and addresses of bookstores, gift shops, etc., in your area would be appreciated.

_____

_____

_____

_____

_____

_____

_____

_____

_____

_____